With best Wishes from Sir John M. Clark and Mr T. G. Clark

WAITING UPON GOD

Waiting upon God

BY THE LATE

A. B. DAVIDSON, D.D., LL.D., Litt.D.

PROFESSOR OF HEBREW, NEW COLLEGE, EDINBURGH

EDITED BY

J. A. PATERSON, D.D.

PROFESSOR OF HEBREW, NEW COLLEGE, EDINBURGH

EDINBURGH: T. & T. CLARK, 38 George Street

1904

Printed by
MORRISON & GIBB LIMITED,

FOR

T. & T. CLARK, EDINBURGH,

LONDON : SIMPKIN, MARSHALL, HAMILTON, KENT, AND CO. LIMITED.
NEW YORK : CHARLES SCRIBNER'S SONS.

PREFACE

———◆———

THIS volume contains a final selection from the sermons of the late Professor A. B. Davidson. The first series, entitled "The Called of God," had as an Introduction a Biographical Sketch of the author, and all the sermons in it were chosen as having themselves a biographical colour. This, of necessity, somewhat restricted that selection; but that the idea was not unwise, has been shown by the immediate success of the book.

In the present case, however, there has been absolute freedom of choice; and, as a result, among the fifteen sermons selected as the best, there is a remarkable variety of subject. It was a surprise to find, after the selection had been made, how greatly the discourses on New Testament subjects outnumber those from the Old. Of the eleven New Testament discourses, seven are from the Gospels, three of which describe the main crises in our Lord's earthly life; other three show how He bore Himself in word or act towards three distinct classes of the community, the common people, the rulers, and the disciples; and the seventh gives us Christ's own conception of the growth of the Kingdom of God.

The other books of Scripture laid under contribution for topics are those on which Dr. Davidson specially loved to meditate, namely, Isaiah, Job, the Psalms, Hebrews, and Revelation. His earliest publication was on Job; to the study of the Psalms and the second half of Isaiah he invariably devoted a part of each session; his Commentary on Hebrews is an acknowledged masterpiece of exposition; and the Book of Revelation, on which he published nothing, though his library is rich in commentaries on it, was chosen by him as the subject of an Introductory Lecture to the students of New College. There is but one sermon on a text from the Epistles of St. Paul, but it treats of "The Power of Christ's Resurrection," and enables a reader to grasp the author's view of Pauline Theology. There is thus in this single volume a most varied selection of the author's choicest work.

The exegetical element, while more manifest in some of the discourses than in others, pervades all, but burdens none. It is indeed always made a help to the vivid and searching presentation of truth. The manifold practical applications, the suggestive illustrations from nature, and the subtle analysis of human character and motive, prove that this scholar, at least, walked through the world open-eyed.

Moreover, this volume of sermons, while revealing on

every page to a skilled eye the patient work of the trained thinker, is written in such a clear and simple style, that it may be read with pleasure by plain people, and by none with greater profit than by the thoughtful among the young.

The title, "Waiting upon God," is to be regarded as applicable not merely to the first sermon, but to the whole series. It also indicates how this book contrasts with its companion volume, "The Called of God." The earlier gave prominence to God's relation to man; this gives prominence to man's relation and attitude to God.

May the blessing of Him, whose Word it was the author's joy to interpret, accompany these sermons still.

J. A. PATERSON.

NEW COLLEGE, EDINBURGH,
December 1903.

b

CONTENTS

I

WAITING UPON GOD

ISAIAH xl. 27, 31

"Why sayest thou, O Jacob,
And speakest, O Israel,
My way is hid from the Lord,
And my judgment is passed over from my God?
.   .   .   .
They that wait upon the Lord shall renew their strength;
They shall mount up with wings as eagles;
They shall run, and not be weary;
They shall walk, and not faint."

THESE chapters of Isaiah, from the 40th to the end, are spoken to Israel, the Church in captivity. Jerusalem is in ruins, the cities of Judah are without inhabitants, the land is wasted, the people desolate and in exile. That is the state of things assumed. And to the Church, in this condition, the comforts and promises are spoken: "Comfort ye, comfort ye My people. Speak ye comfortably to Jerusalem, and cry unto her that her warfare is accomplished." The Exile is nearly over, the redemption draweth nigh; the glory is ready to be revealed, a glory twice as

3

high as the sin into which she had sunk herself is deep.

The prophet represents Jehovah as declaring: " I am the Lord that confirmeth the word of His servant; that saith to Jerusalem, Thou shalt be inhabited; and to the cities of Judah, Ye shall be built : that saith to Cyrus, He is My shepherd, and shall perform all My pleasure: even saying to Jerusalem, Thou shalt be built; and to the temple, Thy foundation shall be laid." Now, this state of things did not come about till nearly two centuries after Isaiah's time ; and that a prophet should direct his consolations to a state of the Church, not of his own day, but so far future, has been thought by some so wonderful as to be quite incredible. And they therefore suppose that not Isaiah, but some prophet living during the Exile, was the author of these prophecies. That is a question, however, which does not in the least affect the meaning of the prophecies. These prophecies are directed primarily to the Church in captivity, whether by a prophet contemporary with the Exile, or by one living a century and a half before it.

The state of banishment and desertion had lasted long ; it had become chronic and ordinary, even almost matter of course. The people seemed hardly to expect release. They had long ago concluded, struggling against the conclusion, but forced to conclude that God had given them over, saying : " My way is hid from the Lord." Suddenly, unexpectedly, a voice falls from heaven :

"Comfort ye, comfort ye My people." It is hasty and peremptory, as if the Lord Himself had suddenly come to realise the position of His people, and repented of His indifference toward them; and was hurried on by the force of His own regrets to lose no time, and move both Himself and others now at last in behalf of them. "I have too long holden My peace. Comfort ye, comfort ye My people." There is almost a tinge of self-reproach in the words *My* people—*Mine*; and I have neglected them, refrained Myself from helping them, been silent about them among the heathen; heard them reviled, seen them afflicted—My people; therefore, now comfort them. Cry to Jerusalem that her warfare is over, that her hard service in exile and bondage to the nations of the earth is done; that her iniquity is pardoned; that she has received of the Lord's hand double for all her sins; that the height of glory to which God's mercy is now about to raise her is twice as high as the depth of sin into which she has fallen. "Not as is the offence, so also is the free gift; but where sin abounded, grace did much more abound."

The passage from ver. 27 contains one of the many remonstrances of the returning God with Israel over her despondency and want of faith: "Why sayest thou, O Jacob, My way is hid from the Lord?" For Zion had said: "The Lord hath forsaken me, and my Lord hath forgotten me." God expostulates with the Church concerning this despondency and hopelessness, and the passage might be described as God's answer to religious depression; and the answer in brief is this: "They that wait upon the Lord shall renew their strength."

The answer is given in the shape of a remonstrance. God wonders at men's faithlessness. He couples His teaching with a reproach—"Have ye not known, have ye not heard? Can ye not be taught?" But it is in sorrow, not in anger; He is grieved for the hardness of their hearts. It is more in the tone than in the words that the reproof is carried: "Why sayest thou, O Jacob, and speakest, O Israel, My way is hid from the Lord." He goes over the cry of depression and takes it asunder, and holds it up before the desponding sufferer to show its real contents, and what such expressions of despondency when looked at closely amount to— far more, perhaps, than the depressed heart imagines; and then, having probed the disease, he administers the cure: "They that wait upon the Lord shall renew their strength."

It is not quite easy exactly to express these words— Why *sayest* thou? It means, why art thou always saying —murmuring, continually concluding: My way is hid? My *way* means my condition, my fate, my manner of being treated, is hid from the Lord, is unseen by Him, unobserved by Him, escapes His notice. Either He cannot see it, or He does not care to look at it. And my judgment is passed over from my God; my *judgment*, that is, the judgment which should be done, or at least which used once to be done, in my behalf—my defence, the help I need against my foes, the rights and protection due, or at least once afforded me—is passed over from my God and neglected by Him. This is what Israel, a solitary slave, far away in Babylon, kept talking, muttering, murmuring to herself in feeble, despondent, half querulous tones, her mind full of memories of former times—of her land, her history, her God. I am fallen out of the view of my God now; He is occupied surely with other interests that absorb Him; He has become forgetful, or at least weary of me; and my history is tame and unattractive to Him; and His promises to me have been forgotten. If not, surely if He means to save, now is the time, if the time be not already past. Thus she brooded over her state of desertion, ran over its details, and ever as she realised her miseries, darker from the light of her former joy, and thought of that former joy, more bright from the gloom of her present depression, she concluded, and kept murmuring to herself : "My way is hid from the Lord, and my judgment is passed over from my God."

In sorrow the mind does not set very clearly before itself the meaning of its feelings. It is blinded by mists, and does not think so much as feel in the dark. And not seeing clearly, it may not be always quite responsible for the real meaning of its complaints. Sorrow and desertion are to be tenderly handled and judged of. We may not pass judgment on the language they utter, but we may in tenderness lay bare its real meaning. God here takes asunder, in His reply, this complex, dreary, dim complaint. Put into thoughts, that vague murmur of the depressed heart amounts to this : either that God was not aware of Israel's fate, that His observation was limited, and did not extend so far ; or, if aware, that He could not or did not care to save ; or, if He cared and could, that He surely could not judge rightly when salvation should be shown.

God's answer shows that, in His view, Israel's complaint could be so resolved. To the first supposition, that He was not aware of Israel's condition, He answers that He is an eternal God, Creator of the ends of the earth. This mission extends to all parts of the world, for He made it all. To the second supposition, that if He knew, He was unable to help, He replies He can save—" He fainteth not, neither is weary." He is not absorbed, overpowered with other interests, His arms wearied with the reins of government, and glad for a time to let them slip to ease Himself. And to the last, that if He can and will, He surely cannot discriminate well when to interfere, it is answered, He well knows the right time ; "there is no searching of His understanding." He will seize the right juncture to make bare His arm, that all the ends of the earth may see His salvation ; and Israel herself will yet confess that in folly and in impatience she clamoured for a premature deliverance.

I am far from saying that religious depression may always be resolved into one or other of the above three things. It is too complex a thing, perhaps, to be

capable at all times of being analysed at all. But here
at least is one analysis of it. This religious depression
of Israel was so analysed by God. And we may well
fear lest our own may be resolvable into the same
elements. For, if we were to convert those dark, dim,
gloomy forebodings and fears, out of anticipations
into thoughts, might we not find ourselves saying in
effect some one or more of these things? God cannot
save, or God does not care to save, or God does not
know the right time to save. And that is not the
spirit, surely, of those whom God ever will save. "They
that wait upon the Lord shall renew their strength."

And now, having analysed this depression, God gives
His answer to it. This depression is certainly a state
of feebleness. It may also be a state of sin, and, when
looked at closely, of downright unbelief. But at least
it is one of feebleness, of weakness. And there is only
one way to renewed strength—"they that wait upon the
Lord shall renew strength." This truth is the burden of
the passage; but it is stated in several ways, and even
the reason of it is given. The Lord is the strong; He is
Creator of the ends of the earth, He fainteth not, neither
is weary. Since He is strong, they who wait on Him
become strong. Lying beside Him, they imbibe His
strength. From sympathy, if from nothing else, they
themselves grow strong. The child is strong beside the
Father: fear not, for I am with thee; I hold thee by
My right hand, as one leads a little child. When the
child feels our stronger hand grasp his, his fear subsides,

and he shares our strength. The Lord fainteth not, He giveth power to the faint. It is natural at first sight, without inquiring very deeply into the reason, that they who are in sympathy and fellowship with the Omnipotent should themselves be potent. It makes us strong to feel ourselves beside power. But it is the fact, rather than the reasons of it, that is the chief thing shown here : "they that wait upon the Lord renew their strength." This fact is shown on two sides : they who wait are strong, and they who do not wait have no strength. The youths faint; but they who wait renew their strength. The truth taught is: *the weakness of all strength which is not divine, and the strength of weakness when it waits for God.* " Even the youths shall faint and be weary, and the young men shall utterly fall : but they that wait upon the Lord shall renew strength."

On the one side, all strength which is not divine is weakness : the youths faint. Natural strength has no permanence; there is no power of self-renewal in it when it fails. It is speedily, often suddenly, exhausted. Youth, lavish of its energy, becomes feeble; overwork exhausts it; years bring it to infirmity; the strongest in a few years may be seen tottering to the grave; and it utterly falls, comes too often to the ground even in the midst of its days. A fever, an accident—how little physically; a surprise, an emergency, a sudden perplexity, a temptation—how small a thing morally, puts an end to it, and makes it utterly fall. But they who wait upon the Lord renew strength, draw out of Him new moral and even mental energy. A surprise, a temptation, but brings to light their hidden strength; every new term of life evolves new reaches of capacity; and if it seem to contract and be for a moment spent, the reaction but develops greater energy.

It is a great mystery, this fainting and wearying of the youths—premature death—the exhaustion and burning out of greatly endowed but passionate natures that utterly fall. The loss of strength, the expenditure of life and power in the universe, is incalculable. Nature is very prodigal of her means. She flings countless seeds into the soil that she never vitalises; and of the countless seeds that she brings to life she takes the trouble to mature but a very few. She brings myriads of human souls into existence, a crop thick and fresh, and then she neglects them. Like a thriftless housewife, she wades about among her resources and lavishes them, indifferent alike to pain and hope and loss. The youths faint and are weary. The vital energy subsides in them, and they die. The world is filled with vain efforts that realise no effect, with great promises that are not fulfilled. It is somehow the greatest promises that are oftenest broken. It is the choice young men, as the word means, that utterly fall. We have seen some young spirit, endowed with wondrous gifts, rise like a star upon the horizon of our day, and move among other lights in the sky, easily to be detected from all others, with a light like none else—a colour of

power peculiar to himself, a complexion of luminous-
ness the world had seldom seen, but longed to see and
retain and rejoice in; and, when the eyes of many
worshippers were being turned to it, it was seen to
become troubled and obscured, or suddenly to shoot
away into the darkness. We comfort ourselves by
thinking that it is not extinguished, but gone to rise
and shine on another horizon than ours. But that does
not solve the mystery why it became dark to us; why
we were promised the comfort and the shining of its
light, and the promise was utterly broken; why so many
great beginnings are made, that reach nothing.

The youths become weary, and the choice young men
utterly fall. It is the choice young men that utterly fall;
their fall is often signal; like a brilliant meteor, they
come down. This is oftenest seen in moral falls. It is
in the choice young men that these are most notable—in
the finely endowed, in the generous, in the lofty-minded,
in the ardent and adventurous. When the fire of the soul
burns most brightly, men see clearest when it burns out.
There are, indeed, some young men who cannot be said
to fall. For only those can fall who have reached some
elevation. There are men who can hardly be said to
have ever been young, men who come into the world
with all the ways of age about them — calculating,
scheming, imperturbable men, who never knew a
generous impulse, who were never guilty of any folly,
—men who always know their whereabouts, who will
rigidly audit and tax even their dubious pleasures lest

they pay beyond the market price for them. These are men of whom Scripture does not say that they fall. They can hardly fall. It is the choice young men, the men of strong natures, but uncontrolled; the men of impulse, carried away by their passions like a reckless rider—capable of all powerful and beautiful and noble deeds, if they were but controlled by Heaven; it is they who utterly fall.

They who wait upon the Lord renew their strength. This is the victory that overcometh the world, even our faith. Whatsoever is born of God overcometh the world. Men are so made that only the love of God rules their whole nature. As the heavens draw the ocean from its farthest shore, and lead it on in rising tides, so God alone can move the nature of man to its deeps, and command it all. Other affections sometimes move it for a time. Appetite will promise much to human love, and it will perform something. It will for a time deny itself. But after a brief space it will generally break its vows, and even be mad and brutal to the object to whom it once promised all things.

And there are many perplexities arising from the world which nothing at all in any way meets except God. Doubts, the darkness of life, this very thing,— that men give way to evil,— the world furnishes no clue to penetrate this mystery; only waiting on God can clear it up. Only men of faith are victorious over all things. Other men are men of power on some sides, often on many sides, but never on all sides. They are always weak somewhere, vanquished somewhere by some passion, or failing, or want of self-control, or excess. They have all some weak point—some place exposed in their armour of strength. Only the men of faith who wait on the Lord are strong all round. They overcome all—the world. All things are under their feet.

Now, this leads to the other side of the truth of the text : that weakness which waits on God becomes strong. "They that wait on the Lord renew strength." To wait is not merely to remain impassive. It is to expect—to look for with patience, and also with submission. It is to long for, but not impatiently ; to look for, but not to fret at the delay ; to watch for, but not restlessly ; to feel that if He does not come we will acquiesce, and yet to refuse to let the mind acquiesce in the feeling that He will not come. And weakness that so waits shall be made strong. God will give it strength. For you have seen how strong this kind of weakness is among ourselves ; how it has the power of winning all the strength of the strong to itself. This weakness is attractive, lovely ; and what of power we have, though it should for ever exhaust ourselves, we will expend for it. Weakness that leans and waits, and is not importunate or clamorous, but only looks with confident, beseeching eyes, that weakness has at its command all the strength of the strong. And that which is lovely to men may be so to God. Dependent, waiting weakness is beautiful in His eyes—trust wins Him. " Without faith, it is impossible to please God." All other things are defective without it—this beautiful, confiding weakness. And He bestows upon it all strength. For this is just the condition that He asks—*faith*. Faith is confidence in one that he will do what it is his natural position to do. It is the confidence, the trust of weakness in strength. It is that which binds all society together— the servant to the master, the child to the father, the wife to the husband, men to God.

And to reward such trust is that which men love most to do. It is sweet to look into the upturned childish face of depending weakness and help it; to fulfil its desires, nay, far overpass them; to expend one's strength in making it strong. And this is the delight even of our Father in heaven. His existence, as far as He comes out of His eternal placitude, is passed in helping weakness, waiting weakness : " They that wait upon the Lord renew strength." And is this not the natural place for us to take to the blessed God, who gives us all ? Surely *He* is one on whom we may wait; surely what we desire is something we may wait for : to wait on Him as for the morning. It is His to give; and ours to wait, that He may give.

But if this that we see among men leads us to hope that if we wait on God He will give us strength, there are things about waiting itself that make us hope that if we wait we shall become strong. God gives us strength, by causing us to become strong. They who wait renew, put out new strength. It is good that a man hope and quietly wait. We gather strength by waiting. The very waiting leads to strength. It is not well for man to succeed too soon. It is not a disadvantage to be unrecognised for a time. Precocious growths are rarely permanent—are often lank and rickety. There are two mistakes that men commit: they gather the fruit ere it be ripe, or they hasten it into premature maturity. It is good to mature slowly and alone, to become at home with our own power ourselves first of all. It is good to know ourselves, to measure ourselves; and it is sweet to feel, at least at certain periods of life, that we have a power, and that, though men do not acknowledge it now, they shall one day be found doing homage to it. But it is the greatest of powers to be independent of outward recognition. And it is especially dangerous to receive it too soon. For it becomes needful. The mind grows up along with it, and cannot want it. And it is sickly and irritated when it is withdrawn, and falls into premature incapacity and pettishness. Those who have exercised the greatest influence on the world have worked long in the dark —struggling on with themselves. Disappointments, defeats, repulses are the education of strong natures.

There are, indeed, some delicate natures that are destroyed by failure. Fruits that ripen only under sunshine are soured by chills. But strong natures are mellowed by the frosts of fortune. Waiting prunes their too hasty and merely leafy outgrowths. To wait throws us in upon ourselves; lets us know what we are made of; what we can endure if put to it, and what we cannot. "Tribulation worketh patience, and patience experience." It reveals to us our resources; makes us ransack and pry into every corner of our nature; or it reveals to us if we have no resource but to wait upon the Lord. Waiting is the way to strength —to find our own strength, if we have any; to find strength in God, if we have none within ourselves.

It is, no doubt, often a great mystery to us why we have to wait so long. The fruitlessness of our efforts is a wonder to us. It seems often as if our life were to be consumed in waiting, and in the end receiving nothing:

> "Dropping buckets into empty wells,
> And growing old in drawing nothing up,"

as if we had to exhaust ourselves looking. As the Psalmist wrote, " Mine eyes fail while I wait for my God." He became blind, looking for God! He looked so long that he lost the only power he had—the power of looking. What oftentimes do our mental conflicts come to—our efforts to pierce the darkness? We wait for light, and behold obscurity. We are beaten back, and seem weaker than before. And what do all the world's efforts come to, in the way of thought? System displaces system, and nothing seems gained. Things are without result. We have the same complaint to make as the preacher of old: "All the rivers run into the sea, and the sea is not full." Nothing comes of anything. Things seem in an eternal flux; but they

2

flow nowhere.   But surely they who wait upon the Lord
shall renew strength.   That harvest of our hopes and
thoughts, which year after year comes up, and has not
power to ripen into fruit, is not without use; it is not
lost.   It falls and withers ; but it falls about our own
roots, and feeds the soil, which shall yet yield a harvest worth the gathering.   Let us be assured that we
shall reap if we faint not.   They that wait upon the
Lord shall renew strength—shall put it out anew as
the tree in spring.   This is the figure conveyed in the
word.   The promise is beautiful as well as blessed.   It
sets the winter and the spring in contrast—the winter
of chill, and feebleness, and desertion—the spring of
light, and power, and returning sunshine.   The winter
is the time of waiting ; the spring the time of putting
out strength.   It is the absence of the sun that makes
winter, and you who wait for the light of God's face
know how it is.   When the sun moves low around the
horizon, and gives no quickening, but is choked by fogs,
the very light about him seeming to make the gloom
more terrible ; when his face is not clear but fiery, and
the heavens do not shine but lower—this is the winter
of God's distance.   But it does not always last.   It
shall surely and speedily come to an end.   As infallibly
as one season follows on another, shall they who wait
through their winter of desertion put out new strength.
The time of quickening shall come, the fresh power shall
begin to move and throb in all their pulses with the
fulness of spring, and every withered limb shall be green

and fruitful; and the shining of God's countenance shall be upon them down from an unclouded heaven.

Now, just look at the ways in which God puts this promise, to make it certain that they who wait shall put forth new strength. In the first place, this waiting is just *faith*; and this is all that God asks. To this He promises, to this He gives, everything. If thou canst believe—to him that believeth, all things are possible. And then again, He puts it into a law of our own minds —they that *wait* shall renew strength. We know that it is the law of our minds that waiting gives us strength; helps us to resolve our difficulties; to look about us, and become familiar with our condition, and thus reach, through reflection, assurance and hope. We begin to apply to our case great laws which we know, great principles regarding God's love to men in Christ; and thus, out of weakness, through God helping us, we gather strength. And, once more, God has given another wonderful confirmation. He has put this spiritual process into the terms of a law of the outer world, saying, that as He acts in nature, so He acts in grace; that as certainly as the joy and strength of spring follow on the darkness and weakness of winter, so certainly shall He return in light and power to the sinner, who waits patiently through the winter of His distance. And to all who do so there is the promise— "They that wait upon the Lord shall renew strength." Surely further confirmation of the truth is not needed; but if it were, Scripture is full of it. There is hardly

any word so often read as *wait*, or such things said of
it. "The Lord is good to them that wait for Him.
Blessed are they that wait for Him. They that wait
on the Lord shall inherit the earth. Let none that
wait on Thee be ashamed. They shall not be ashamed
that wait for Me. I will wait on the Lord, who hideth
His face, and will look for Him. I waited patiently
for the Lord; and He inclined unto me, and heard my
cry. To them that wait for Him shall He appear the
second time without sin unto salvation." And Scripture
is likewise full of examples of men who waited—who
waited so long, that the power of waiting seemed
exhausted; but who, after all, put out strength. One
impotent man lay a long time—a lifetime in that case,
eight-and-thirty years—waiting for the moving of the
water—a wintry life; but at last the Lord came to
him, and he renewed his strength. There are examples
even of men who waited not in conformity with the
promises of God, but in spite of His threatenings, in
spite of appearances, and what seemed plainly visible
methods of God's dispensational providence.

It is a distinction made much of by theologians, that
God is not obliged to fulfil His threats; but He is
obliged to fulfil His promises. That means that God's
mercy is to be hoped in against all things whatever that
make any appearance to the contrary. His mercy in
Christ is general, all-embracing, deep; His threats can
but apply to particular cases. The faith of the Syro-
phenician woman is often extolled as wonderful, and

of this kind. And perhaps it is; but I think there is
greater faith shown more than once in Old Testament
history. For the Lord surrendered to the woman
everything, when He conceded to her and her maniac
child the position and relation of the dogs. Jesus said
unto her : " Let the children first be filled : for it is not
meet to take the children's bread, and cast it to the
little dogs." The Lord must have expected to be
entangled in His talk here. A mind less acute than
a woman's in misery, must have seen its advantage.
In a great house like His, the little dogs under the
table have a place, and rights; they, too, shall be
satisfied, fed—not first, but certainly some time ; perhaps
not last. The woman and her child are safe when in
such a house ; they are assigned the place where the
children drop their crumbs. There is no want there.
And she saw it, and answered : " Yes, Lord : for the little
dogs, too, under the table, eat of the children's crumbs."
Perhaps the advance the woman made upon the Lord's
concession just lay here—He admitted she might
receive after the children. She, by speaking of the
children's crumbs, put in a plea for not waiting till
they were done ; but for receiving a little, a falling
crumb even, in the meantime. And the Lord wondered
at the keenness of her faith ; and He said unto her :
" For this saying, go thy way : the devil is gone out of
thy daughter."

There is a case of waiting in the Old Testament—
cited also by the Lord, and wondered at by Him, as

was this woman's faith—which goes beyond all prece-
dent. It is the case of the Ninevites. Everything was
against them. They were a heathen nation—beyond
the pale of God's dispensation of mercy. They lay
under an express and definite threat of destruction—
"In forty days Nineveh shall be destroyed." The Lord
had even gone out of His way to threaten them. Had
they a single spar of hope to cling to? Not one, except
this, that God had threatened them—that He had gone
out of His way to threaten them. And their faith was
very marvellous. They turned His threats, and their
very extraordinariness, into a kind of promise. They
did not believe His threats. They felt what we are
entitled to feel, that when God threatens, He is promis-
ing; that when God comes near us in anyway,—if we
hear of Him, if He is at the trouble to threaten us,—
He comes near for our salvation. Look how they
reasoned. They proclaimed a fast, and put on sack-
cloth, and cried mightily to the Lord, saying: Who can
tell if God will not turn and repent; and turn away from
His fierce anger, that we perish not? Their only argument was, Who knows—who can tell? Everything
was against them; their great sin, their heathendom,
the peremptoriness and marvel of the prediction against
them; but they waited: they would not have it so—
who can tell? Unless someone can say for certain
that God will not turn and repent, they will wait.
That is the length faith will go. It will hold on by a
thread so slender as that; it will hope in God's mercy,

when there is nothing to be said for it, and everything to be said against it, short of this, that no one can say *for certain* that it may not be shown ; who knows—who can tell if He will not turn ?

Finally, it is said how this renewed strength manifests itself. It does so in every variety of way.

They mount up with wings like eagles ; they soar in moments of ecstasy, in clear thought and feeling, breaking the cords that bind them to the earth, and pressing towards God Himself—upward with strong wing and eagle eye. They have moments of joy and vision.

They run and are not weary. In the struggle of life, in its race and battle, they are girt, and succinct, and strong ; and, when others fall off the course, to hide their defeat and die, they are victorious. In the crisis, in the hurried moment of swift decision and prompt action, they are strong. The youths faint and are weary, but they run and are not weary.

They walk and do not faint. In the dull, plodding, weary journey of life they faint not ; over its monotonous, hard-beaten, uphill, uninteresting way, in which there are few glimpses of earth beautiful enough, and few glimpses of heaven clear enough, to cheer them ; and few enough travellers met that have any sympathy to enliven them ; when the way to come is like the way gone—hard, monotonous, uphill,—in the dull, grey walk of life they faint not.

These three—soar, run, walk—might seem a falling

climax, but they are not; they rise. It is easier to mount heavenward with eagle's wing, taking short, rapid, upright, strong, far-piercing flights of thought, direct toward God's throne. This, which is oftener a gift than a virtue, is easier than to run the race of life—the hot, dusty, keenly-contested race of living well, which needs a steady eye, and a strong breath, and a practised foot, and calculation of the distance, and measuring of one's strength, and coolness, lest a seeming defeat should lead to too hasty and exhausting action, and one be forced to retire. But even this is easier than the *walk*—the lonely, cheerless, lifelong, monotonous tread, when a man is cast quite on himself, without excitement, or emulation, or immediate gain and prize. It is then that one most surely faints. To live an ordinary life well is the greatest of all deeds. To utter noble thoughts at a time, to do noble actions in the heat of emulation and on the field, that is less severe. To do well the common things of life, to do them always well—that is hardest. It is just then, in the walk of life, that men are most liable to faint. "But they that wait upon the Lord shall renew strength; they shall mount up with wings as eagles; they shall run, and not be weary; they shall walk, and not faint."

II

THE SERVANT OF THE LORD

II

THE SERVANT OF THE LORD

ISAIAH xlii. 1–4

> "Behold My servant, whom I uphold;
> My chosen, in whom My soul delighteth:
> I have put My spirit upon him;
> He shall bring forth judgment to the Gentiles.
> He shall not cry, nor lift up,
> Nor cause his voice to be heard in the street.
> A bruised reed shall he not break,
> And the smoking flax shall he not quench:
> He shall bring forth judgment in truth.
> He shall not fail, nor be discouraged,
> Till he have set judgment in the earth;
> And the isles shall wait for his law."

THE prophet presents to us here one whom Jehovah calls His servant, or rather he represents Jehovah as presenting him to us: "Behold My servant." And He particularly specifies the service in which He employs him: "He shall bring forth judgment to the Gentiles." By judgment is meant very much *religion*, practical true righteousness and godliness. The office this servant of God has before him is this,—and it is not a small service—to make the Gentiles righteous, to set judg-

27

ment, justice, and truth in the earth. That is not a small service even if we look at the present condition of the world, where iniquity and injustice and false methods of action and untrue ways of thinking are still prevalent, after so long a leavening of the world with Christian opinion and Christian living. But it might seem a greater service then, when this prophet lived, when the gigantic monarchies and institutions of the time were mere embodiments of force or human passion ; when "judgment," that is, the practice of law and equity, and right feeling, and just discrimination, and sympathy for the weak, and a due sensibility to all the various sides of human character and life, and a proper or any sense of responsibility, in what was done, to God above—when judgment in this sense was almost universally absent from the world, when darkness covered the earth and gross darkness the people, and only on a small speck of land and the insignificant community of Israel had the Lord's light arisen, and His glory been seen.

It is in these conditions that the servant is introduced and his mission declared, and also the triumphant certainty of its success : " He shall not fail, nor be discouraged, till he have set judgment in the earth ; and the isles shall wait for his law."

I. We have here presented to us one called servant of the Lord ; and we have the declaration of God regarding him, that He holds him fast, and that His soul delighteth in him ; and we have a statement of the

service which this servant of the Lord is to perform
for Him : he shall bring forth judgment, or right, to
the Gentiles, to the nations of the earth, the world
universally.

This prophecy was written certainly not less than
five or six hundred years before Christ. And it may
not be quite easy to discover whom the prophet had
in his mind, when he spoke of the servant of the Lord.
If we look at the end of the preceding chapter, we find
the Lord passing a judgment of condemnation on the
Gentile nations and their false gods: " Behold, they
are all vanity ; their works, that is, their idols, the works
of their hands, are nothing: their molten images are
wind and confusion." The nations are vanity ; they have
no power within them, or destiny before them ; at least,
if they have a destiny, it is one which they cannot
reach by themselves; for that which should enable
them to reach it, the god among them, is but wind
and confusion. If they have a destiny before them,
as they have, they must be helped to reach it from
without. Then, in opposition to these nations, the
servant of the Lord is introduced, who shall enable
them to reach the blessed end set before them by
God : " Behold My servant: he shall bring forth judgment to the Gentiles."

It certainly seems from this, and from the general
scope of these chapters, that the prophet spoke of
Israel under the name of servant of the Lord—Israel
as God's missionary and prophet among the nations ;

or, if not of Israel as a whole, of those in Israel who
truly represented the idea of Israel, and to whom the
name Israel attached. Israel had a mission to the
world ; Israel had an ideal character. As true to that
character, and as fulfilling that mission, Israel was to
the prophet's mind the servant of the Lord. But this
was never more than a splendid conception. Israel
never realised her true character, never rose to the
idea expressed by the name, and, therefore, never fulfilled the mission set before her. At last there came
one who gathered together in himself all the bright
lines of Israel's character and endowments, who truly
rose up to the height of the ideal Israel, and was in
truth the servant of the Lord. In him all the things
said here were fully verified. He is the true servant
of the Lord. His own consciousness bears testimony to
the perfection of his service : " I do alway those things
that please Him." He is kept hold of and sustained
by the Father : " He that sent me is with me." " I am
not alone, for the Father is with me." And God Himself hath testified of him on His side : " This is My
beloved Son in whom I am well pleased." The ideal
conception of the prophet, sketched so long before, was
realised at last.

The prophet so conceived Israel, and not wrongly ;
for all its forces and all its endowments, like vital saps,
were moving on to form this glorious fruit. Is it not
strange that such ideas should have risen in the prophet's
mind so long before? and strange that at the last

they were verified? In what other lands had such conceptions birth? or in what other land had they verification? But stranger than anything else are the ideas themselves—one whose consciousness testified to him that he was a true servant of God—one of whom the Lord Himself testifies that His soul delighteth in him. And this testimony of the servant's mind was not that of a fanatical mind whose enthusiasms and warmth prevent a calm verdict; nor was it that of a superficial conscience whose moral depth was small and its moral censures lax. It was the testimony of one who judged himself no less strictly than he did others, and whose judgment on the ordinary run of morality was this: "I say unto you, Except your righteousness shall exceed even the righteousness of the scribes and Pharisees, ye shall in no case enter into the kingdom of heaven."

And such testimony from God as that He is pleased, is not easily extorted. God *is* an austere master. He docs not lightly applaud; "He trieth the hearts and the reins." No doubt He might say He was pleased in Israel, imperfect though Israel was, because Israel contained within it forces and vital energies that were yet to combine themselves in the true servant. No doubt He is graciously pleased with His Church now, though very deformed and wrinkled, and with each soul that believes, because they are one with His true servant. But, to begin with, only absolute purity will please Him; He will abate no jot of His demand for perfect

service.   And He testifies here that He is pleased—" in
whom My soul delighteth "—pleased to the very soul.
This is the testimony of Him of whom aforetime it was
said: "The Lord looked down from heaven upon the
children of men, to see if there were any that did understand and seek God.   They are all gone aside : there is
none that doeth good, no, not one." Well might He
direct our attention to this person : Behold My servant!
—one with a clear conscience towards God ; one with
whom God is pleased.   It is the wonder of wonders, the
most transcendent of miracles to anyone who knows
himself, to anyone who has broken through that
which is merely sensible to any thought of a spiritual
God.

What it was in the servant which made God delight
in him, we need not inquire.   Our minds can suggest
many things.   The Lord was pleased with the servant
because of what the servant was in himself.   But He
was pleased with him because he was, as His servant,
undertaking so great a task—to bring forth judgment
to the Gentiles.   It was a chivalrous task that the
servant was undertaking, to set *right* in the earth,
if we will only think of it.   Only a very lofty spirit
would face it, only one endowed with great resources
and conscious of them, and yet, if we might say so,
altogether prodigal of them, ready to fling away himself and all that he was upon a splendid but almost
impossible enterprise, with entire forgetfulness of himself in the fascination of his object.   To God as well

as man such an unselfish enthusiasm must be a delight. Apart from all other things, which our minds, now enlightened by further revelation of the relations of this servant to God, can discern,—apart from all else, this self-abandonment of the servant, this readiness to fling himself alone, when of the people there was none with him, upon an enterprise so humane, yet so vast and dangerous, must have made him dear to God : " Therefore doth the Father love me, because I lay down my life, that I may take it again."

II. In vv. 2–3 we have presented to us the servant's method of fulfilling his great task of setting right in the earth : " He shall not cry nor lift up, that is, lift up his voice, nor cause his voice to be heard abroad ; a bruised reed he shall not break, and the smoking flax he shall not quench." The second verse describes his way of presenting himself to others, and the third his way of treating those who present themselves to him. There is no loudness nor violence ; no contentiousness nor aggressiveness nor undue assertion of himself : "He shall not cry nor lift up his voice." He feels it enough to present himself, to appear among men like a light that shines in silence, and yet draws all eyes to it. He assumed that the truth had an attractiveness of itself, that it made its way best, or only, by its own force ; that all other means of propagating it, as by violence or compulsion, or even of giving it a forced prominence by loud and artificial methods, or by anything other than its simple self, did not help, but rather

3

detracted from its effect.   The good shepherd's sheep
follow him, for they know his voice ; but it is its *tone*,
not its loudness, that they recognise.   " Everyone that
is of the truth heareth my voice."

That is about the hardest and the deepest word in
Scripture. If we are of the truth, we will hear him ; and
if we hear him not, it is because we are not of the truth.
That word may be no solution of our problems, of our
faith or our unbelief; it may be no solution, but it is
the last word that can be said of them in lieu of a
solution—" Everyone that is of the truth heareth my
voice."   And, again, an apostle says : " By the manifestation of the truth commending ourselves to every
man's conscience."

It always gives a clearness to the words of Scripture
to realise the circumstances in which they were spoken.
If the prophet is here thinking of Israel as a people,
and of the methods which, when restored and become
the servant of the Lord, it shall employ in teaching the
nations and in all its intercourse with them, he is pre-
dicting a complete revolution in national feeling, and
in the relations of nations to one another.   In his day
each nation thought of all others as its natural enemies.
It could only prosper at their expense and by their
defeat.   And there was only one instrument by which
influence could be gained, namely, the sword.   The
empires of Assyria and Babylon, with which this
prophet was familiar, were incarnations of violence and
force, of everything that was not judgment or right, of

oppression and cruelty. Israel shall inaugurate a new
era among the nations, shall originate and realise among
the peoples a new conception of the relations of nations
to one another. Her swords shall be beaten into plough-
shares. Her voice shall not be loud in contention; she
shall not strive. "The remnant of Jacob shall be in the
midst of the peoples as a dew from the Lord, as the
showers upon the grass." Her mission as a people
shall be not to devastate other peoples, but to render
them fruitful, and quicken all the powers of growth and
life within them. Force and compulsion shall have
had their day, and another influence will be supreme:
" Arise, shine; for thy light is come, and the glory of the
Lord is risen upon thee. And the Gentiles shall come
to thy light, and kings to the brightness of thy rising."

The evangelist sees a fulfilment of these words of the
prophet in our Lord's manner of presenting Himself
while on earth: "Then the Pharisees went out and held
a council against Him; and when He knew it, He
withdrew Himself from thence. And great multitudes
followed Him, and He healed them all; and He
charged them that they should not make Him known,
that it might be fulfilled which was spoken by the
prophet: He shall not strive nor cry." He shunned
violent encounters with His enemies; He disliked the
loud applause of His friends. Controversy had no
attractions for Him; He cared less to attack error than
to exhibit truth. He believed more in that which was
positive than in negations. He did not go out and

fight with the darkness. The darkness, like most forms
of evil, is too impalpable to be fought with. It can be
overcome only by letting the great light shine, which
rolls it back, fold upon fold, till it has no more place.
And the popular incense rather stank in His nostrils.
He knew that the popular applause was not given to
Him on account of what He really was, or because
His real aims were understood. His works raised a
conception of a Messiah in men's minds, a false conception; and it was their own false conception that they
applauded and cried hosannah to. He did not misunderstand the nature of the task He came to perform,
to set right in the earth. That was not a task to be
accomplished in a moment. He was a sower. He
came to lodge seeds in the heart of humanity, which
would take long to germinate and long to bear fruit.
He came to commit principles to men's minds. Hence
He shunned all contention with His foes, and disliked the precipitancy of His followers. The truth
and the love needed neither to commend it; it worked
by a native energy of its own; it found in the world
something that it appealed to, something that was
waiting for it, and which would accept it and rejoice
in it, which would rise up with an instinctive energy
to meet it and lay hold of it.

The power of quietness is very great. Yet we are
always forgetting this, and are liable to great uneasiness in consequence. Rumours of great efforts of
other persons reach our ears, great efforts of speech or

labour in behalf of the truth, and we feel we are nothing and are doing nothing; and we are paralysed even in the small efforts which we had been making, and we either drop them altogether, or, what is almost worse, we are tempted to make unnatural efforts, and to enter on undertakings either beyond us or unsuitable to us. We are constantly tempted by the noise, whether genuine or fictitious, of those about us to do something convulsive, in order to show to ourselves and to others that we are a power, and for our own comfort to assert our place in the world or in the Church. But if all these extraordinary spurts are vain, the motive of them is often bad, and they are not fitted to advance righteousness. What we have to do is to live natural and godly lives, to let our light shine; whatever its natural colour and its natural brilliancy may be, to keep it burning. It is a mistake to think that nobody will see it. It will be seen both by those who despise it, and by those who will rejoice in it.

The world is full of observers. There is a keen outlook among men; many times, alas! it is directed to trifles, and attracted by what is superficial and evil, but it is observant. It is wonderful how we are watched, how men take knowledge of us, how our affairs are canvassed, our doings noted, and our histories conned,— all this many times from trifling motives and with malicious purpose, but not always. There are hearts open to the truth, eyes longing for the light, ears keen to catch even whispers from an unseen world. We do not need to cry nor lift up. Genuine godliness, however modest, will make itself felt.

There is a kind of godliness that only develops itself in the presence of the minister. It then becomes highly demonstrative, and lifts up its hands and shakes its head, and utters religious maxims and sentiments with a volubility resembling inspiration. Yet it is only acting. But there is another kind that does not cry nor obtrude itself, and yet cannot be hid. You have sometimes seen in some sorrow-stricken circle, when every other one was helpless, some person put out his hand to do some little service, or utter some simple reflection, which at once went to the hearts of all present, and not only approved the genuineness of his own religion, but went far to impress others. Genuineness, true sincerity, cannot be hid; it will as by an instinct make itself felt. And often it will do much. The effects are sometimes out of all proportion to our estimate of ourselves. The faith of the little Israelitish maid in the house of Naaman had great results. Her faith in the prophet of the Lord prompted her to speak, but her naturalness and modesty prompted her first to break the matter to her mistress; and she spoke to her husband, the great Syrian officer, and he was healed. We are all of us heard of, and referred to, in places that we never think of; and sometimes when we have been doing a simple duty, and only trying to do it well, and thinking nothing of it, we meet someone years after who will refer to it, and gladden us with some words of thanks regarding it. Do not cry nor lift up, nor let your voice be heard in the streets; do not cry, but *live*: let your light shine.

This was the servant's manner of presenting himself; similar was his manner of receiving and treating those that presented themselves to him: "The bruised reed he shall not break, the glimmering light he shall not quench." In order to see the real force of the passage, we must attend particularly, as we always should, both to the exact words, and to the precise circumstances in which they were spoken. The words are a bruised reed and a glimmering light. The reed was once whole; but something has fallen on it and crushed it, and it bends; and little is now needed completely to break it. The flame once burned more brightly; but the oil that fed it is well-nigh consumed, and it flickers in the socket. And when it is said that he will not break the one nor quench the other, the figure of speech implies that he will strengthen and set erect the reed, and feed and nurse into a flame the light.

The time in which the words were uttered was many hundred years before our Lord, when Israel was in exile, and the great empires of the world, Assyria and Babylon, were crumbling to pieces through their licentious and enfeebling idolatries, and their violence and want of judgment. In these circumstances the appli-

cations of the words 'a bruised reed' and 'a glimmering
light' might be, as they might still be, very many; to the
world, in which the primeval light of religion and truth
was burning more and more languid, and the sterner
virtues of simplicity and frugality and endurance were
growing more and more feeble, luxury and voluptuousness taking their place; to an exiled, oppressed people
—weary saints, far from the sanctuary, worn out with
waiting, crying, "The Lord hath forsaken me, and my
God hath forgotten me"; to men whose energies sin
or excess has undermined, and whose resistance to evil
is becoming less energetic; to those in whose hearts
the love of God is dying out, or in whose minds faith
is struggling to live amidst difficulties. The application
of the words may be manifold, but the principle is one;
and it is this: that the servant of the Lord, he on whom
God has put His spirit, has come into the world to save
it; to reinforce whatever of strength or light there
remains in it, or in any soul in it; that there is a power
now manifested among men, a divine power, with a love
and an affinity for whatever there is of strength or light
in them, and an irresistible desire to increase it till it
become perfect; one desiring truth in the inward parts,
one righteous and loving righteousness, one who looks at
men—at all men—on that side of them in which there
is any remains of good.

The words, "a bruised reed shall he not break, and
the smoking flax shall he not quench," do not mean
merely that if anyone came to him bruised, with all

the moral strength well-nigh gone out of him, or with the light of religion or conscience or grace flickering and ready to expire, he would deal mercifully, and strengthen such a mind. They do mean this; they meant it then, and they mean it now. If you are a bruised reed or a glimmering light, if you feel your strength not what it once was, that your resistance to sin is growing less, that the feeling of shame, which the commission of it was once followed by, is less acute, that the compunction and bitterness is shallower and of shorter duration, that you are giving in to it more and more as a matter of course; that the aspirations and nobleness of the old youthful days are dying out of you, and that, though you may be prospering, and cultivating some æsthetic tastes, there is a vital feebleness in your hearts, and a relaxation in your moral nerve,—if you feel this, or if you feel that the flame of faith or divine love in your heart is burning low; if the oil that fed it seems withdrawn, and there is a dryness, a worldly dryness about it; or if you are crushed and almost utterly broken under the sense of your sin, and the impossibility of doing anything to master it, and the awful weight of responsibility which the past lays upon you; if having been betrayed into evil your compunctions are stirred, and you go out and weep bitterly,—the words mean that he will not break but strengthen that bruised reed, that he will not quench but kindle that glimmering flame — the words mean this, because they mean more. They express rather the general view the servant took of his task, and of those among whom he came to exercise it. They were all bruised reeds, all glimmering flames. It was not one here or there; this was the universal condition. It was the condition of the world into which he came. The moral vigour of mankind was enfeebled; the universal conscience was shedding but a glimmering light.

This was the aspect the world presented to him, and into this world he flung himself—not a dead world, but one dying; not a cold burnt-out fire, but one smouldering under a heap of its own ashes; not a state of the human mind when all moral effort was beyond it, but when its efforts were becoming feebler and feebler, and there now remained but little more than the consciousness that all its efforts were hopeless. A dead world would have been beyond even him to resuscitate, and would have had no interest for him; a broken reed, even if healed, would have been another reed; an extinct fire, if kindled, would not have been the same fire. For this was precisely the thing that attracted him, the yet existing good that was in the world, the very life, languid as it was, that still beat in men's hearts. For this is love, mercy, pity—whatever name you call it—this attractiveness of life. Virtue, goodness, is the love of life; mercy, pity, is the love of struggling life.

Ah, it is life that binds us together—our mysterious, common, conscious life. It is this that binds us to one another, and binds God to us. One wonders many times at the unwearied devotion shown by a physician in

nursing, through all the vicissitudes of sickness, some
feeble life. The very feebleness of the life seems to
stimulate his ardour, and call out his energies; and he
will expend all his resources of knowledge and of art
in tending day and night the lingering vitality, and
breaking the mortal grasp of disease upon it. It matters
nothing to him that the life, when taken into the account
of the great sum of life in the world, may be really
worthless. It may be but an infant in some poor hovel,
which after its recovery may never be heard of again,
and may contribute little or nothing to the stock of
good in the world. Such thoughts never rise to his
mind; rather do its poverty and its infantile years and
its very worthlessness in all but this, that it is a life,
move his pity the more, and call out all his humanity,
and make the exercise of his office a sacred joy to
him. The joy of saving life arises from the feeling that
there is a responsive life to save; the poor bleached
check and the colourless eyes speak to him.

And such a feat it is which the servant of the Lord
is undertaking, but on a universal scale; and such feelings
animate him and sustain his efforts. The bruised reed
he will not break; it is the sympathy of life with life,
of full life with struggling life; the sympathy of
truth with truth, of the clear unclouded truth for the
dim, misty, choked, and labouring truth; of goodness
for goodness; of that which is all good for that which
has in it anything of good—in a word, the sympathy
and love and pity of the pure, unclouded, blessed God,

for the stained and darkened and troubled spirit of man.

There is no doubt that Jesus Christ inaugurated a new way of looking at men; that He taught us moral discrimination; that He habitually looked at any human character before Him not in the general, but with an eye that analysed it, and fastened on whatever element of goodness there was in it. All other things about a a man or a woman were to Him irrelevancies—the question for Him was whether there was one streak of goodness in the character, one avenue through which He could enter, one point in common with Himself which He could make a vantage ground. In His days, as in ours, men were judged in the gross, and general epithets applied to them,—they were publicans, and all publicans were avaricious and unpatriotic. They were harlots, and their touch was contamination; they were Samaritans, with whom no dealings could be had. Men had ceased to think, as we are always ceasing to think or feel, under the narcotic of general terms. But to Jesus Christ such general terms had no meaning. What He understood was a bruised reed, a glimmering light; that was what He looked for, what He was irresistibly drawn by, a failing, stricken, dying, but not dead, human spirit. He Himself announced as His motto: "The whole need not a physician, but they that are sick." The men and women saved by Him when upon the earth are all specimens of His method, a method which He still pursues.

One was a publican. Now the very reprobation of this class in the public opinion tended to bruise any better mind in it. No doubt, the very depth of the contempt shown might in the long run utterly extinguish all better feeling. But, until this was done, every mind among this class of a higher kind must have had many moments when very crushing sensations filled it. Sometimes after any act of cruel extortion, perhaps the judgment of the public would be acquiesced in, and the poor publican would feel himself sunk in unfathomable degradation. Sometimes, on the other hand, under the consciousness of better feelings stirring in him, and of a capacity to do well but for his circumstances, there would rise up a protest against the undiscriminating sentence of the world, and then would follow the crushing sense of injustice and the appeal of the heart to be understood. Jesus Christ understood this; and He recognised in Zaccheus that deeper goodness, covered up and buried by avarice and worldliness, yet bubbling up out of his deepest nature, like a pure spring through the heavy crust of earth, that deeper goodness which made him outrun the crowd to catch a look of Jesus — He recognised it, and He broke not the bruised reed, " for he also was a son of Abraham."

The same skill or rather divine instinct of fastening on what is good shows itself in Christ's treatment of the woman of Samaria. It might be doubted whether there was any good whatever in this woman beyond this, that she was a woman. She seems, indeed, to have passed through one stage of degradation after another till she reached the lowest. Yet there was this good about her, and it was perhaps the very thing that explains her badness. There was about her a certain openness and frankness of character, a certain give-and-take manner, which in youth must have been attractive, even though it then approached to levity, as later it grew coarse and immodest. She has none of the Oriental female's dread of a strange man ; she is too downright even to pretend to it. Everything is above board, and everything she feels she must express. When the Jewish stranger asks for a drink, she will not refuse ; but, instead of complying in silence, she goes to the root of the matter, and recalls to His mind what is implied in His asking it. And when He bids her call her husband, she lets in the light upon her history with a kind of self-mockery, saying she has no husband. One might run back through stage upon stage of this poor woman's history, from that last stage of it when she is allied to one who is not her husband, back, each stage becoming fairer and purer than the last, till one reached a bright, vivacious, open-hearted, spirited girlhood ; just as you scrape off year upon year of dust and daubing from some picture, and there comes out, at last, a precious masterpiece. And so the Lord did. He saw what was beneath—the glimmering light, the remains of innocency, a quick mind and an ingenuous, open, womanly spirit ; and to this He attached the truth, and thus He nursed the light into a flame.

The two figures, a bruised reed and a flickering light, might well express—the one, decaying spiritual strength; the other, a waning knowledge or faith. But it is not necessary to press the figures so as to imply merely that which is declining. They express that which is weak—power that is weak, faith and light that is feeble, whether it has once been stronger, or whether it be but yet in its beginnings. Whosoever of you is bruised with the sense of sin, with the sense of power-lessness, with the sense of a want of deepness and reality; bruised with the feeling that you are not bruised enough; troubled lest your trouble on account of sin should be too superficial; fearful lest the light in you should be but a false and transient flicker,—to you is the word of this salvation sent: "He will not break the bruised reed, he will not quench the smoking flax."

III. Third, a few words on what is said of the servant's success in his work: "He shall not fail, nor be dis-couraged, till he have set judgment in the earth; and the isles shall wait for his law." If there is anything more astonishing than another in the Old Testament, it is the faith of its prophets and writers. This prophet lived when Israel had ceased to exist. He operates not with Israel, but with the idea of Israel. Israel had vanished before the conquering world. Yet Israel, or something that would come out of Israel—the idea of Israel—

would rise and bring forth right to the nations, and the isles would wait on his instruction. And our Lord's enthusiasm is not less: " All power is given unto Me in heaven and in earth; go ye into all the world." The power given to Christ is just the kind of power required. He does not refer to the power that can launch a world into space, as the child spins his toy on the pavement; nor yet to the power that could raise up children to Abraham out of the stones. It is a different power which is His, and the use of which He has in some way committed to us. It is the power or powers suggested by the two figures—the glimmering light, the bruised reed. That which reinforces and moves into a flame the glimmering light is oil—symbol of something wholly divine—the unction of the Holy One. But though a tender divine hand may bind up the bruised reed, it is not immediately made whole. Only by accumulating toward the weakened part the natural forces of the whole plant, from the root upwards, can the weakness be healed.

Religion should be the concentration of all the powers of the mind. Our Lord uses words which will never cease to be astonishing: " The earth bringeth forth fruit of herself." The earth has powers of her own, which the seed calls into operation. The harvest is just these forces and natural powers concentrated, determining towards one point by the seed. We must endeavour to awake and carry forward the whole mind, the whole life of society, so that religion shall not be, as it were, an exotic cultivated on the mind, but the natural flower and fruit of man's whole mind and life. It is not only a great task, but it can only be accomplished in one way—a way that takes much time. The bruised reed cannot be healed at once. Suddenly to straighten it would but break it wholly. It must be gradually lifted up.

The process of healing is a long one, and embraces a multitude of appliances. We speak of the *power* of God as if it could effect anything and at once. The power of God is a power of many kinds. His power can kindle in the sun a fire so great that we may warm ourselves at it a hundred million of miles away from it. But this kind of power will not heal the broken reed. The power that does this is of a different kind, and works by different methods. This kind of power will not convert a mind to Himself, nor fashion it into His own image. It is another kind of power—love, patience, goodness, and continual fellowship—moving in the sphere of mind, and using the appliances proper in that sphere.

The statement that he shall not fail, is so made as to imply that there might be danger of his failing. The words, a bruised reed he shall not break, the smoking flax, *i.e.* the glimmering lamp, he shall not quench, are taken up and said of himself. He shall not fail or be quenched; he shall not be discouraged or broken, till he set judgment in the earth. Like those flickering, expiring lights among which he shall

4

walk, feeding their dim flame, he shall many a time feel dim, as if amidst all this darkness the light in himself must go out. Like those bruised reeds which he is engaged in healing, his own spirit will often seem bruised, as if, before the steady and powerful currents running against it, it must break. Yet he shall hold out. He shall bring forth judgment unto victory.

In another passage he is found expressing fatigue and despondency: " I have laboured in vain, I have spent my strength for nought, and in vain." The task seemed too great for him,—to set judgment in the earth. It is not the extent so much as the particularity of it that is immense. To make every human mind just, true, sensitive, sympathetic, godly; or even to make all the ruling minds, the outstanding, influential minds of this character, so that society on the whole shall be under this influence; or even to select and lay hold of one single human mind, and so change all its faculties as to subdue its whole nature to the colour of righteousness,—consider what a task this is. It might well seem hopeless.

Does it not often seem hopeless to ourselves, when we consider the subtlety in evil of our own minds, and their backwardness, and the delusiveness many times of what we thought improvement, and the disheartening relapses that occur, and how we turn even our good into evil, and when we have made some progress pride ourselves upon it, so that we only change the form of our badness, and a refined spiritual wickedness takes the place of a coarser sensual wickedness, and our last state is worse than our first? Indeed, when we consider all this, we are ready to despair.

And all this was plain to Him; and it is the case not of one mind only, but of the millions of minds which He has to perfect, each most subtle in evil, and each with its own manner of subtlety. If we were but able to read off to ourselves His mind, while upon the earth, it would be a startling page. And we should have the spectacle of a boundless enthusiasm, paired or alternating with a paralysing weakness; one with a sense of impotency making it His task to make others strong; one binding up broken hearts, while His own bled; one wiping away tears, while He wept Himself; one preaching the ever constant presence of God, while He cried out: My God, why hast Thou forsaken Me?

But He is far exalted above all this now, and remembers it only as waters which have passed away. And all power hath been given Him in heaven and in earth—all power of the kind that is necessary. And He is able to save unto the uttermost all them that come unto God by Him, seeing He ever liveth to make intercession for them. He will bring forth judgment unto truth. He that hath begun a good work in you will perfect it unto the day of His coming. He will so control your mind; He will so discipline it; He will so show you to yourself, and enable you to know your secret faults, and give you power over your springs of action ; He will so make all things to work for your good ; He will so keep His own most pure and blessed image before you, that at the last evil shall be overcome in your mind, and your whole body, soul, and spirit shall be blameless at His coming.

III

DAVID REPENTANT

III

DAVID REPENTANT

PSALM li. 1, 3, 7, 10, 13, 17

" Have mercy upon me, O God, according to Thy loving-
  kindness:
According unto the multitude of Thy tender mercies blot
  out my transgressions.
For I acknowledge my transgressions:
And my sin is ever before me.
Purge me with hyssop, and I shall be clean:
Wash me, and I shall be whiter than snow.
Create in me a clean heart, O God;
And renew a right spirit within me.
Then will I teach transgressors Thy ways;
And sinners shall be converted unto Thee.
The sacrifices of God are a broken spirit:
A broken and a contrite heart, O God, Thou wilt not
  despise."

PSALM li. is headed a psalm of David, when Nathan
the prophet came to him. This is the tradition regarding the composition of the psalm. There are
many, however, who consider that it belongs to a much
later time than this. Perhaps there are not materials
at hand for settling with certainty the date of the
psalm, and I shall assume that the circumstances in

which it was composed were those described in the heading.

It is not known very well how long David remained hardened and sullen after his great and double sin. At least he remained a certain number of months, unawakened, it would seem, to the exceeding badness of his act. Perhaps no one in the kingdom knew quite the full details of the affair. Some may have known or surmised the part of the transaction that occurred in Jerusalem, and some may have known the part that occurred in the field with the army. But perhaps not many were able to connect the things together, or saw through the intrigue from beginning to end. And the king himself, drunk with illicit pleasures, seemed dead to every feeling of a nobler kind, whether of shame or of remorse. But proportionate to his hardening in sin was the softening and break-down that came on him, when the prophet's words found their way to his heart. After a severe winter, the thaws of spring come with the greatest violence. When the earth is bound with an iron frost, and the streams are locked in ice, it is then, when the thaw-wind sweeps over the fields, that the freshening is wildest, when the ice breaks in pieces, and the rivers roll like mountains to the sea. And when the quickening spirit breathed upon the king's heart, it broke, and dissolved into the wildest sorrow.

The remorse or the repentance of a strong man is a thing worthy to be seen. If the man be very strong, he may remain master of himself, and, in the view of others at least, give no sign. But the repentance may be so strong as to master him; and then he will lie, as David here, convulsed and shaken like one in the grasp of a fit, uttering the sorest cries of sorrow, careless who is looking on, thinking only of Him against whom he has so grievously offended.

It is difficult to trace any order in the psalm, and the disorder and disjointed nature of it may be due to the very strength of the mental disturbance of the suppliant. An extreme emergency does, no doubt, sometimes give something like a supernatural balance and calmness to the mind, but many times the agitation betrays itself in the abrupt and fragmentary character of the exclamations. And this seems the case here. Everything is heaped together—confession and description of sin, entreaty for forgiveness, hopes of a new life of active goodness that break in, like gleams of light, upon the present gloom and helplessness — all come forth together from the penitent's heart, mixed and confused, like the tumbling waters of a flooded stream.

Let me seek to present to your minds some of the thoughts or feelings which at this moment filled the mind of this penitent. This may be of use both to help some of us to know what thoughts we should have of our sins; and, if any of us have these thoughts in some degree already, to lead us to take the right course to find relief and escape.

First, the petitioner begins his prayer with what we might call a *burst*—" Have mercy upon me, *pity me*, O God." The cry suggests much. It suggests a terrible back-lying misery, now become unendurable, out from beneath which the penitent must cry at last, *Pity me*! This cry had long been repressed. His feelings had chafed behind his closed lips, demanding an outlet; but he stubbornly kept silence. With a determined, sullen energy he sought for long to keep them in, with a stubborn unbroken heart refusing to let escape from his lips one word of confession or one cry of repentance. Many cries came from his heart, cries of shame, cries of despair against the irrevocable evil he had wrought, bitter cries of a lofty human soul that had by its sudden, ungoverned impulse dragged its glory in the dust—" he watered his couch with his tears, he roared all day long." But even while roaring all day long he was keeping silence, steeling his heart and sealing his lips, that no cry of penitence, no appeal for pardon, should escape him. But now his heart was broken, and its imprisoned impulses, thus set free, speedily burst open the barrier of his lips: " Have mercy upon me, O God."

Now the chief question for us is: What was this great back-lying misery from beneath which comes out this cry for pity? It was, in a word, his *sin*; but the feeling of sin in his mind was complex, embracing various feelings; and we can best learn what they were, by looking at some of the expressions in the psalm. Perhaps there is really only one petition throughout this psalm—that for forgiveness, for the removal of the consciousness of sin, for a word from God, either spoken to the ear or to the heart, that He has nought against the struggling soul before Him. Even the expression, 'a clean heart,' seems to me to have this sense: it is a clear conscience, created by God's word of forgiveness.

First, we have such expressions as these: "Wash me throughly from mine iniquity, and cleanse me from my sin; Purge me with hyssop, and I shall be clean; Wash me, that I be whiter than snow; Create in me a clean heart, O God; Deliver me from blood, O God of my salvation!" These expressions imply that sin is an *evil*. It is a pollution. It is a stain upon the nature of man. Perhaps the figures used imply more. The words, 'wash me throughly,' refer to the method of washing and fulling cloth into which foul stains had passed, which required to be kneaded and wrung, ere the impurity could be removed. And the expression, 'purge me with hyssop,' refers perhaps to the practice of declaring clean the person afflicted with leprosy. And both figures seem to imply not only that sin is an evil, but that it is a deeply seated one; that the very threads and tissues of our nature are coloured by it; that, like a subtle and tenacious dye, it has ingrained itself in all our faculties and in the very elements of our constitution; or that, like a disease which more than any other is constitutional,

the very distressing and loathsome form, in which it
manifests itself outwardly, is but a proof how completely it has seized and corrupted our blood.

But the thing most prominent here is the idea of its
foulness; it is a blot upon our nature. Sin is in itself
evil.   It is a perversion of the nature of things.
Apart from the evil consequences of it, which are
incalculable, especially of such a sin as David's, apart
from any verdict man or even God may pass upon it,
sin is in itself evil, foul, corrupt.   On the nature of
man, which is, in its true condition, also the nature
of God,—on the nature of man, sin is like a stain of
blood upon the linen garment clean and white.   It is
like a black footprint upon the unstained snow.   That
is the penitent's own thought of it : "Wash me, and I
shall be whiter than snow."   Here one hardly ever
sees snow in its purity ; but among the mountains, up
among the Alps or on the fields of Norway, one comes
upon drifts of stainless snow.   Its whiteness is dazzling ;
its beauty is beyond the mind's conception.   I have
wondered that the Creator scatters with so profuse
a hand so much that is of matchless beauty in
regions where there is no human eye to behold it,
where it has lain for so many ages unseen.   But
there are other eyes besides man's to behold it ; there
is God's own eye.   And He is, as it were, careless
should none else discover the riches of His glory.

But if God looks with delight upon a stainless snow-
drift, solitary and unseen, and He must, or else it would

not have been formed, how must His eye be fascinated
with a pure spirit, an unstained human soul, free from
every lust, free from all guile! How our own eye is fascinated by it, when we see it in some child yet ignorant of
evil, whose soul is as pure and unwrinkled as her cheek,
and to be near whom seems to take out the scars and
stains that disfigure our own! or how we feel it even
more, when we meet one who has grown up amidst
the untrodden ways, far from the haunts of men, never
having known temptation, nor having had her mind
made common and beaten hard by the innumerable
feet of that round of petty trivialities that fill up
life in populous places, and whose spirit is as pure
as the summer robe that folds around her. That pure
soul fascinates; yet of what a richer glory it is capable,
when it shall be washed in the blood of Christ!

It was the feeling of the evilness of his sins that
helped to work such a disturbance in this man's soul.
This evilness is felt by all lofty minds. It does not
need that a man be godly, to feel that sin is evil and
degrading. All better natures feel it. All noble souls
strive, if even in their own strength, to avoid it. Even
when giving way to it, they lament it. The strong
passions of strong natures are always, the moment
they have been indulged, loathsome. We hate ourselves every time that a passion overcomes us, and
cry out in our bitterness and helplessness: "Wretched
man that I am, who shall deliver me from the body of
this death?" Even apart from the grace of God, which

David had, his sin would have appeared loathsome ; and how much more, having that grace ! For David was a man of the noblest nature. This must be our final verdict, if we take in all the elements of his history.

This is the traditional view, and it is the true one. No doubt, the current runs a little the other way at present. Men have taken to making heroes of men certainly not according to God's own heart. And in the new pantheon, not David, but Saul, not Jacob, but Esau, not John only, but also Judas, are to find places. This is but a temporary revolt,—one of the reactions of which history is full,—when even goodness and truth, because long enjoyed, weary men ; and they rise up and demand a change, even if it should be for the worse :

"And the old order changes, giving place to new ;
And God fulfils Himself in other ways,
Lest one good custom should corrupt the world."

David, I say, was a man of the loftiest soul. Consider what elements of misery, in view of the evilness of his deeds, were at hand. He had wrought an unworthiness. He had done an injury. It was an irrevocable calamity, like the loss of a limb, marking him and maiming him for ever. His mind was filled with moral pain and self-torture. How sad a sight it is to see one once high in place, and from his youth looked up to, and held before the eyes of others as a bright example of self-restraint and activity and devotion to the highest things ; one whose name has long been quoted and dwelt upon with admiration,—to see one like this suddenly and greatly fall, and tarnish by some shameful vice the brilliancy of a hitherto clear reputation! And, if the sight be sad to onlookers, how more than sad is it to the man who looks upon himself so fallen! What feelings of regret rush into his mind, making him feel at one time utterly crushed, and at another filling him with despair that dashes itself against the irrevocable past, like some poor, wild, captive creature against the bars of the cage that confines it! For he remembers how he has done an unworthy thing, and thrown away all the power which a long life of purity and nobleness had gained him; and, by one single act, taken the lustre from the splendid life he had in many ways hitherto led. And now he must no more shine, or fill men's mouths with terms of admiration, or stimulate the young to follow his career, but shrink away into obscurity, his highest hope being to be forgotten. These were some of that crowd of dark thoughts that filled David's mind, and caused him to roar all day long, and at last to find refuge in the goodness of God: " Pity me, O God, according to Thy goodness."

But, again, there is another class of expressions in the psalm, which show another feeling in the penitent's mind: "Against Thee, Thee only, have I sinned, and done this evil in Thy sight; Behold, Thou desirest truth in the inward parts; Cast me not away from Thy presence; Hide Thy face from my sin." The additional feeling was this: that sin was against God. David's first

feeling was the evilness of sin. His next was that it
was against God. I wish that this feeling about sin
prevailed more among us, whether we be religious men
or no. I wish we felt that to give way to vice, or to
excess of any kind, is to dishonour ourselves; that
to swerve from the right in anything, whether in
business or in intercourse with men, is a shame. I
wish that we stood high above cupidity, sharp practice,
and taking an advantage—regarding all such things as
degrading and foul; that we were delicate, sensitive,
scrupulous, as if the touch of evil would defile us.
But our minds are so blunt naturally, and the practice
of the world is so extremely low, that it ordinarily needs
falling, like David, into some flagrant sin, to awaken
in us any keenness of touch. Then we go back upon
the past, and what, while we were leading it, seemed
to us a very respectable life becomes full of shameful
spots and stains, at which our eye sickens.

Much of the evilness of sin arises from its being
against God, but not it all. It is evil in itself. But it
is doubly evil from being done against the commands,
and in the face of the goodness, of God. When the
penitent breaks out with the exclamation, 'Pity me, O
God,' it may be little else than the exclamation of one
who feels himself all evil, as he flings himself into the
arms of one whom he feels to be all good. But when
he has flung himself there, he begins the confession:
"*Against Thee* have I sinned." This *only* in the confession: "Against Thee, Thee only, have I sinned," is

remarkable. It is not the expression of reason; for he had sinned against men as well as God. It is the voice of feeling, of conscience; it is the religious estimate of sin, in which all human things give way, and God alone stands out; or rather, in which all human things and relations become transformed into God. The cry is the voice of conscience; but, as often, the sentence of conscience is true in reality, and may be sustained by reflection.

All sin is against God only. Not only sins directly aimed at Him, such as blasphemous thoughts, or infidelity, but particularly sins against men. For the whole order of things, and, above all, human society, is an outcome of God Himself. God is behind all; laws are but formulas that express some parts of His will—rather some aspect of Himself. Each human creature is God's; rather, is God; is a manifestation of God, a revelation of His image; and when we offend against it, it is upon God that we strike; it is against Him that we thrust ourselves; it is He whom we offend. Ah, if we could but learn to meet God everywhere, to feel that it is He that is moving in all the motion that we see; that it is He that is the power in all force that we behold; that His will is the essence of all that we name law—particularly, if we could learn to identify our fellow-creatures with their Maker; to think of the men and women that work in the same field with us, or that dwell in the same house, as each of them an outcome of God, an image of God,

5

behind which is God Himself; how lofty, and pure, and divine would our intercourse with one another grow! We should meet God everywhere, and we should fear to sin against men, feeling that it was only against God that we sinned. We should reverently serve one another, and receive the reward of our service: "Inasmuch as ye did it unto one of these little ones, ye did it unto Me."

But though the feeling expressed in the cry, "Against Thee, Thee only, have I sinned," may be shown by reflection to be true, it was certainly not reached by reflection. It is the cry of an awakened conscience; and the conscience, so soon as it awakes and opens its eyes, beholds God. For God is always an object, almost the only object, in the range of vision of the conscience. When it sees aught, it will see Him. And God is directly present with this penitent. He felt himself in the hands of the living God. There was a face, full and luminous, bearing direct upon him and his sin. It is a fearful thing to fall into the hands of the living God; to see rise up before us this dread, living person, and to feel that we have sinned against Him, and that it is with Him that we have to do.

And shall not some such sense of God yet take hold of us all? For is not this what is meant by the judgment and the sentence? Shall not judgment be passed upon us chiefly through our conscience? Shall not God enter in and fill out our conscience, giving it quickening and knowledge? The things which God has made, and which gather about Him and prevent

Him being seen, as clouds about the sun, will pass away, and He will break forth. For even to the righteous the place of His presence is often rather guessed at. But to them He will one day shine out with a blessed light, so great that all other things will be swallowed up in it, and He alone will be seen.

But He will be the same absorbing object to the wicked. He will break upon them with such an intensity of realisation that the universe will contain but Himself and them. But He is on His way to meet us all. It cannot be that He will suffer any spirit whom He has made to remain without the knowledge of Him. He will bring Himself close home to all of them. Time and place and relations and affections may hide Him here, but He will one day break through, and burst upon us in awful nearness. Then we shall cry: "Against Thee, Thee only, have I sinned, and in Thy sight done this evil,"—happy if we shall also be able to cry: "If God be for us, who can be against us? It is God that justifieth, who is he that condemneth? It is Christ that died, yea rather, that is risen again, who is even at the right hand of God, who also maketh intercession for us."

There is one other class of expressions, which adds something more to the elements of this penitent's feeling of sin, to which I will refer very briefly—"Cast me not away from Thy presence. Take not Thy Holy Spirit from me." This expresses the penitent's feeling of what the possible consequences of sin may be, namely, casting away from the presence of God. This prayer, you observe, comes late—many petitions have preceded it. Perhaps ere now the penitent had a feeling that he was establishing his case before God. The very next petition shows that the suppliant was beginning to feel he was making way, for he ventures to conceive of a restored life, and to forecast what should be his employment in it: "Restore me the joy of Thy salvation, then will I teach transgressors Thy ways." Perhaps he would hardly have dared to name such an awful possibility as being cast out of God's presence altogether, if there had not been rising within his heart the blessed hope and assurance that it was no more to be dreaded. The words are rather a reminiscence of what he felt in his state of impenitent hardness. Then it seemed to him to want but little that he should be cast out of the light of God into the outer darkness.

The expressions, "Cast me not away from Thy presence," and, "Take not away Thy Holy Spirit from me," mean very much the same thing. Perhaps to an Old Testament saint the phrase 'Holy Spirit' had a wider meaning than to us. We use it to express that supernatural influence which precedes and causes conversion, and which sanctifies the heart. It is a somewhat narrow and technical use which we make of it. But to an Old Testament saint the Holy Spirit was almost a natural possession of the mind. It was the name for all the promptings of the mind to seek God, and for all its strivings after God, and for the very idea of God in the mind. Its taking away leaves a blank where God was. The mind falls back into a condition in which God, or the thought of God, has no power to move it. And this penitent felt that there lay in sin the possibility of bringing the soul to this.

There had come into his mind the idea of an existence without God, and that he was entering upon it; he felt the beginnings of this state in his sin, and the hardening that followed upon it. Perhaps this is further than many go. Yet, perhaps, you have felt a recklessness and alienation come upon you after some sin, when you were in such a state that you wilfully, or not unwillingly, chose the darkness rather than the light; or at times you have felt as if the moral light were going out of your mind, and the restraining power of the thought of God was growing weaker. Then you sought the pleasures of sense with a greater avidity, and had a certain impatience and scorn of what is called spiritual. And you could see from this the tendency of sin to overbear and encroach, and, like an advancing darkness, to swallow up even the natural light of the soul. And you shuddered at your own experience; for you were like one leaving a great and lighted city, and going out upon the solitary road. Every step one takes, the lights become fewer; and at last the darkness alone will prevail.

Or you have in your recollection, perhaps, a period of deadness in your own history, out of which you are now happily awakened. But in that state God was hardly present to your mind, and His influence over you was none. Your first thought on waking was not of God, but of the daily newspaper, and of the state of parties or of the funds. By day, if you had a spare moment from your business to look forward, you perhaps thought of the evening, and where you were to spend it, and hoped that it would be pleasant and not wearisome. And when the day was over, and you retired, your only thought was that you might have good rest. And in the morning it was again the newspaper, and the state of parties and of the funds. It is the tendency of sin, even though not flagrant, to push God out of the soul, so that His Spirit withdraws, and men are cast out from His presence.

Now, though I have said enough, we should leave with a very inadequate idea of this man's character if I did not allude—I shall do no more—to another petition : " Restore unto me the joy of Thy salvation . . . then will I teach transgressors Thy ways, and sinners shall be converted unto Thee. O Lord, open Thou my lips ; and my mouth shall show forth Thy praise."

This petition comes among the last. The suppliant could not have begun with it. He is at first too much occupied with what needs to be done to him, to think of what he himself shall do. But as his mind calms down, and as there rises to him the hope of pardon and restoration, he cannot help thinking how his pardoned life would be spent : " I will teach transgressors Thy ways." Observe the connection : " Blot out my transgressions; then will I teach transgressors Thy ways. Cleanse me from my sin; and sinners shall be converted unto Thee. I was dumb; for Thou didst it. Open my lips; and my mouth shall show forth Thy praise." What seals his lips is the sense of unpardoned sin. What he will teach to transgressors is God's ways—His pardoning way. What seals his lips is not shame or backwardness,—lest men, when addressed, should quote the old proverb against him, " Physician, heal thyself." He does not pray that this dislike of coming forward publicly amidst the still fresh memories of his sin should be taken away from him, and boldness be given to him.

What he wants is not an audience, but a theme. What can an unpardoned transgressor speak to transgressors about? Platitudes about God's goodness, not one of them felt? Men who have never felt God's goodness will perhaps speak specious generalities concerning it, but not one who has felt it, least of all one who, having once felt it, has, by his own sin, come into a condition where he no longer feels it. His very past experience will make it the more impossible for him to refer to it. What seals his lips is the sense of sin unforgiven. What will open them will be the sense of sin forgiven. This will both open his lips and furnish him with a theme for speech: "Then will I teach transgressors Thy ways,"—Thy way with transgressors and transgressions. "Who is a God like unto Thee, pardoning iniquity, and passing by the transgressions of the remnant of Thy heritage?—and sinners shall be converted unto Thee." There is a splendid sincerity about this man. If he do not know God's ways, he will not speak of them.

It is not always easy to say whether silence on religious subjects be a good sign or a bad. If you cannot draw a man into conversation at all on these things, there must be something wrong. Yet too ready speech may be only proof of a shallow mind that is too superficial to feel the hollowness of speaking about that of which it has no experience. This man was too open to simulate anything. God's favour was a thing too sacred to speak of and commend, when he knew he had it not. And, in like manner, as he cannot speak generalities among men, he cannot pray in generalities to God. His prayer is most specific: " *Open Thou my lips.*" He does not seek power in speech, he seeks only to be able to speak. He directs his prayer to what he feels lacking. His prayers do not outrun his sense of need. And he prays for essential things only, not any manner of them—" Open my lips, and sinners shall be converted unto Thee." If he can but speak, however rudely, however feebly, if *truly*, the effect will surely follow—" sinners shall be converted unto Thee."

This is his outlook. Many here have sometimes had a sickness that threatened to be mortal. Your first prayer, if you were conscious, was perhaps that God's will might be done, though along with that—that you might recover. Perhaps you were so distressed that

you hardly thought of anything — your whole powers
being put forth in the struggle of nature with the
disease. But you remember when the crisis was passed,
and the thought broke on you that you would yet
live, what a crowd of feelings burst into your mind!
thankfulness, and a tenderness that quite broke you,
and a happiness all round about, and yet such a thrill
of life stirring every nerve! And your mind reached out
to what your recovered life should be, and devotion and
intelligence combined to sketch a brave and patient
and high life, one out of which all littleness and all
evil should be cast. Perhaps in human life, especially
if one be young, there is no such full moment as when,
in great sickness, we realise that we shall yet live. But
the moment in a sinner's life, when he realises God's
mercy, and that his sin is not mortal, must be fuller
still; the joy deeper, the feeling of life more powerful,
the yearning to go forth and act more intense.

These are some of the thoughts of sin which this
penitent had. They are true thoughts. Would that
we had them! or that we had them more and more!
It is not, of course, needful that we should have them
all; to have one of them is enough, though one will
perhaps give rise to others. Some minds of the higher
kind may be most afflicted with the feeling of the
baseness and stain of sin, and most drawn by the lofty
moral life of Christ. Others of a devouter turn may be
most alarmed and agitated by the thought that sin is
against God; and when He sets their sins in the light

of His countenance, the terrors of the awakened conscience may be overwhelming. Others again may feel
most strongly the power of sin to increase and invade
the whole nature, and put out one after another the
lights of the soul, till the light that is in us become
darkness. This suppliant before us seems to have experienced each of these feelings. Yet such a thing
cannot be necessary. To have one true thought of
sin will be enough. I say this, because we sometimes
agitate ourselves by the fear that we do not feel rightly
about sin, because our feelings may not coincide with
those of some others of whom we have heard.

Yet this suppliant, besides thoughts of sin, had
thoughts of God. If we abide by thoughts of sin,
and do not rise to just thoughts of God, our last state
shall be worse than the first. In this penitent's petition
the thoughts of God precede the thoughts of sin. And
the thoughts of God which he had were that God was
loving and merciful. " Pity me, O God, according to
Thy loving-kindness ; according to the multitude of
Thy tender mercies blot out my transgressions." Great
as sin is, love and mercy is greater. There is not
only mercy, but tender mercies ; yea, an innumerable
multitude of tender mercies. And it is the way of
mercy to forgive. " Pity me according to Thy loving-
kindness." It is the nature of love to pity ; it is also
the practice of it. And you can use this argument
with more full assurance than David. Perhaps he had
his own experience chiefly to go on, though also, no

doubt, that of the Church before him,—and he had an innate human belief in God's mercy, which no speculative sophistry can drive from men's minds,—but you have the manifestation and the words of Christ: "God so loved the world, that He gave His Son, that whosoever believeth in Him should not perish, but have everlasting life. I beseech you by the mercies of God that ye present your bodies a living sacrifice, holy and acceptable. The sacrifices of God are a broken spirit: a broken and a contrite heart, O God, Thou wilt not despise."

IV

I KNOW THAT MY REDEEMER LIVETH

IV

I KNOW THAT MY REDEEMER LIVETH

JOB xix. 25–27

"But I know that my Redeemer liveth,
   And that He shall stand up at the last upon the earth :
   And after my skin hath been thus destroyed,
   Yet from my flesh shall I see God :
   Whom I shall see for myself,
   And mine eyes shall behold, and not another.
   My reins are consumed within me."

IN some respects the problems of one age can never be the problems of another; or at all events the problems, though perhaps fundamentally the same, enter into new combinations of life and thought in each different time; and this makes them look, and indeed be, different. But it sometimes happens, when problems come before us which we think new, that aged persons among us tell us they are not new. They were the difficulties and objections current in their youth; and they remember how, in their intellectual strength long ago, they exploded them; and they wonder that men of this time should be moved by them. They did not explode them. They only hid them in the sand, or hid them-

79

selves from them, or were enabled, in the exercise of a higher trust and in active deeds, to disregard and forget them. But being only buried in the sand, the periodic winds of time and life and the circling earth blew them bare again, and we are called upon to face them. There are some problems, indeed, which are not those of any time, but belong to the individual mind, which every earnest person has to face for himself, such as the question of his own relation to God. But this question may be wide or narrow, according to the character of the individual mind. Sometimes it may be narrowed to the single point of one's own sin, but sometimes it may broaden out so as to be as wide as the world itself; and instead of its being a straight, clear line which connects him with God, at one end of which he stands, and God in the full blaze of His own light at the other, the man may feel himself beneath a shower of influences and forces, a pitiless shower, all beating down upon him from heaven; and, whether he look around him or above him, with only thick darkness before him. Such a condition was that of Job.

The author of the book lets us know what was the meaning of Job's sufferings. They were meant to try him—to prove whether he was truly a righteous man. Satan had insinuated that Job's religion was selfish. God had answered, Let him be tried. Neither Job nor his friends knew this.

Both they and he had a theory about affliction, namely, that it was sent by God upon those whom He held

guilty of great sins. The three friends, assuming that
God was righteous, immediately concluded that Job had
been guilty of great offences against God, and that he
was suffering the consequences, and they earnestly
entreat him to repent. Job, however, knew he had not
been guilty, and yet he concluded from his afflictions
that God was holding him guilty. Hence he is brought
into great perplexities regarding God, and into great
darkness of mind.

Let me endeavour to show, first, what is the most
probable meaning of these words; second, how this
extraordinary profession of belief arose out of Job's
circumstances; and, third, let me draw some lessons
from the whole relations of the parties to one another.

1. The general meaning of the passage. If you look
at the margin in your Bibles, you will perceive that
almost every clause in these verses is susceptible of
more than one meaning. The margin ought to contain
meanings which are possible, but less probable than
those in the text. But it is well known that this is
not always the relation which the margin bears to
the text in our version. The readings given in the
margin often appeared to the authors of our Bible
more probable than those in the text; but as they were
not translators but only revisers, and as there was a
text already in possession, they considered themselves
bound by their instructions not to disturb it, unless
they could put in its place something, of the correctness
of which they were absolutely certain. But absolute

6

certainty in a passage like this is hardly to be expected ;
and hence we are left with parallel translations in the
text and margin between which we must ourselves
make choice.

Ver. 25 begins with the word *for.* Perhaps the word
but would bring out better the rapid changes of feeling
in Job's mind. In ver. 21 he made an appeal to his
friends : " Have pity upon me, have pity upon me, O
ye my friends"; but he could discern no sign of re-
lenting there. Then suddenly the thought seized him
that he could make his appeal to the future, to the
generations to come, whose judgment would be calmer
and unimpassioned, and no longer excited by the personal heats of controversy : "Oh that my words were
written ! oh that they were inscribed in a book ! that
they were graven with an iron pen and lead in the
rock for ever ! " But even if the generations to come
should pass a more gentle sentence upon him than
his own time, being better able to estimate his circumstances, and more inclined, amidst the acknowledged
mystery of his life, to allow weight to the persistent
testimony of his conscience as that behind which it is
impossible to go ; nay more, if the generations to come,
moved by the spectacle of his awful miseries, and
swayed by that wider sympathy which the human race
does seem to be acquiring as its years advance,
should even reverse the judgment of his contemporaries, how small a thing that would be to him ! It
is something to have the esteem of men while we live.

And when the sensibilities are not indurated by blows from without, nor blunted by vice that] hardens all within and petrifies the feeling, the esteem of men is, next to a good conscience, what gives the widest and most satisfying pleasure to the mind. And Job keenly enjoyed it while he had it, and bewailed with the most pathetic lamentations the loss of it. And it is something to think that, when we die, our memory shall live in some stray corners, and in some hearts here and there, and that it shall be blessed. Yet this is but little. And Job felt it to be but little; and it could not satisfy him. His mind rebounded from it, and grasped the greater treasure which it possessed. "But I know that my redeemer liveth . . . whom I shall see for myself, and not another."

There is not much to alter in the translation of ver. 25. Perhaps the expression 'at the latter day' would more fairly be rendered 'afterwards,' or as 'one coming after me.' It is a fundamental assumption of Job's that his present sickness will be fatal. The hopes that the friends hold out of recovery, he calls mere delusions. He knows better; he shall die. But though he dies, there is One that doth not die—his Redeemer liveth; and, though he pass away, and return to the dust, he leaveth One after him who shall stand upon his dust. He dies, but he does not all die,—his history does not die, his problem does not die, the relation into which he has entered with God does not die. God does not die, and He must yet make

manifest Job's relations to Himself. Obscurity hangs
over these relations here. Clouds and darkness are
about Him, but He will yet shine forth; and the
travailing, troubled spirits that He drew to Himself,
and that spread out their hands towards the darkness, and refused to believe that the darkness which
they could not penetrate was hollow, or filled only by
their own idea, but clung to Him that was in it
amidst all the confusions of brain and life,—these spirits
shall see Him, and be acknowledged by Him; and
their true relations to Him shall be set forth before
the eyes of a congregated universe.

The word 'Redeemer' has become so sacred and
special in its use among us who are Christians, that
we are averse to any different application of it. Yet
we must remember that Job is represented as living
in the patriarchal age, perhaps two thousand years
before the birth of our Lord, and that the book must
have been written many hundred years before His
coming, and that the term Redeemer is applied many
times in the Old Testament to God; as, for example,
in one Psalm: "Let the words of my mouth, and the
meditations of my heart, be acceptable in Thy sight,
O Lord, my Strength, and my Redeemer"; and in
another: "When He slew them, then they sought
Him . . . they remembered that God was their Rock,
and the high God their Redeemer." A prophet also
declares: "Thus saith the Lord, your Redeemer, the
Holy One of Israel; For your sake I have sent unto

Babylon, and I will bring down all of them as fugitives, even the Chaldeans, in the ships of their rejoicing." And again: "Doubtless Thou art our Father, though Abraham be ignorant of us, and Israel acknowledge us not: Thou, O Lord, art our Father, our Redeemer; Thy name is from everlasting." And so in many other passages.

Now, Job had no idea of a distinction in the Godhead, such as we have. This was not yet revealed to him. And what he says of his Redeemer, he says of God generally. A fuller revelation has taught us that God the Redeemer is God manifested in His Son; and what Job says here of his Redeemer standing on the dust is fulfilled in the Son. Yet this distinction, as I have said, was not one known to Job. God is his Redeemer. In the next verse he himself explains this to be his meaning: "I shall see God." He shall vindicate him against the wrongs which he suffers, against the suspicions of men, against the aspersions of Satan—nay, against another thing: against the hardships that have fallen upon him from the general providence of God, where evil and disease and death are now elements of the current of events.

God is his Redeemer—He who shall vindicate his innocence before men; He who shall smite the accuser on the mouth; He who shall clear away the darkness, and remove the terrors and perplexities amidst which the spirit of His child sobs and wails, and who shall press it to His fatherly heart,—it is God, the inner God, the heart of God, the God of grace and consolation. For one of the most singular positions into which Job is driven by the riddles of his history is this : he divides God into two. One God, the God of outer providence, who rules, and whom events obey, persecutes him, holds him guilty, and refuses, with ears obdurately closed, to listen to the appeals of His creature for a hearing and an adjudication: "Oh that I knew where I might find Him! that I might come unto His place! I would fill my mouth with arguments. Wherefore hidest Thou Thy face, and holdest me for Thine enemy?"

But behind all this is a God who knows his innocence, a heart conscious of his rectitude : "My witness is in heaven, and He who can bear testimony to me is on high." And the suffering saint appeals to the one against the other, from the providence of God to the heart of God, from the Ruler of the universe to the gracious Redeemer: "Mine eye poureth out tears to God, that He would do justice to a man with God, and between a man and his neighbour." There are strange riddles in life, strange mysteries of providence, irreconcilable with our ideas of God, the miseries of the just, early deaths, earthquakes and shipwrecks swallowing up innumerable lives. Our spirits are bounded by iron walls on every side, cabined and confined ; and we are mostly content to have it so. We are so familiar now with mystery that we are scarcely stirred by the

most appalling occurrences; we are so used to the
inexplicable, and so absorbed in what is around us,
that the narrow limits of our knowledge hardly trouble
us. But to an eagle spirit like Job's this caging was
unbearable; and he spread his wings and dashed
himself against the bars of his cage demanding knowledge—resolved to come even unto God's place, and
pluck out the mystery from the darkness; demanding
that the events of God's providence should be made
to correspond with his idea of God, and sure that if
he know not now he shall know hereafter, when God
will descend from the heavens, and stand upon the
earth, to unravel the mysteries of his life here, and to
proclaim his innocence and God-fearing way.

The 26th verse is susceptible of a good deal of alteration, as you perceive from the margin and the great
number of words supplied in the text. The words
'though,' 'worms,' and 'body' are not in the original.
Further, while the text reads, "Yet *in* my flesh," the
margin, you observe, reads, "Yet *out of* my flesh shall
I see God." It may seem extraordinary that senses
directly opposite should be afforded by the same words.
But this arises from the ambiguity of the words *out of.*
The expression is: Out of my flesh shall I see God.
But this may either mean: In a disembodied state,
having laid aside my flesh, I shall see God. Or it may
mean : *out from my flesh*—in my flesh, but looking out
from it,—I shall see God. The ambiguity is one that
is found in our own language as well as in Hebrew.

There is, therefore, only the context and general scope
of the book to decide.

Now I have already said that Job resolutely scouted
all ideas of a recovery from his malady in this life.
His disease was mortal. But his disease was due to
the immediate hand of God; it was the proof and
signature, both to him and to his friends, of God's
anger. That anger, therefore, he was well assured,
would pursue him to death; the darkness, that to his
eyes encompassed God now, would not clear away on
this side the grave. Here in his present body, at least,
he should never see God for himself. He would go
down to the grave in darkness and amidst mystery.
This certainly makes it probable that the words mean,
without my flesh, that is, disembodied—when disease has
wasted the flesh, and death has severed the cord that
bound the spirit to it: "Away from my flesh I shall
see God." Already, in ver. 25, he had said that his
Redeemer would come after him, and stand upon the
dust where he should be laid.

No doubt the other sense is possible, namely, looking
out from my flesh, clothed anew in flesh, and beholding
from that new body, I shall see God. And this suits
well what was said in ver. 25, for his Redeemer seems
going to be visible to human eyes, when He stands
upon the dust. And there is one very singular passage,
in an earlier part of the book, where the idea of a
resurrection is certainly found. In chap. xiv. 13 we
read: "Oh that Thou wouldst hide me in the grave!

that Thou wouldst keep me secret, till Thy wrath be past! that Thou wouldst appoint a set time, and remember me! If a man die, shall he live again? All the days of my appointed time would I wait, till my release came. Thou wouldst call, and I would answer Thee; Thou wouldst have a desire to the work of Thine hands." Here there is certainly the idea of a return from the grave, a living again; and, when God's wrath is past, a reconciliation anew with God, who should have a desire to the work of His hands, and call him again to His heart. And the meaning might be the same in the passage before us: "Yet clothed anew with flesh, and looking forth from it, shall I see God." This would certainly give a unity to the representation, for God, standing upon the dust, would be God whom the suffering saint should see; while, on the other view, the vision is only a spiritual one after death. Still the words, *out from my flesh*, form a rather small expression to put so large a meaning into; and, upon the whole, the other sense is more probable.

The sufferer's ideas may not be complete, and he may not see the way clearly to that which his faith demands. His expressions are exclamatory and disjointed; but this is his assurance, that though he die in darkness, as he will, though the riddle of God's dealing with him remain unsolved here, though God's face be resolutely hidden from him till, under the ravage of his disease, his flesh be consumed and his

bodily frame dissolved, yet that shall not be the end
of all. He shall not be dissolved, and God cannot be
dissolved; and this darkness is not an eternal darkness. On this night of estrangement and mystery,
however long it may be, a morn shall break at last;
and through the clouds there will shine out a face, a
reconciled face, that I shall see for myself; and mine
eyes shall behold, and not another's: and my reins
within me are consumed with longing. Thus the whole
passage will read:

> "But I know that my Redeemer liveth,
> And that afterwards He shall stand upon the dust:
> And after this my skin is destroyed,
> And without my flesh, I shall see God:
> Whom I shall see for myself,
> And mine eyes shall behold, and not another's.
> My reins within me are consumed with longing."

Hence the two things that Job *knows* would be these:
first, after his disease had worked its final effects on
him, and he should be laid in the grave under the
stigma of wickedness and the reprobation of men, God
would appear to clear him. His name should not be
left in dishonour. But God in human form would stand
upon his dust, and make known his rectitude, redeeming
him from the injustice which he had suffered.

And, second, he himself, though not in this life,
should see God; see Him for himself, see Him on his
side, reconciled, and all clouds cleared away. In that
world beyond, whither the spirit went, the mysteries
of this life should be cleared away, and those who felt

separated and estranged from God here, but longed for His face, should see it there in peace.

2. Now, look briefly how this singular profession of belief was pressed out of Job's heart. The whole contest between himself and his friends was about the meaning, in God's providence, of his great afflictions. The friends had a short and simple explanation : his afflictions were for his sins. All affliction is for sin ; great affliction is for great sin. Whom God is angry with He afflicts: "God is angry with the wicked every day." Job went so far with his friends ; he, too, believed that God afflicted only in anger. But he could not take the other step, that He was angry only with the sinner. Job's conscience rebelled against this. And thus, to him, God's anger and his own afflictions were a mystery.

The passage before us follows that hardest of all speeches in chap. xviii., in which Bildad, with scarcely concealed insinuations, pictured the awful fate of the sinner. Under his terrible picture he wrote: "These are the habitations of the wicked"; and he held it up before Job. It was meant for him. The terrible distemper, the firstborn of death, which consumes the sinner's limbs, was too plain an allusion to Job's leprosy to be mistaken by him. The brimstone that burns up the sinner's habitation was, no doubt, the fire of God that fell on Job's cattle and consumed them. The tree withered at the roots, and cut down, reminds Job too easily of his own wasted state, and the sad calamities that had lopped off his children from him. He is the sinner. To every sentence of his oration Bildad adds: "Thou art the man."

Against this application Job's whole soul protests. He resolutely maintains his innocence. But while maintaining it he realises with new distinctness his dreary isolation, God and men having alike turned against him. This he describes in most pathetic words. Yet so profound and unalterable is his conviction of his own innocence that, as with a desperate leap out of the depth of his misery, he rises to the assurance that his innocence shall yet be revealed; that God will publicly declare it; and that he himself shall hear the declaration, and see the Redeemer that makes it. "I know that my Redeemer liveth." The joyful anticipation overcomes him, and he faints with longing: "My reins are consumed within me."

It is the lowest ebb of sorrow that precedes the flow of this full tide of faith. God not only afflicted Job with trouble, but removed from him all human sympathy: "He hath put my brethren far from me; and my familiar friends have forgotten me." There is something more breaking to the heart in the turning away of men from us than in the acutest pain. It crushes us quite. We steel ourselves against it for a time, and rise to it in bitterness and resentment. But it breaks us at last, and we soften and are utterly crushed. And this seems the way, whether men frown on us with justice or no. And there came on Job,

when he drew before himself his complete casting off
by men, by his friends and his household, and even
by the little children, who mocked his vain attempts
to rise from the ground, a complete break-down, and
he bursts into that most touching of all his cries:
"Have pity upon me, have pity upon me, O ye my
friends. Why do ye persecute me like God?" But his
appeal is in vain. Those pharisaic muscles will not
move. The rigidity of that religious decorum no
human feeling shall break. Secure in their principles
and their piety, their countenance shows but austere
reprobation of their wicked friend. They will be more
austere because he is their friend, and because they
feel it a sacrifice to be austere. And, looking into
their hard eyes and set faces, Job reads only their
unalterable verdict against him. Then, turning away
from them, the desire suddenly seized him to make
his appeal to posterity—to the better informed and
calmer judgment of the future; to record in writing his
protestation of his innocence; to grave it in the rock,
that it might last for ever, and that all generations
to the end of time might read, when they listened
to his story, the solemn denial of his guilt. "Oh that
my words were written! Oh that they were graven in
the rock for ever!"

But if that were possible, how small a thing it
would, after all, be! Job needs more; he shall have
more. This invincible confidence in his innocence
and in his godliness makes him feel that behind all

the darkness there is a face that looks kindly on him—
the face of a living God with whom he has walked in
fellowship, who knows his innocence, and who shall yet
make it manifest to the world: "But I know that my
Redeemer liveth, and that afterward He shall stand
upon the dust: and after my skin is consumed, and
without my flesh, shall I see God: whom I shall see
for myself, and mine eyes shall behold. Oh, my reins
faint within me!"

3. Now let me draw one or two lessons. First,
what belief does Job express here, when he says: "I
know that my Redeemer liveth, and that afterward He
will stand upon this dust"?

We must consider what Job was—his righteousness,
which is the very basis of all: a just man, fearing
God and eschewing evil; a man in union with God
—living by faith in God, justified by faith, and having
peace with God. In the general providence of God,
which embraces all, and where each unit is made to
contribute by help or suffering to the advance and
good of the whole, great calamities had fallen on him.
He was maligned by Satan; he was suspected by men.
Even God's countenance seemed to him withdrawn
from him. This life became a riddle to him; he
shuddered with awe at the problems regarding God's
character and government, which the universe and his
own experience presented to him: "It is God that
makes my heart weak, and the Almighty that troubles
me: for I am not afraid before the darkness that

covers my own face." It was not his calamities, it was
this, that they were due to God, that frightened him.
The world seemed to him to be dissolving into disorder,
and the moral governor of it becoming a mere arbitrary
force, whose attribute, if he had one, was cruelty—
"righteous and wicked He destroys alike." The universe
was becoming a machine that inexorably gnawed to
death the creatures upon it, regardless alike of their
lamentations and their protests in the name of righteousness. It is out of this lowest depth that the sufferer's
mind leaps to its highest height. He knows that this
cannot be so; he recalls the past—his fellowship with
God—the months past when God's candle shined upon
his head; and this God still lives, and still is what
He ever was. And out of his very necessity, his heart
projects a scene that shall yet be enacted on the
world, when God, his Redeemer and Deliverer, shall
descend from heaven and stand upon the earth, and
shall clear up the mysteries of life, and acknowledge
publicly those that are His own, and give unto all
according as their work shall be.

What Job craved, and what his faith enabled him
to say he knew, was that the unseen God should
become visible; that God, whose dwelling is in heaven
amid clouds and darkness, should descend and stand
upon the earth; that the great problem between God
and man, and between men and men, should be un-
ravelled by God in human form, and in human speech;
that the riddle of the painful earth, the mystery, the

misery, the wrong, the bitter wrestlings of mind with
mind, should be removed for ever and composed, and
that all those who clung to God amidst darkness and
misconceptions of men, or of their own, should pass
out of darkness into an unclouded light, in which their
eyes should see God.

You see here the peculiarity of the Old Testament
revelation.   It came in fragments; it was given in
sundry portions and in divers manners; it arose bit
by bit through the pressure of circumstances upon the
hearts of God's ancient saints.   They lived into the
truth which they uttered for all ages.   And the truth
was oftentimes anticipations, presentiments, clutches at
the unseen by the outstretched nervous hand of faith.
In the Old Testament, truth has not yet reached a unity.
The temple of truth is not yet reared, nor the idea of it
yet conceived in its full proportion.   Yet everywhere
workmen are engaged preparing for it, and all around
lie the exquisite products of their labour.   Here you
may see one laying a foundation, and there one carv-
ing a chapiter, and there another wreathing a pillar,—
working singly most of them, each able only to take
in the idea of the one piece on which he is himself
engaged, till the master builder came, in whose mind
the full idea of the temple bodied itself forth, and at
whose command each single piece of workmanship
arose and stood in its proper place.

Might I add another lesson, taught us very sharply
by Job's friends?   Both Job and his friends were wrong

in the construction they put upon this providence. They all failed to take a right view of the meaning of God's dealing with this saint. But the error of the friends was greater. Job erred only speculatively. The friends, in addition to their error of this kind, judged their brother. Job's friends were good men ; but good men are not always wise men. There is a wisdom in goodness, —a calmness and breadth, and repose and moderation, and many times an insight which only piety gives,—and there looks out from the eyes of goodness a benevolence and a tolerance, and a readiness to make allowance, which in a world like ours, where there is much uncertainty and such a conflict of mind with mind, and where we are all so liable to be warped by evil, is the truest wisdom—a wisdom, indeed, that cannot be attained except by the mind that is godly.

Yet one sometimes sees something different. It almost seems as if piety sometimes made men more unwise, and intensified their narrowness, and took away from them the very elements of judgment and the form of moderation, and instead of that "spirit of power, and . love, and of a sound mind" which the apostle declares God to have given us as Christians, we see feebleness and rancour, and a mind the prey of every distemper. This is perhaps not unnatural, for the powerful convictions of religion, taken into the mind, add intensity to it ; and if there be any narrowing in it, these will tend, before they have had time to work a general softening and mellowing of it, to make it more narrow.

7

This was the religious condition of Job's friends. In some respects they were more intractable and mischievous, just from being religious. But that we may avoid falling into their faults, it is well to notice where they erred. They erred, first, in drawing inferences of their own from certain and revealed truth ; and, second, particularly in making inferences about God, and by means of them overbearing the conscience of their brother. They started from the foundation that God was righteous,—and there they were right. Next, they laid down the maxim that no man could be righteous in God's sight ; here, too, they had both truth and experience on their side. Then they said the Lord is righteous in all His ways, and giveth unto all according as their works shall be. But here they began to infer. On this latter statement they put the construction that God will in this life punish the sinner according to his sin, that calamity is in proportion to sin, and that where men are seen to suffer severely, they must have sinned heinously.

Job's friends offended where men are always exceedingly apt to offend—in judging others ; and their history did not teach their countrymen wisdom, for Christ even in His day had need to warn His contemporaries against the same error. " Or those eighteen, on whom the tower in Siloam fell, and slew them, think ye that they were sinners above all men that dwelt in Jerusalem ? I tell you, Nay." They thought they could measure providence. They forgot that it is a complex scheme ; they did not consider that God deals not with

men only, but with mankind, and that each is used by
Him in the interests of the whole. They forgot the
incomprehensibility of God. "Thinking themselves to
be wise, they became fools."

But has not the history of religion been a series of
scenes where their conduct has been copied to the
letter? Regarding what thing have men professed
themselves so sure as regarding God? They have ever
been ready to take Him in their own hand,—to speak
for Him and in His name, to lay down what things
are consistent with His authority and His nature and
His will, and to beat down the resisting consciences
of their brethren, also His creatures and children, with
His so-called authority, which is nothing but their own.
We do know God,—God the Father of our Lord Jesus
Christ. "He that hath seen Me hath seen the Father."
We behold His glory, full of grace and truth. We
know the God of salvation. We believe that, in knowing Him thus, we have got the key to all the knowledge of Him that is possible. But do we yet know
Him wholly? Is there not another side of Him that
we do not know at all? "Who can by searching find
out God?" He transcends us.

It is not amiss for us sometimes to dwell on that
transcendental side; and if we do, then we shall be
more tolerant, one of another, when we differ regarding
Him. Our reasoned thoughts of God are mostly sure
to be false. A few great reverential thoughts, or rather
feelings, about Him is our truest knowledge. Think of,

or rather feel, His majesty and sovereignty, His holiness and love and grace; but be slow to reason upon them beyond what is written; and slower still to dispute regarding Him. Let every thought be a feeling, let every exercise of mind regarding Him be worshipful. Feel like Moses, that you are entering on the mountain, which is all on a smoke and in darkness; and you will come out from it full of awe, and in no mood to contest with your fellow-men points regarding God.

I cannot close without pointing you to the power and grandeur of faith. The human spirit is the greatest thing in our world; but that which is greatest in the human spirit, or that which makes it great, is faith. Stoicism may rise superior to suffering, but Christian faith rises superior both to affliction and to the speculative perplexities of the universe. Nay, it sometimes seems to measure itself even against God, and to claim to be greater than He. But this is only appearance; for its whole strength arises from its feeling itself in harmony with God as He really is. Behold its greatness in Job.

Job was not one of the covenant people. He lived outside the community of Israel. He had not much around him to fall back upon—no public life embodying God's relations to men, no great society of believers on whose experience to lean, little except his own history, his consciousness of what God had hitherto been to him. He was alone. And this crisis that had occurred in his history was a new point of God's dealing that had not occurred before. He had his view of it, and others had theirs. Or rather he had reached to no view of it, beyond denying that it was to be explained as others thought. He had nothing but his conscience to fall back on. All else was against him. His friends, one and all, took another side; they quoted revelation against him; they adduced the immemorial consent of mankind against him. Nay, they pointed to the testimony of God—and he admitted it—against him; for his calamities he believed to proceed immediately from God's hand, and to be proof of His estrangement from him. All this—one and every external testimony—proclaimed him wrong and guilty; but there was one testimony for him, a testimony within him, the testimony of conscience to his fellowship with God. He knew he was the friend of God. He knew he was this before, and he knew he was this still.

Job had the witness in himself. And that is an invincible assurance. Human opinion is feeble before it; calamities and afflictions, regarded even as providences from God's hand — the riddles of time and life and thought—all break themselves into dust upon this immovable rock. The human spirit comes into relation with God,—they meet, they have fellowship,—and the human spirit is assured of it; and no mysteries or obscurities can shake this faith. Is there any other thing certain? Is there any other principle or tradition of men that will enable us to live well, and weather the storms of life? There is naught else—nothing but this:

"an anchor of the soul, both sure and steadfast, and entering into that which is within the veil."

This was the anchor of the Old Testament saints. They knew God, they had found Him. In His grace He had come near to them, and removed their transgressions far from them. They had His fellowship. They walked with Him. They were His friends. They were even His children. He loved them,—and He was life, and He gave them life,—and they felt it to be impossible that He could cease to love them, and, therefore, impossible that He could let them die. Here was their hope of eternal life—to know God. He could not break this tie of love between Him and them, for He loveth with an everlasting love. He could not let them ever go from His heart, any more than a father could let go his child. "Can a woman forget her sucking child, that she should not have compassion on the son of her womb? Yea, these may forget, yet will not I forget thee."

The saints of the East were not speculative men— they had no philosophy. They did not reason that the soul was immortal from its nature. They did not lay stress upon our instinctive hopes of immortality. They could not, with the patient eye of inductive observation, gather up what we call analogies to the passage of beings from a lower to a higher life, such as we conceive our own death to be. They did not reason; they felt. They *knew* that their Redeemer lived. They were safe in the arms of God. Death

could not assail those who were folded to the bosom
of the Everlasting Life. " I have set the Lord ever
before me; because He is at my right hand, I shall
not be moved. Therefore my heart is glad, and my
soul rejoiceth; my flesh also resteth in hope. For
Thou wilt not leave my soul to hell; neither wilt
Thou suffer Thy godly one to see corruption." In
God the man felt himself safe, all safe, safe as a
man, heart and soul and flesh,—the man whom God
made, and as He made him, no thing of elements,
but one being—safe for ever: " Thou wilt show me the
path of life : in Thy presence is fulness of joy; at Thy
right hand there are pleasures for evermore."

These were the hopes, the certainties of the Old
Testament saints. Certainties! yes, certainties of faith.
Ah, but these subjective assurances, what do they
come to? What availed them all their ecstasies, and
their protestations against death, and their confidence
that they should never be moved? " The fathers, where
are they? and the prophets, have they lived for ever? "
Has not all their assurance remained but an unverified
feeling of the mind and heart? Is there any fact that
bears it out? There are facts. The Old Testament
has not remained the mere record of the emotions and
hopes of ardent and pious souls. If it had, it would
still have been a distinct contribution to our belief in
immortality—a contribution in a region altogether
different from those made by other nations, grounded
on reasons altogether distinct, namely, not the nature

of the soul, but the relations of the reasoning, loving,
religious creature to his reasoning Creator and God,
and embracing within its demand the immortality of
our whole nature, body and soul.

But it has not remained an unverified record of
faith. In the case of those of whose faith it is the
record there was no verification, because they were
not truly one with God. Their faith was the perfect
faith of imperfect men. But there came a perfect
saint, the Holy One and the Just, one truly the
Friend, yea the Son of God; who, indeed, set the
Lord ever before Him; who loved as He was
loved, and who therefore could not be left to death.
He died, indeed, but it was for our offences; and
He could not be holden of death. In Him, the
true Saint of God, all these hopes of eternal life
were verified,—" He brought life and immortality to
light."

Subjective hopes, ecstasies of joy, energies of faith,
became real, outward, tangible facts in Him; they
passed into history in His career. And thus He fulfils the law and the prophets. For if He was the
beginning of the New Testament, He was also the
end of the Old, and a part of it, and is the seal that
confirms the truth of it. And, looking backward, all
who went before Him and had such hopes, now realise
them in Him; and, looking forward, all who believe in
Him shall receive the fulfilment of them too: " Whosoever believeth in Me, though he were dead, yet shall

he live: and whosoever liveth and believeth in Me shall never die."

Unless Christ came and was what we hold Him to have been, unless His history was real, the Old Testament not only loses its meaning; it is worse, it becomes a terrible book. Its earnestness, and its faith, and its tenderness, and its cries after God and life,—in all which it expresses in a higher way than aught else the hopes of man's heart,—all are delusions, and only the miserable human soul mocking itself. And we look on them as we do on a withered flower, or rather as we do on the face of a dead child of our own, beautiful, doubly beautiful now, but dead, with death sitting in mockery over the loveliness. They are delusions; and if they were delusions that would continue, it might be well. But delusions cannot last. We shall know that they are delusions. But these hopes of ours are not delusions. "If Christ be not raised your faith is vain. But now is Christ risen from the dead, and become the firstfruits of them that slept. But every man in his own order: Christ the firstfruits; afterward they that are Christ's, at His coming."

V

THE TEMPTATION

V

THE TEMPTATION

MATTHEW iv. 1–11

THE Temptation of Christ is a subject of very great difficulty. It is difficult almost in every aspect in which it can be looked at. There is very great difficulty, although this perhaps is the least of the riddles connected with it, in understanding the details as to places and circumstances given in the narrative. We have difficulty in conceiving how Christ should be at one moment in the wilderness, and the next on a pinnacle of the temple, and the next on some exceeding high mountain from which He could see all the kingdoms of the world, even though the last expression should be used in a general way. And if we conclude that it was only in imagination that He was there, that He felt Himself in such positions, and saw mentally the glory, and felt under the sense of His Father's protection, as if He might expose Himself to any risk, even fling Himself down from the summit of the temple,—we instinctively feel that this is not the fair sense of the narrative.

.   And when we pass from the form to the matter, the difficulty appears even greater still. There is the difficulty of believing that the devil, daring though he be, should dare to measure himself with the Son of God, if he knew Him to be so in the fulness in which He was God's Son; and if we suppose he did not know Him in the fulness of His Godhead, the mysteriousness of the transaction is none the less.

There are some things in the narrative that seem to imply that Satan had not a full idea of who the person was that he was in collision with; he seems to handle our Lord with muffled fingers that carried no true sense of touch to their owner's mind. In the first two temptations he addresses Him as Son of God, though in a doubtful way: "If Thou be the Son of God"; but in the last he drops this appellation, as if in real perplexity how to address Him. Perhaps those words uttered from heaven at the baptism, "This is My beloved Son," fell on Satan's ear too; and though they conveyed to him no very distinct idea, yet he instinctively felt that He who was so named must be a decided foe of his; and so he ran blindly against Him, seeking to eject Him, as the eye does an unknown mote that troubles it.

And then passing from what is comparatively difficult to what is so in the highest degree, how shall we account for the Son of God being susceptible of temptation at all? Temptation to evil seems to imply not only the understanding of evil, and the conception of it in the mind, but also, one would say, the feeling of the desirability of the evil thing — an attraction so far towards it. For if it stop short of this, it is hard to see how it is a temptation. And can He who is God be so drawn towards what is evil? or, if He be so far drawn, is there not already sin?

These and many other difficulties beset this history. But there are mysteries everywhere, even in the histories of minds so simple as our own; and much more may we look for them in the career of One of whom an apostle has said: "Great is the mystery of godliness." In spite of all that is mysterious, this great fact remains, that the Son of God was in all points tempted like as we are, yet without sin.

There are two things in the passage:

1. The circumstances of the Temptation.

2. The Temptation itself, and Christ's manner of rebutting it.

1. The circumstances of the Temptation.—We must be very careful in noticing these. The Temptation came close on the back of the baptism. The turning-point of our Lord's career had arrived. Impulses which He had felt at times, perhaps, during the last thirty years, had at last become so frequent and powerful that they could be resisted no longer. He had come to a decision to take a public stand. With what precise views and purposes He put Himself under John's baptism is not easy to discover. But at that baptism

there occurred events which must have opened up the
way to Him, even if it had not been clear before,
and given His own mind a certainty and a direction,
even if we should suppose it to have been confused
with great emotions and conflicting purposes at the
time immediately prior: " He went up straightway
out of the water: and, lo, the heavens were opened
unto Him, and He saw the Spirit of God descending
like a dove, and lighting upon Him: and lo a voice
from heaven, saying, This is My beloved Son, in
whom I am well pleased." He was now born into
His Messianic office. And He felt it. The voice from
heaven interpreted Him to Himself, and came like
God's call to Him. Henceforth hesitancy, if ever He
had hesitated before, was impossible.

But there now fell upon Him even a greater disturbance of mind than ever lay on Him before. He
was in a new world. And the sights and forms of it
thronged in upon Him. The meaning of the Messiah-
ship flashed upon Him like lightning, rather than
dawned like the breaking day. He was the Christ
of God. And thoughts took possession of Him that
mastered Him, and left Him no power either of
resisting them, or of attending to anything besides.
He was weary or unaware of the common relations
of life. He was entranced. He wandered away abstracted, absorbed, fascinated by the awful forms of the
moral world that had suddenly been created around
Him. When He came up out of the water, and heard

the heavenly voice, "immediately the Spirit driveth Him into the wilderness."

Thoughts of what is beautiful seem to lose their intensity by being familiar. The beautiful strain of music, at first passionately admired, grows flat by repetition. The scene that struck us once as grand or charming, we pass by at last as tame and uninteresting. This may be true of these things. If it is, the reverse seems true of moral things. Familiarity seems rather to give new power to truth and godliness. At least there comes a moment when truths of religion, held separately in the mind perhaps for long, acquire a new intensity, and gather themselves together with an irresistible force. As you have seen on a sultry summer's day the heavens clear, except here and there a small electric cloud, yet each of these separate clouds seems impelled by an instinct to join itself to the others, and speedily they all combine, and the heavens grow dark, and the storm breaks with ominous sounds ; so in the mind the separate truths that lay apart at last gather into one, and cloud its sky, and the tempest breaks with destructive fury.

There is such a tempest in the history of many minds. There was one in Christ's. In some it is more intense than in others. In Him its intensity can be measured by this, that it raged for forty days, during which time He was in the wilderness with the wild beasts ; and in those days He did eat nothing. Why His was more intense than any man's we may readily guess, and also

8

in what respects His differed from that of any man.
Yet virtually the tempest is the same in all, and its
causes are the same. It is a moral tempest. It comes
through the revelation, to the mind, of the condition
of mankind. It is the realising of this. Its elements
are the same in all. It rises when the Spirit con-
vinces of sin, of righteousness, and of judgment. Sin,
righteousness, judgment,—these are its elements.

Ah, what elements of awful trouble lie in the souls
of us all, and in the world about us! Ordinarily we
are placid and calm. It seems impossible that these
smooth, indifferent, gay, hopeful, busy minds of ours
should be the scenes of anything unpleasant. They
resemble that sleeping ocean, cradled between islands,
charming in its repose, giving back to heaven its
peaceful smile. Of elements of evil it appears to have
none; even the little child might play with it. Yet
behold it at another time, furious in its passion, and
greedy in its lust for human life. So are our minds,
ordinarily placid, hardly movable, the circumstances of
our life peaceful, apparently with no elements in our
characters or our sphere of existence out of which
trouble can arise. Yet how the sweep of a wind from
heaven may stir them, lashing them into awful tempests!

The agony of men under the sense of sin is familiar
to us. We know what effect this one feeling produces. We may not wonder, therefore, at the profound
effects produced in Christ, when through the avenue
of His baptism He entered upon His Messianic work;

and there broke upon Him all the terrible forms with which the moral world is peopled,—sin, wrath, suffering, and His own awful personal interests in it, with its sharp pains and bitter cross, and He could see, behind all, the breaking glory as a sunrise beyond a tempestuous sea. We do not wonder that such thoughts —thoughts we can neither enter into nor conceive— held Him spellbound, as one entranced, for forty days. The absorption was not unnatural. And though the extent of it was such as to seem hardly credible, reaching even to forty days' fast, yet we know how great the power of the mind over the body is, even among ourselves ; and we can well conceive how much greater it was in Him. Let the intensity of it help us to understand in some measure the real meaning of the situation in which the Lord was.

To see a mind working in any circumstances is interesting; to see it arrested by thoughts or themes that fill it and almost master it, whether it be the statesman's mind or the moralist's, or the merchant's deeply involved in ventures on many seas, yet most profoundly interesting is the sight of a mind laid hold of by spiritual things—when God and truth, and evil, and death, and all those things that people the spiritual world stand out in more awful clearness than material things. And to no mind did they ever stand out so clear as to Christ's ; and in none were they so vividly reflected in the emotions that accompanied them. There was in Him a spiritual freshness and youthfulness, almost like the state of a child, in whose countenance, from its greater flexibility than that of a grown up person, every emotion and feeling shows itself very clearly.

The spiritual in Christ shone almost outside of Him, not only on great occasions, as on the mount of transfiguration, but at all times; and to an eye with any insight it revealed itself. And this is what makes Christ Himself, in the things that He did and the ways in which He showed Himself affected in the particular circumstances of His life, so great a study. No doubt we must always have recourse to His words, for they are plain, and we cannot be mistaken in them; but He Himself is deeper than His words, and what we might call His involuntary revelation of Himself —the feelings He manifested, the way in which He showed Himself moved and affected on occasions—is almost profounder than the things which He formally spoke. This strange absorption or almost fascination, which fell on Him at the threshold of His mediatorial work, casts a clearer light on the meaning of the situation to Him, than any words He ever let fall.

And we must not think that the way in which He was affected was something peculiar to His divine nature or due to it, and therefore something with which we cannot, or need not, sympathise. The opposite is truer. For He was now going to be indeed the son of man. He was entering into the life of mankind, taking up His place in the situation in which men stood, accepting their responsibilities and charging Himself with their destinies. It was just to His being in man's place that His agitation of mind was due; and it was an agitation which would overtake us all, if we were only able to feel, as He felt, man's real condition before God. We are generally occupied most of all with considering what Christ did for us. That He gave Himself up unto death is so wonderful that it almost entirely absorbs our attention, and enchains our gratitude. Yet even the meaning of this will become clearer to us by the study of Christ's own mind, the way in which He looked at it, and the way in which He viewed the whole position in which He was placed. Christ taught us by words; but He was Himself the great lesson. His consciousness, if we could but unfold it, and read it off, is the great revelation.

It is necessary, also, to note the condition in which Christ was at the time when the temptation took place. The moment the tempter chose was the most perilous moment possible for Him who was tempted. It was the moment when the reaction came after the great spiritual elevation and tension. After a fast of forty days and forty nights, reaction, mental as well as physical, was inevitable. The spiritual elevation traceable to His baptism and its attendant revelations could be sustained no longer, at least at such a height. Bodily weakness impeded the spirit's further flight. The pressure of ordinary needs came back, very intense from being so long denied. This also was natural.

The cravings of human nature cannot be eradicated; if too long repressed, they are apt to assert themselves with more than their due force. Human nature, innocent or sinful, seems subject to these laws. If sinful, then repression by the spiritual inclinations, long indulged, may cause these cravings, when the spiritual pressure is relaxed, to reassert themselves in an excessive and flagrant outbreak. But even in innocent human nature there must be danger of reaction. As undue exertion may exhaust the body, so spiritual tension may exhaust the mind; and as Christ sat down weary at the well of Samaria, so He seems to have awakened out of His abstracted condition in the wilderness, with His mind weary also. His human nature, the needs of which had been so long neglected, now rose in its strength, and urgently demanded help — "afterward He hungered." And this was the moment chosen by Satan to tempt—a most perilous moment; the moment when Christ could be taken at most disadvantage; the moment when, if I may say so, the spiritual part of Him was weakest, being exhausted, and the natural strongest, having just reasserted itself in all its might. No fair foe would have compelled his adversary to give battle in such circumstances. But one hardly looks for chivalry in the leader of evil. Yet Christ, at His weakest, proved stronger than Satan at his strongest.

2. The Temptation and its rebutting by Christ.—"And
when the tempter came to Him, he said: If Thou be
the Son of God, command that these stones be made
bread. But He answered and said: It is written, Man
shall not live by bread alone, but by every word that
proceedeth out of the mouth of God."

Looking about Him in the wilderness, under the
gnawings of hunger, the Lord saw nothing that could
minister to His wants. In that dry brown waste not
a tree could be seen, not a bush even, from which a
wild berry could be gleaned. Only stones lay thickly
scattered on the hot ground. And the wish entered
His mind: Oh, that these plentiful stones were but
bread! And after the wish the thought: Might they
not be made bread? Have I not the power? I feel I
have. Need the Son of God suffer such keen pangs
of hunger?

This was the temptation. But after this other
thoughts came — the thought about Himself, that
though Son of God, He was a man, having voluntarily
entered into the dependent condition of man, within
which it was above all things necessary that He should
confine Himself. And then this thought of Himself
was followed by thoughts of God, of God's will and
God's power. It is not for man to choose by what
means he shall live; it is for God. I am God's. I cast
myself on God. I shall not perish. God will preserve
me in the way He pleases: "*Man* shall not live by
bread alone, but by every word that proceedeth out

of the mouth of God." Men do live by bread; yet God can dispense with bread. He can keep men alive by other ways, by many other ways, by any creative word that proceedeth out of His mouth.

This was the repelling of the Temptation. The general object of all the temptations was to introduce something amiss into the relation subsisting between the man, Christ Jesus, the Son of God, and God His Father—to confuse these relations, to sow in the mind of Christ some thought or some feeling that would break up His due relation to God. The devil sought to make Christ play once again the game he had played himself; he sought to detach Christ from God, to make Him take up an independent position. He harped on His being Son of God, and what rights and powers such a great person must possess. Christ, on the other hand, fought against this idea with all His might. He put Himself down. When Satan dexterously insinuated that He should take His proper place, He set up God. He put down every temptation by naming God.

To the first temptation Christ answered, Man shall live by every word that cometh out of the mouth of God; to the second, Thou shalt not tempt God; to the third, Thou shalt worship God. I think a sting of madness must have gone through Satan's mind at every one of these answers. Whether he betrayed it or no, it must have been like a sword at his heart, this mention of submissiveness to God. Every reply of Christ's was not only a protection of Himself, but an assault upon His adversary. He not only parried his thrust, but cut him to the ground at every stroke.

The first temptation was a temptation to distrust of God, to impatience under the restraints and privations imposed by Him, and to undertake to supply His own needs independently of Him—"Command that these stones be made bread." It was a temptation to gratify the needs and cravings of our ordinary nature, without waiting for God to give the means, and to indicate the time.

This was a temptation to which the man Christ Jesus was susceptible, just as we all are. He had a human nature. This nature had the ordinary qualities of our own, its appetites, its impulses, its necessities. These belong to innocent human nature. They belong to sinful human nature in a disordered and excessive state. To be righteous is to hold these appetites and impulses in hand, and regulate them by God's will. To sin is to give way to them in forbidden circumstances or forbidden degrees. The temptation to which Christ was subjected was to indulge them in circumstances where God had denied the lawful means. There were means, but not lawful means. The man Christ Jesus, in the condition in which each of us is as a mere man, restricted within the ordinary laws of human life, had no means of appeasing His extreme hunger.

But the Son of God had means—He could command the stones to be made bread. Satan suggested that He should. And thus the temptation became not only

beyond measure complicated, but diabolically subtle.
It was a high game that Satan was playing.   Suppose
Christ, under such strong pressure as His hunger brought
to bear upon Him, had supplied His own needs in this
supernatural way, He would immediately have lifted
Himself out of the plane of an ordinary man ; His life
would have been no human life, and His whole appearance for our salvation would have gone for nothing.
That great purpose of God, that a godly and pure life
should be lived upon the earth in human conditions,
would have been frustrated a second time.

But more than that, there would have been a human
God upon the earth, independent of God in heaven.
There would therefore have been two Gods.   This was
perhaps what Satan aimed at, to disrupt the Godhead,
if that could be, by creating in it two disagreeing wills.
But, in addition, see how complicated the temptation
became ; it was a temptation to Christ not merely to
gratify His lower wants in circumstances forbidden, but
to use even His spiritual powers for this purpose,—the
temptation to make His spiritual powers useful in pro-
viding gratifications for His lower nature.

Satan's argument was in effect this, that it was fitting
and proper that Christ should use the power He possessed to minister to the needs He felt.   Such a gift
or power as Sonship gives may surely be employed in
emergencies like the present, or for purposes in themselves good and lawful, above all, to prevent or remedy
evils—the pains of hunger, the lawful cravings of human

nature. But these are natural and not evil. Nature has her rights, her desires, her necessities ; unfortunately they cannot always be gratified, but surely they may justly be gratified, when it is possible. Spiritual powers of an exceptional kind, which are above the ordinary, need not make one blind to advantages of another kind, even though it be through these spiritual powers that they come. If one can change the spiritual into the currency of the temporal, if the temporal be good and innocent, surely that is both lawful and praiseworthy. Could an argument be more plausible in itself, and in the circumstances ? Christ had fasted forty days. It might be said that food was not only a mercy, but a necessity. It was even doubtful how far it was right, considering what the consequences might be, to refuse to employ the powers He possessed. It is possible to be over-scrupulous. At any rate, when life is at stake, men do not scrutinise too closely the means they use to preserve it, if means there be.

This was Christ's temptation. Does anything like it befall any of us? Much like it befalls us all. "He was tempted in all points like as we are." There is no moment, no act of that life of His, but is full of meaning, if we could fathom it. Does not our human nature many times cry for 'bread' in circumstances when God has denied it? I do not speak of the mere natural hunger, though there are many that cry for bread, and cannot lawfully find it; for that is the evil of our present civilisation, that while many surfeit, many at the same time starve. But I speak of the general desires of our human nature—its hunger and cries for bread in conditions where it can find only stones to put into its mouth. It is a hungry thing, our human soul. It is full of appetencies, it is agitated with longings, it craves and cries and pants with desire, and opens wide its mouth for bread. And there are generally means, though not always lawful means, of gratifying it.

The expense of living and the unequal distribution of wealth many times prevent men from entering into those relations, or taking that place, which they long to do. Around them is the wilderness of life where no bread is, only stones. And they cry for bread, for food to their natural desires; and they hunger for position and distinction. They cannot want. They cannot wait. They will use the power they have, the power of self-command with which God has endowed every man; that free will which God has given as the highest gift to man, and which makes them in some sense sons of God; they will use this to create bread for themselves. Unlawful indulgence, fraudulent trading, and much else, are but specimens of the mad efforts of men to create bread for themselves when God has denied it, and is trying them by making them wait.

And not only in this broader, coarser way are men tempted to use their power to create bread for themselves without the concurrence of God, but also very often in that subtler way they are tempted to use their spiritual gifts or attainments as the means of ministering to the desires of their lower nature. The variety and subtlety of such temptations is very great. Regard, for example, the hothouse civilisation in the midst of which we live—the nervous enfeeblement from an easy and effeminate life through several generations, and the excitability of the emotions prevalent among the wealthier classes — the craving among all classes for what is sensational showing itself not only in professed works of fiction, but even in our religious magazines, not one of which appears able to exist without a romance or two in its pages.

Fancy a person with a spiritual gift of any magnitude in such a sphere, in which effeminacy has taken the place held by superstition in the dark ages—fancy such a person exerting a very wide influence, courted, run after, the subject of all the blandishments which enfeebled natures so lavishly bestow. How he is tempted to use his gift from God to further any lower ends he may have! and no one is altogether free of them ; to accumulate property, for example, by setting his spiritual power up to auction, to work his way into social connections of a useful or gratifying kind, to gain himself a place in general estimation flattering to vanity, and thus to acquire an influence not specially for good, but just in general an influence. These are all things craved for by human nature. They are the bread for which it cries; and the spiritual power may be made to minister to them. Or, again, in business a man is sometimes tempted in the same way. He has a spiritual gift, a power of exhortation, a gift of prayer, a place of influence in the counsels of the Church, a name for earnestness; and it *is* possible to put out these talents a little to usury in the world's bank. A man may be tempted to consider whether it would not be professionally a better thing for him, if he were to go over to this communion or that Church rather than remain in the somewhat obscure place where he is; and he may not perhaps be ill-pleased to think that the rather prominent part his gift has enabled him to take in religious movements, and the kind of people this has made him intimate with, may possibly by and by react favourably on his prospects in another direction.

Or perhaps the temptation might show itself in another way. You have undergone, say, a change of mind, and in circumstances rather remarkable, — if, indeed, anything could be called remarkable in comparison with the fact that *you* should have undergone such a change. There is naturally a tendency to make much of you, to bring you out and play you off, to draw attention to you as a monument. It is a process certainly full of peril to you. Your attention is drawn to yourself, to the wonders of your case. You are made to look great to yourself, to seem something uncommon. You say, indeed, "By the grace of God I am what I am"; yet is there not a tendency, which grows by repetition, to put more stress upon *I am* than upon the *grace of God*? Our sense of self-importance will obtrude itself even here. The craving of the lower nature for bread will manifest itself, and try to make bread even in these unpromising conditions.

To all these attempts of Satan to raise in Christ the idea of Himself, of His high place in the universe, of His needs, and His rights, and His capabilities, Christ replied by naming God—God's mouth. He put Himself down; He set God up. Ah, how difficult it is for us to estimate and use ourselves rightly! How hard to take our proper and just position in reference to other men and before God, to act always becomingly, in a way suitable to our place and to the kind of ability and mind God has bestowed upon us, to exert the influence that we should naturally exert, and to exert it just in the natural way! Most men, perhaps, think too highly of themselves. Yet by no means all men. There are men who habitually estimate themselves too low, and all of whose mistakes in life arise from this cause, men who are only awakened to a proper appreciation of what they really are by the public voice pronouncing their acts unworthy of them, or declaring that they have not in some crisis come forward to take the place and say the things they ought. It is very difficult to analyse human nature, and find the true causes of its defects. Yet it is possible that there may be, in such cases, some hidden vice or badness which paralyses action, and of which the public judgment is unaware.

And if it be difficult to take our right place among men, how much more difficult is it to take it before

God! Not to trust God was Christ's first temptation;
to presume upon God's goodness was His second. Not
at all, or too much altogether, are the two extremes
between which we oscillate. When our Lord proceeded
to wash the disciples' feet, Peter said : Lord, Thou shalt
never wash my feet. Our Lord replied, It I wash thee
not, thou hast no part with Me. Whereupon the apostle
exclaimed, Lord, not my feet only, but also my hands
and my head. To which the quiet answer was, He
that is washed needeth not save to wash his feet.
We pass from extreme to extreme. A right place
before God is difficult to take. The right place is
that our sense of Him should overbear, and almost
obliterate, our sense of ourselves in His presence, that
He and the intimations of His will and the assurances He has given — the assurances of His love
directed to our good—should make us lose ourselves
in complete dependence upon Him.

Now one lesson that may be impressed on us by this
narrative is this : that we must beware of religious
reactions. It was at the moment of the reaction, in
Christ's mind, from the spiritual to the natural that
Satan intervened to tempt. We are all subject to this.
After spiritual excitement there comes a dulness over
the soul, and the old desires that had been kept down
rise again, and demand their accustomed bread. The
old man whom we thought crucified and buried with
Christ is but half dead. He is apt to rise to life
again. It is then that Satan tempts. He uses the

opportunity. He must use the laws of our mind for his purposes, just as we use the laws of nature for ours. Satan has no creative power more than ourselves. And just as for our mechanical operations we employ physical laws of nature, so he employs with rare skill the laws of our mind. The Spirit of God can use our minds otherwise. He can create. Satan can only use. But his use is full of skill. Beware of the moment when the old nature rises up again with fierce demands for its accustomed bread. Give no way to it. To its cry for bread, answer with the Son of God: "Man shall not live by bread alone."

Christ's first two temptations were indirect efforts to seduce Him. The third seems altogether different. Satan now throws off all disguises, and makes a direct proposal to Christ. With that shamelessness which only natures wholly evil, and unable to believe in good in others, ever show, he assumes that Christ has only been pretending piety all the time. He says to Him in effect: Let us have done with this fencing. Let us understand one another. We do understand one another. Your position is, it cannot but be, my own. We have common interests against *Him*. Let us make common cause, and the crown of the universe is yours. Satan recognised the power of our Lord, the vast spiritual range of His mind, His royal nature. Here was an instrument, a mind of such capacity, that through Him alone the kingdoms of the world, a consolidated universe, could be arrayed against the

9

sovereignty of God.   If He could be detached from
God, the scheme was accomplished.

But what I wanted to say was this : Our Lord's
temptations are not only types of those which we
have each to go through as individuals, but types
of the temptations which mankind, the human race,
has to pass through as a whole. His first temptation
was to distrust God and provide for Himself.   This
might correspond to the age of barbarism in human
history, when, with little sense of God above, each
man's hand was for himself.   This age is past.

The second temptation was to over-trust in God, to
presumption on His interference.   This corresponds
to the age of superstition ; and that age is also past.
His last temptation was to assume, in the consciousness
of His own powers, the rule of the world, as none
but He could do, not in subordination to God, but
as a rival to Him.   And is not this the temptation
towards which mankind is drifting in these last times?
Not towards the brutalities of barbarism, not to the
abjectness of superstition, but towards a moral un-
godliness.   Gradually bringing the world under subjection, learning the secrets of things one after another
and turning them to account, and with every new stride
of advancement acquiring a new consciousness of itself
and the range of its powers, this consciousness being
accompanied at every step with a diminution of the
sense of dependence upon God,—does not mankind
seem moving on towards that sovereignty of the

world which was opposed to Christ, and in a way that fulfils the condition on which it was offered to Him—the renunciation of homage to God? Is not this the temptation to which mankind is now subjected?

At all events this is sure, that in all the temptations that come to us, whether as single persons or mankind as a whole, our strength against them lies in God—in naming God, in setting God before us. In our straits, we should say: We live by the word that cometh out of the mouth of God. In our high moments, when we feel capable of anything, and think we could cast ourselves from the pinnacle to the ground with impunity, we should not neglect the natural safeguards with which God has surrounded us, but use them wisely. And when, feeling our own powers, a sense and consciousness of ourselves rises in our mind, we should set ourselves in the light of God, and walk humbly with Him: "Thou shalt worship the Lord thy God."

Again, Christ resisted temptation. "He was in all points tempted like as we are, *without sin.*" Think of the meaning of such a statement. Look into your own minds, and consider the infinite troop of thoughts, feelings, and desires that rise continuously up out of the heart. The myriad atoms of dust that are seen to fill the air, when you send a ray of light into a dark room, give but a faint idea of the million emotions that crowd the soul. And in Christ these were quicker, deeper, wider far than in our narrow hearts. Yet of them all not one was amiss—not one erred by

excess or by defect. There was not one irregular
desire, not one inordinate affection, not one unjust
judgment, not one resentful feeling. You do not
believe it. You cannot conceive it—" tempted in all
points like as we are, without sin."

If such a thing be true, then this world on which
it happened is no more the sinful world it was. It
is another world. A change deserving to be called
infinite has come over it. In God's eye it must have
become new. I think this earth must since then have
seemed a brighter star to heavenly eyes. It is another
world. "Behold, the Lamb of God, which taketh away
the sin of the world!" We have not a High Priest
who cannot be touched with the feeling of our infirmities, but one that hath been in all points tempted
like as we are, without sin,—touched with the feeling
of our infirmities, able to sympathise and to help. We
make much of Christ's suffering, and His understanding
us, and His sympathising with us. We are glad of His
sympathy. But have we ever sympathised with Him
away down in that dim desert, taken no account of
by men, not upheld by God, face to face with the very
principle of evil, with the wild beasts, carrying on in
absolute conditions the mortal struggle of mankind,
the fight of faith—for us? Have we ever sympathised
with Him whose sympathy we are so glad to claim
for ourselves? Ah, well, we are weak, and He is strong;
yea, but He was strong in the Lord and in the power
of His might.

But He was tempted, *without sin.* "He did no sin, neither was guile found in His mouth." It is possible to pass through temptation without falling — to be tempted, without sin. But somehow both men of the world and Christians seem to think that falling before temptation must happen—that it is inevitable. The man of the world, when youthful irregularities are brought to his notice, will say as little as possible on the matter. He will not defend them ; but neither, knowing what he knows, can he very heartily condemn them ; and he sums up his views of fatalism and free will in the comprehensive sentiment that young men will be young men. Fathers, guardians, men of the world, men of influence, this is the devil's formula in another shape.

Finally, the joy that comes when temptation is overcome. It is said: "Then the devil leaveth Him ; and behold, angels came and ministered unto Him." Neither man nor angel helped Christ when tempted. God seemed to stand aside and watch the struggle. A father will watch with intensest absorption the trial of his child ; he will mark the higher principles called out by the emergency, and exult as he sees these principles wrestling with the lower desires, and finally rising to preponderance and gaining the victory. Joyful will be the moment when he clasps his victorious child in his arms ; joyful the moment for the child — joyful from the sense of power and the feeling of higher sympathy.

The angels ministered to Christ ; they brought Him that which He needed. Perhaps the truth to be learned is that when the unlawful gratification of the desires of our nature is resisted, the lawful gratification is a divine thing. We feel that Heaven is giving it to us to enjoy. Or perhaps the truth is this, that when we resist unlawful pleasures, God compensates us by sending into our souls, through His heavenly messengers, divine joys and a spiritual fulness. It is sweet to have resisted temptation ; the mind is filled with a heavenly satisfaction.

When we have carried on a long struggle, and have been pinched or in distress, and have felt as if we must give way, and have only been upheld by naming God every hour, saying, God is able, God will not fail us ; then, when the relief comes at last, there is a strange sense that it has come direct from God. Angels come and minister to us. The joy of resisting temptation is the highest joy men can feel. It is a moment when our little life here grows larger, and we feel ourselves lifted into a wider sphere: we have a sense of fellowship with higher beings, and are somehow conscious of their sympathy. All God's creation smiles upon us, and appears made for our joy. Every pore of our nature seems opened, and there rushes into us a stream of joys that lift us into another world. At such moments angels do minister unto us.

At other times, however, even the Christian, worn out with the struggle against old habits, loses heart, and

gives in to the evil, and regards falling before temptation as a thing inevitable, however lamentable and
humbling. But when the fit of passion is over and the
appetite sated, there comes a moment of utter loathing
both of the sin and of one's self; and the higher mind
rises to its place, and seems to have its foot upon the
neck of the grovelling desires, and we resolve anew
that in God's strength we shall never give way again.
The evil desire appears drowned in our tears, or put
to flight for ever before the moral power of our shame
and contrition. But by and by the torpid thing shows
vitality again; and what looked hideous gains a new
and strange attractiveness, and the resisting mind is
drawn into concurrence and overcome, and we feel
that we cannot resist, that we must give way — and
again we fall. Thus we grow weaker and weaker, and
come to think that sinning is inevitable, and all that
we can do is to be as sorry as possible about it. But
it is not inevitable. Temptation may be overcome.
An unstained youth may be lived. The fight of faith
may be fought victoriously. The youth, Jesus, passed
through life pure. The Author of the faith was also
the Finisher. From end to end He overcame—tempted
in all points like as we are, without sin. And in His
strength and His name, we may conquer also. "Be of
good cheer, I have overcome the world."

VI

THE TRANSFIGURATION

VI

THE TRANSFIGURATION

MATTHEW xvii. 1–8; MARK ix. 1–8; LUKE ix. 28–36

To understand this subject fully one would need to know, *first*, what this transformation or transfiguration which passed on Christ was in itself; *second*, what the meaning of it was to Christ Himself, what purpose it served in the chain of His experience, or what its meaning was in connection with the progress of His life—how it helped Him, how it bore on what He now is, and the like; and, *third*, what meaning it had for His disciples. This last may be in great measure the meaning which it is intended to have for us. No doubt, if we could understand its meaning to Christ Himself, and could perceive its relation to His whole history and life, this would add much to the deepness of its significance to us. But perhaps this is beyond us.

Yet there are many things which, though imperfectly apprehended intellectually or in themselves, leave, nevertheless, a great impression on us; and even though we suppose the disciples had no very clear idea of its meaning, still it was a very glorious condition this in which they saw Jesus; and it may have suggested to their minds deeper thoughts of Him than any which they had yet had. And it is fitted to do the same for us, even though we make no attempt to understand it in itself. My object at present is to make two or three practical remarks, suggested by the whole circumstances, rather than enter on the question of the transfiguration in itself. There is one point, however, which touches this subject itself, to which I cannot but allude.

The transfiguration or metamorphosis, to use the original word of two of the evangelists, is described by Luke as follows: " As He prayed the fashion of His countenance was altered, and His raiment was white and glistening"; and by Mark thus: " He was transfigured before them; and His raiment became shining, exceeding white as snow, so as no fuller on earth can white them." There shone a glory out of the countenance of Christ; and all His body seemed to shine with the same glory, so that His raiment became exceeding white, as no fuller on earth could white it. Now it is manifest that this glory was no reflected light. It was not a splendour that fell on Him from without, and lighted Him up. The glory came from within. It corresponded to something going on in His mind. The incident was not a spectacular exhibition, enacted for the sake of the disciples; for though Jesus, perhaps with some presentiments and feelings that we cannot analyse, took the three disciples with Him, this was not done with the purpose of

impressing them, but from the same craving for fellowship which made Him take them with Him into the
garden. Neither can we consider that it was a mere
foretaste of the joy that was set before Him which
the Father already gave Him ; as if, in order to uphold Him in view of His approaching death, He had
enveloped Him for a moment with the glory that
was to come. For this would be to conceive that
glory which was to come, and which is now His, in
too external a manner. We must by all means hold
that the external change that passed upon Him was
but the reflection of movements in His own mind and
heart going on at the moment.

It may help us a little if we remember the general
circumstances in which Christ was placed, and His
immediate posture when this occurred to Him. It
occurred soon before His death, when it was now nigh
at hand, and after it had begun to occupy so large a
place in His own mind, that not distant reference to it
had broken from Him. Indeed, He had made a formal
statement regarding it to His disciples : " He began to
teach them that the Son of Man must suffer many
things, and be rejected of the elders . . . and be killed.
. . . And He spake that saying openly. Six days after
He taketh with Him Peter and James and John into
an exceeding high mountain apart, and was transfigured
before them." These were the general circumstances.

And the immediate posture of Christ was that of
prayer. " As He prayed, the fashion of His countenance

was altered." We cannot doubt that the subject on which
He drew near to the Father was His approaching death.
This was the subject on which Moses and Elias spake
with Him—the decease which He should accomplish
at Jerusalem. Exercised in some way on this subject
in prayer, holding communion with God, and this the
subject of the communion, the fashion of His countenance altered. From the intensity and the nature
of this communion, He became outwardly glorious.
There came a radiance from His mind within, that
lighted up His face and all His form. Joy makes the
face to shine. There is a power and a light in the
countenance, when a pure thought or a noble resolution fills the mind. Sorrow is supposed to darken the
countenance, and lay the shadow of a cloud upon
it. But there is often a deeper joy in sorrow, the
feeling as of a new birth and a new consecration,
and of a refining and quickening of all that is highest
in us, and an enlarging of the meaning of all things
and of human life, that causes the face to shine with
a subdued but heavenly light.

It was perhaps no particular thought that filled the
mind of Christ at this moment. It was that indescribable tumultuous crowding of emotions which
rushed into His heart, as He lay on His Father's
bosom and saw, now standing close before Him,
His death, and all its meaning. The elements of
such a condition of mind are hardly to be taken
apart. Some part of it, perhaps, was love—love to

the world, meeting the Father's love and intensified by it, and no longer able to be confined to His heart, but breaking out and beaming with a divine glory in His face and form. We have seen the radiance of a human love that bends over and falls on the worn face of a sick child. What would be the radiance of the love of the Son of Man falling upon the face of a sick and restless world? Or perhaps some part of it was of another kind. Suffering gives men a dignity. We go into it with a firm step and a light in the countenance; the loftiness of the resolution lightens up the face, and deeper feelings of many kinds rush into the mind, and look out from the countenance.

Now the hour of Christ's sufferings was at hand, and He had to gather up His mind to face it; and this resolution taken anew, and taken with such steadfastness, must have shed an awful light over the Redeemer's face. Yet the light does not appear to have been awful merely. Many elements went to compose it. But it arose most probably from His mind taking in the full meaning of His death and that which should follow it. Standing now in full view of the Cross, having forced on His mind the approaching realities, yet also looking beyond to the joy set before Him, and straitened till all should be accomplished, and in the fellowship of His Father, these multiplying thoughts and emotions, thronging into His heart like the rushing waters of a swollen river, glorified Him by anticipation even here. It was a mental rehearsal of His work and history,

a more full and complete taking of it in than had
before been possible to Him; and this full mental
realising of it, with the emotions accompanying it, reflected itself externally in an anticipation for a moment
of something like the glory that was to follow. For
what is the glory of Christ now? or what is the glory
of God? or what shall be the glory of redeemed men?
Shall it not be the spiritual nature clothing itself with
a spiritual body that fitly expresses the mind? Is not
Christ's glory that halo which surrounds Him, bodying
out His blessed mind and nature, and expressing all
that He has done, His grace and truth and love, His
merciful patience and self-sacrifice, and the lofty place
in the universe to which these have raised Him?

And all these things, gathered together in Christ's
mind, realised to themselves for a moment a fit
expression in His earthly body, even the glory beforehand which now is His eternally. And surely it is a
great sight to see, more wonderful far than that bush,
burning and not consumed, which the prophet went
aside to behold. Would that we were found looking
on it with a more adoring curiosity! This is one of
the few incidents, such as the Temptation, the Agony,
and the occasion on which it is said that Jesus rejoiced
in spirit, which enable us to detect the moral tensions
in the mind of Christ, and see the waves of thought
and feeling that rolled in His heart under a calm and
placid demeanour.

But I wish rather to refer to some ideas which are

more practical, and which the passage as a whole suggests.

The first, which scarcely needs to be stated, is that if we are to see anything of this glory of Christ, or of Christ in His glory, if we are to have anything more than mere ordinary views of it, we must go apart with Christ. He led the disciples into a high mountain apart, and was transfigured before them. He does sometimes reveal Himself to men even in the crowd. There are moments when there breaks in upon us amidst our ordinary occupations, when we are at the receipt of custom or in the moving crowd, a divine face of majestic glory and beauty, such as appeared to Matthew and to Zaccheus. But though Jesus showed Himself to Zaccheus in the throng, that full view of Him that turned the rich publican into a liberal disciple was reserved for his own house.

We must lay aside our employments, and follow Him where the world's sounds do not reach, if we would see His glory in any fulness. I do not mean merely that we must lay aside our worldly occupations, but all occupations in which we are ordinarily engaged. The early disciples, under pressure of occupations, exclaimed: It is not meet that we should leave the word of God and serve tables; take the management of these things upon yourselves, that we may have leisure to preach the gospel. But Christ said more. He said to these preachers, Come apart with Me and have a short respite from preaching. He said this in words more than

10

once : "Come ye yourselves apart into a desert place, and rest awhile." He did not, however, bid them go apart themselves, but come apart with Him. He took them apart, that they might fill the sinking fountain of their life out of Himself. And what He more than once said in words, He was always saying in effect by His own example and practice. Rising up a great while before day, He was often found alone, with the Father, by the seashore or on the mountain side, replenishing His own life out of God. We must lay down our tools of whatever sort they be. We must throw aside our sermon-making no less than our money-making. We must lay down the teacher's art, that we may take up the learner's. We must cease to point to Christ, that we ourselves may have leisure to look at Him. Activity should give place to contemplation.

No doubt the fountain, when not drawn from, grows stagnant and sour, and ugly things gather on its surface. The heart and life cast up all kinds of foul weeds and scum, when their waters are not drained off in the sympathies and activities of love. But the drain may be too exhausting. When you dip the pitcher too often, the water becomes disturbed and turbid; when you use the same weapon too long, its edge gets turned and blunted; or, if not, the arm becomes weary, and the blows fall feebly. The truth perhaps does not grow old, but to the mind it seems to grow old; and the mind needs repose as well as the arm.

Of late years the mechanical appliances of religion

have been very greatly multiplied. We have trans-
ferred the exercise and drill which is characteristic of
the time in other matters into the sphere of religion.
And for many years religious literature has been so
abundant, and is always so ready to our hand, that we
can fill up every spare moment by reading. And the
consequence is, that we are always either busy doing
some work or other, or else absorbing into our minds
other people's thoughts. Now it may be true that the
thoughts of others are often greatly superior to
our own, and it may also be true that to anyone who
realises aright the condition of mankind,—their misery
and sin and blindness,—and who also realises what
they might be through the gospel of Christ, it may be
almost impossible to pause in the work of God. And
this also may be true, that in bringing the gospel
before men, and seeing how it is applicable to the most
diverse minds and the most dissimilar conditions, and
what changes it works, we may get views of the glory
of Christ which transcend all conception. Yet this is
also true, that a thought which we think ourselves is
more powerful to us than one supplied by others.

When men withdraw for a time from men into the
presence of Christ, they return among them with a
power and a light around them, of which they themselves are quite unaware; just as Moses came back
from the mount with a glory about him that dazzled
men's eyes, though he wot not that his face shone.
But it only shone when he was newly out of the

presence of God. In a little while, through the wear
and tear of life, it faded away from him, as the sunset
fades from the mountain tops. The Apostle Paul after
his conversion communed not with flesh and blood,
but, before he began to preach, spent three years in
the wilderness in fellowship with God. And there is
a singular fact in his history further on. When his
public ministry was arrested, and he lay for two years
in prison, he was thrown in upon himself and upon
thinking of Christ; and to while away the tedium of
the weary hours, this must have been his most grateful
employment. Now, in all those Epistles, written from
the prison, he makes use of a new word, namely, to
know: "That I might *know* Christ, and the power of
His resurrection. I count all things but loss for
the excellency of the *knowledge* of Christ Jesus my
Lord."

Paul had tasted of the joys of contemplation. He
had had leisure to think; and through reflection the
glories of Christ and the depth of meaning in the
gospel had grown on him, and had fascinated his
mind, so that he longed to enter more and more into
it, both in mind and heart, and to plunge himself into
its unfathomable deeps. Which of us sets himself
seriously and thoughtfully to study the gospel on all
its sides, or to draw for himself a full picture of the
Lord? Perhaps this is beyond the power of any mind.
No picture that you ever saw of Christ pleased you.
And no idea of Him your own mind could form would

satisfy. Yet perhaps if our minds were interested as
they should be, we would be making some effort;
and our little success would impress upon us how
transcendent the subject is.

The defect of our faith lies in its being languid.
There is no enthusiasm in our life. That has partly
happened to us which happened to the Jews. The law
came between them and God. And perhaps the gospel
has come between us and Christ. Which of us ever
sets himself seriously to conceive Christ to himself, to
realise Him as the living Lord? The apostle speaks
of the face of Christ, and I think he saw it daily.

But if to see in Christ anything above the ordinary
commonplaces of our faith, to see Him transfigured,
it be necessary to be much alone with Him, there
is another thing we must bear in mind. Christ has
nothing which He does not share. No experience of
His but may be ours. That which happened to Him
will also befall ourselves. In the fellowship of God the
fashion of His countenance became altered. And so,
in the fellowship of the Father and the Son, may ours.
We too shall be transfigured. The inward elevation
will reflect itself without, if not to our own eyes, to
the eyes of others. Moses came back out of the cloud
where he had been with God, with a light on his
countenance that dazzled every eye, though he himself
wist not that his face did shine. And from the same
presence we too shall come out radiant with a similar
light. And, like every other light, it will remove all

wrinkles from our face and from our disposition. The
greatness of the issues, and the thoughts that have
been engaging us, will reduce to nothing the frets of
life. We shall move among men with serenity, but
with sympathy, tender-hearted, kindly affectioned, for-
bearing and forgiving, not readily ruffled, smoothing
away irritations with a patient hand, meek, doing good
as we have opportunity, not thinking this life too mean
to attend to, but lifting it up, and filling all its offices
with love.

Look at those disciples at the foot of that hill, in the
midst of that crowd with that poor tortured child before
them, unable in the least to help him. There was
Satan, playing his most fantastic tricks before them,
flinging the child into the fire or into the water, so that
he wallowed foaming, and they could not lay a finger
on him: "This kind goeth not out but by prayer
and fasting." Through the multitude of their labours
they had grown exhausted, their faith and energy had
sunk low ; or through their too practical life they had
never attained to the needful power. The lesson is one
which in this practical time we have need to learn. We
must at times cease our work and go into a desert place
apart. We need reflection. Sustained contemplation
on the mysteries of the gospel has perhaps too little
place among us. Follow Christ out of the world 'up to
some height where the world lies beneath your feet.
Make Him the object of observation. Think of Him.
Think of Him only, and of what you know of Him. If

you do, does not this history warrant that you will see Him glorious? Does not what happened to Himself prove it? It was while in communion with God that He was transfigured: as He prayed—as He continued in prayer, the fashion of His countenance altered. And as you continue, a change will come over Him to your eye, you will see Him transfigured before you; the ordinary everyday Christ that you have heard spoken of, and known somewhat before, and lived with, and believed on, will become quite altered to you; He will stand out with a glory very great, so that you will exclaim, like Peter: "It is good for us to be here."

Another truth I must mention, and it is this : The transfigured Christ was not alone. "There appeared unto them Moses and Elias talking with Him."

There gather about the glorified Christ other forms, other human forms. There are *men* beside Him in His glory. The meaning of the presence of these two, Moses and Elias, may be partly this, that the law and the prophets were until Christ, and that all is now gathered up in Him. "He is the end of the law for righteousness to every one that believeth." The past becomes present; the beginnings made long ago now find their perfection. He came to fulfil the law and the prophets. All former efforts are made perfect in Him. Movements and currents that have been flowing since time began, sweeping on with a motion some- times felt and sometimes unfelt, find in Him the point towards which they tended.

Or these two, Elias and Moses, may have performed some office for Christ. "They spoke of His decease which He should accomplish at Jerusalem." Did they help Him? An angel at another time appeared strengthening Him. And it is possible that these two confirmed His spirit by showing Him how long this great event that was before Him had been in preparing, and that He must needs go through with it. The greatest of men know how, when in trouble, the very least and weakest may strengthen them. And these men, representing all the past, and representing to Christ all its meaning and all its tendencies and promises, may have done something for Christ. Wonderful strength in a creature, to be able to strengthen God! Wonderful weakness in the Creator, to draw strength from the sympathy and the representations of a creature! Most blessed community of nature and work between man and God, that thus they can give to, and receive from, one another! And there are moments in our history when we feel that it is needed. But the point I wish to emphasize is rather this, that Christ in His glory is not alone. There were men like ourselves around Him even when He was transfigured, and so there will always be. All the past is gathered up in Him, but the past is not obliterated. Men are not lost or overshadowed in Him, but rather brought out in their full significance.

Now this idea is one we like to dwell upon. For there is no more oppressive or paralysing thought than one that sometimes overcomes us, the thought of the utter nothingness of ourselves and of our life. What do we accomplish? What fruit or gain is there of our lives and the way we spend them? We walk upon the summer road, and see some ant tugging towards the common heap a husk. If it reaches the heap, it will increase it by a husk. But ten to one some foot will crush it, ere it has time. And so death falls on us, ere we have time to do aught. Or if we are spared, what is it that we do? Men's lives seem traced on water, so soon are they obliterated. Even the most brilliant of them seem traced in air, like a flash of lightning whose zigzag illumines the sky for a moment in its descent to the earth where it is buried.

In spite of all the halo that surrounds the heads of these two men, Moses and Elias, theirs was a history not without its sadness, like so many other histories, like almost all histories that have any meaning in the progress of the human race. Have not almost all those who were capable of doing very great things been taken away, ere the half was done which they could have done, or saw it needful to do? Fate is envious. It will permit no man to do very much. If it allows one to found, it will remove him, and give another the glory of building. If one sow, another will reap. Moses brought the people out of Egypt, but another led them into Canaan. Elijah threw down the altars of Baal, but other hands were left to rear the altars of Jehovah. It is oftentimes what we might call the immaturest contribution of great minds that the world receives. Just when they are mellowing, and the ripest fruit is about to be gathered from them, a tempest shakes them, and it falls.

Has the world ever yet got from any of its greatest children the best that they could have given? One has sometimes seen an old man weep, when he witnessed the labours and the prospects of younger men into which he could no more enter. And how deep must have been the longing of men like Moses and Elias to do more, to see more, to know more. What would be the end of that work to which they were permitted to put their hands? Inexorable was the fate that called them away in the midst of it. Yet surely they and their work shall not go for nothing. Compared to Christ and His work, their work was mean enough. Yet they too did something in their day. This Moses was privileged to give to mankind the law, graven at least on stone; Christ came with it, graven on the fleshy tables of His nature: "Thy law is within My heart." This Elias was very zealous for the Lord of hosts. But Christ could say: "The zeal of Thine house hath eaten me up." Yet they are not swallowed up in the greatness of His work, rather they are brought out by it. "He came not to destroy the law, but to fulfil it." He came not to supersede men, but to perfect them. No effort is lost; no man who does work is lost. The effort is perfected in Christ's work, and the man stands beside Him, his fashion brought out by the very light of Christ's glory. How many outlines hover about

Christ if we could perceive them, human spirits pressing towards Him as the perfection of all their own travail. We have no knowledge of them; their memory is gone, their names even do not remain. But they remain. They worked, and longed, and drew rude material forms which Christ has made spiritual, and realised dim shadows of a life which He has perfected. And they are all about Him. And on the day when He shall come to be glorified in His saints, His very brightness shall bring them all into relief, and they shall be seen.

Is there anyone whom you remember and think of, whom, perhaps, no one else remembers, or only one here and there, in whose recollection his memory is blessed; one who laboured too, and set before him such a life as that which Christ fulfilled in perfection, who sought not his own; who pleased not himself; who, though moving within narrow limits, lived according to his lights, and did justly, and loved mercy, and walked humbly with God,—is there such a one dear to you now passed away? or are you yourself one of such a kind, labouring very obscurely, leading a life which, though earnest, shall leave no mark, and looking forward to the time when you shall pass away and no one speak of you, or, at least, when your life and work shall be a shadowy outline and remembrance? Yet, of a truth, that life, if it has been lived in Christ, and for Him, shall not be lost. That shadowy outline shall yet be made bright. Christ's glory shall lighten it up on that day when "they that be wise

shall shine as the brightness of the firmament, and
they that turn many to righteousness as the stars, for
ever and ever."

I cannot refrain from drawing attention to this contrast, though to some it may appear a commonplace,—
this contrast, the glorified Christ above and the convulsed demoniac child below.   There are many contrasts
in this world of ours.   Joy and sorrow sit by turns on
the same brow.   Wealth rears its palace, and poverty its
hovel, side by side.   Life and death jostle each other in
the street.   Marriage and burial compete for possession
of the highways.   The philanthropist and the murderer
meet.   It is a world of contrasts.   Yet, was ever contrast like this?   Up on that hill, in fellowship with the
Father, surrounded with the great of past ages, His
face illuminated with the radiance of grace, and truth,
and love, and great resolves, and vast and comprehensive conceptions, about to give Himself for the life of
the world, achieving the one great moral work of the
universe—the man Jesus.   Below, the maniac child—
man, too—convulsed, distorted, the prey of evil.   Oh,
how wide are the limits of humanity!   What may be
realised in it, both of glory and of debasement!   To
what height goodness may elevate it! and to what
awful depths evil may sink it!   There is the possibility
of this contrast, and of one even more awful, in us
all.

There is still one other lesson—less pleasant, indeed,
but not less true and needful to be learnt—which

may be noticed: The glimpses of glory obtained on the Mount of Transfiguration are of brief duration. We seek in vain to give them permanence. One of the apostles, at least, desired to retain the heavenly visitors. "Peter said unto Jesus, Master, it is good for us to be here: and let us make three tabernacles; one for Thee, and one for Moses, and one for Elias." What his exact thought was, we can hardly say; but he evidently felt the grandeur, the goodness of the scene, and would have retained it if he could. But this was not possible. One evangelist says, almost in apology, that Peter said this, "not knowing what he said." He was intoxicated with the glory of the vision. But the desire to retain it could not be gratified.

Such heavenly figures will not abide permanently on an earthly mountain, nor in tabernacles made with hands. We know that transitoriness marks all such visions. In this respect these revelations of the glory of Christ resemble our glimpses into the more ideal parts of other things. The poet's visions of truth and beauty are but momentary. Sometimes, amidst the commonplaces and the mechanical hurry of our life, we catch sight of a higher purpose in it, and are enabled to set before ourselves a better and nobler ideal. But the commonplaces must be attended to, and the mechanical activities close in about us again, and our ideal is lost. Yet these openings do much to sustain a worthy life, and we owe much to the man who will give us these.

Now the visions of Christ's glory are equally transient. We are shown them for a moment, and they disappear. They are let down from heaven long enough to teach us some one truth, or send one great gleam of joy into our hearts, or impress us with an awe that lies on us till death. They open up to us, as by a flash of lightning in a dark night, one great comprehensive prospect, giving us a broader view than ever we had before, and filling our mind with some fruitful general conception, that unites in harmony many things that seemed diverse. They are let down to teach us this, and are then withdrawn. And how much this is needed! For how apt we are to narrow and make mechanical the very gospel of Christ, and compress it into a formula or two! How apt we are to content ourselves with a very moderate realising of Christ to ourselves — a name which we conjure with, but vague and dim as a glorious person, whom we know! Yet, transient as are such visions of the heavenly glory, our view is not only broadened by them, and the mysteries of the gospel made grander, and its comprehensiveness more immense; but there is a sealing, assuring power in such sights, very precious in such times as these. "There came a voice out of the cloud saying: This is My beloved Son; hear Him." As another apostle described it, who had heard it: "There came such a voice to Him from the excellent glory: This is My beloved Son in whom I am well pleased." These visions quicken faith. There comes a new accession of assurance. There comes to us, as by a voice from on high, a new testimony and corroboration of the truth of what we believe. And we go away, not only knowing more, but feeling surer. And, in truth, it is only such things that give us true assurance. It is not outside proofs or arguments that will sustain us: it is experience, it is direct vision only.

"We all, with open face beholding as in a glass the glory of the Lord, are changed into the same image from glory to glory."

VII

A FATHER'S FAITH AND ITS
REWARD

VII

A FATHER'S FAITH AND ITS REWARD

MARK ix. 14–29

THE Mount of Transfiguration was apparently not a lofty mountain. It was high enough for Christ when upon it to be out of the world, and to feel the presence of His Father only; and thus for His brief earthly life to vanish, and the glory which He had with God before the world was to meet the glory that was to be His for ever, and so make His existence one continuous line of glory. It was high enough for this; and yet not too high for Him immediately to descend from it and enter among men,—to see their sorrows and afflictions, and the impotence of all besides Himself to cure them. And in this way that mount of glory, and this scene of sorrow and weakness at its foot, might be taken as symbols of something much larger—of Christ's glory now in the heavens, and of the sick world lying beneath them. Though Christ may seem far in His unapproachable glory, He is indeed near, and can immediately descend in all His power to heal.

There are just two things in the passage which may

be looked at for a little. First, the scene below, while Christ was on the mountain. And, secondly, the scene when He came down.

1. The scene while Jesus was absent was just the scene that met His view when He descended. He saw a great multitude about the disciples, and scribes questioning with them. This was what had been going on. In the centre were the disciples, and scribes disputing with them; and around them a great multitude, spectators or partisans. And there was the origin of the dispute—a poor sick child; but he seems to have been forgotten in the keenness of the contention that had arisen over him. The disciples had made an attempt to heal him, and had failed; and between them and the delighted scribes a dispute arose. It was possession by the spirit of evil, some said; others, that it was only something natural, such as the falling sickness. They differed possibly as to the diagnosis of the disease; or even more as to the mode of treatment. The scribes had their own formulas for exorcising evil spirits, and each side upheld its own methods. And the crowd pressed eagerly around them, and entered keenly into the dispute; and the practical question was forgotten in the furious heat with which the abstract one was discussed. Who possessed the best formula, and who was the right physician? Meanwhile the poor sufferer lay on the ground, unheeded.

The picture is a miniature of the larger one which we may look upon any day. The patient is the sick,

delirious world itself, lying in the face of Heaven, so
near Christ that the glory that surrounds Him might
almost be seen, as on the mount,—lying in the wicked
one. There are plenty of physicians, infinite diagnosis
of the disease, much conflict of view as to what it is,
though all admit that the patient is not well. There
are nostrums and formulas in abundance, but they are
ineffectual; and all the while the patient is nothing
bettered, but rather grows worse.

Our Lord states the general reason of the failure to
effect a cure in this case to have been the want of
faith. When the father came forward out of the crowd
saying: "I brought unto Thee my son, which hath a
dumb spirit: and I spake to Thy disciples that they
should cast it out; and they could not," Jesus exclaimed,
as if in despair of the whole condition of mind of
His day: "O unbelieving generation, how long shall I
be with you? how long shall I suffer you? bring him
unto Me." Here He charges the crowd, including, no
doubt, the father of the child, with want of faith. But
He probably also included the disciples; for in the
narrative as given by Matthew they asked privately,
Why could not we cast him out? And He answered,
Because of your little faith. In the present narrative
He gives a different answer: This kind can come out
by nothing, save by prayer and fasting. The answers
in the two evangelists are not quite identical; that in
Mark goes a step further back than that in Matthew.
It is faith that works cures, not prayer and fasting.

The power that heals is exerted by faith, and by nothing else; but prayer and fasting are the source behind faith out of which it draws its strength, out of which, indeed, it may be said to arise. Thus our Lord suggests a kind of chain: out of prayer comes faith, from faith power, and from the power healing.

By prayer our Lord does not mean merely formal acts of devotion at stated times or frequently, but along with these a habitual converse of the mind and heart with God, in thought and feeling regarding Him. And by fasting not merely occasional abstinence from food, but that general self-restraint and refraining from sensual enjoyments, the tendency of which is to dull and blunt that which is spiritual within us. We all try to abstain from what is sinful, but we probably seldom go further. We enjoy to the full what is lawful, without calculating the indirect influence which the enjoyment may have upon any spiritual life or power which may exist in us. And yet it may be certain that the enjoyment makes our minds grosser and duller, and tends to damp out and smother the flame of spiritual life which might burn clearly.

At all events we can readily perceive how that which Jesus calls prayer, the habitual frequenting of the presence of God, should be the nurse of faith. For apart from any increase of faith, which may be supposed the direct gift of God in answer to prayers, by being in His presence the mind receives great impressions of God; and by being often in His presence it receives impressions that are very varied, and thus gradually it becomes filled with a very deep sense of God and all that He is. And then, further, through this frequency with which His presence is sought, the sense of His being present with us grows. We are continually with Him, or He abides with us. It was thus that the great prophets of the Old Testament had that faith which carried them through such opposition. Each of these prophets had a great vision of God given to him at the commencement of his career. Isaiah saw the Lord seated on His throne, high and lifted up. And they came out from His presence with an awe upon them which never left them, and a strength of conviction which never deserted them, and a sense of God's presence with them, and a feeling of power which no opposition was able to overcome. When, therefore, we complain, or when the Church complains, of a want of faith, and consequently of a want of power to cope with the evils of the world, to cast out the demons under which it lies before us convulsed and shaken, it might be well for us to raise this previous question of prayer and fasting: whether we have been with God enough, or with the world too much? whether, on the one hand, we have not allowed the fountain of faith to dry up? and whether, on the other hand, we have not enervated it by luxuriousness and sensuous ease?

Yet the want of faith may not be due to these causes alone. In the case of the disciples, it was due partly to this. For, no doubt, the absence of the Lord from them paralysed their faith. Had He been present, or had they had a sense of His being always with them, even though absent to the sight, their attempts at healing would not have been ineffectual. But there was another cause for this paralysis of their faith, and that was the faithlessness of the crowd before them. It was an unbelieving crowd. And its unbelief reacted on the faith of the disciples and unnerved it. For if faith itself be contagious, and passes from mind to mind with an electric touch through a crowd, unbelief is no less contagious, though its influence may be slower. The disciples saw a multitude of stolid, incredulous faces before them, a dense mass of dead matter which they felt they could not quicken into life. The sight killed their faith. Possibly it did not do so consciously, but its effect was all the same. They hesitated, and faltered, and failed.

Now this is a kind of experience which faith has had in all ages, and must have. For if faith influences unbelief, unbelief also influences faith ; and faith, as the more sensitive, feels the influence sooner. Mind reacts upon mind for good, but also for evil. And the greater the mass of mind from which the influence comes, the more powerful it is. Now our faith and that of the Church is constantly exposed to this kind of influence. It is like an air which we breathe every moment, and which touches us vitally at every breath. It is a narcotic atmosphere which we are constantly inhaling. We

begin the day with it in the morning journals. We
go out into life, and the spirit of it, which touches
our minds at a hundred points, is unbelieving. And
just because of the natural sympathy of mind with
mind we feel its influence. We are affected, we
are insensibly changed, we fall into the ways of
thinking and feeling of the mass around us; the
native hue of our faith becomes sicklied over with the
pale cast of unbelief. If it does not die altogether, it
lives a stunted, blanched existence, like some exotic
chilled by unnatural winds. And it is altogether
without power to heal the world.

This has been the history of the Christian mind,—
both of the individual, and of the Church since it began.
Its history has been a succession of periods of decline
and weakness, followed by periods of revival and fresher
life. It succumbs to the powerful influences around it,
and falls into the kind of life of the mass about it. Then
it becomes impotent. By and by it becomes conscious
of its impotence, and awakens to the causes of it.
Then a reaction sets in, led generally by some mind
of more than ordinary power. But these minds, we
find, always go back to the primary fountain of faith
—prayer and fasting, the thought of God, the sense of
the presence and the power of Christ, and an abstinence
from that sensuousness of life which blunts and stifles
the spiritual mind.

These periods of reform have usually been marked
by excesses; they have run into fanaticism, or degener-

ated into mere asceticism. But to us these historical
extravagances are useful, because they enable us from
the very excess to see the better the principles from
which they spring. And these principles have always
been the two named by Christ—prayer and fasting—
the sense of God and Christ, and self-restraint. It is
the former that has really had power to influence the
world—those outside. But how powerful the sense of
God or Christ was to the Reformers themselves, we
may gather from the historical instance of one who
felt himself changed not only into the likeness of
Christ's mind, but of His body, and who took on
him literally the marks of the Lord Jesus.

The lesson for each of us, and for the Church, is
plain enough. It is converse with God, the fellowship
of the Father and of His Son Jesus Christ, that is
the source of faith; and faith is power, and power
gives ability to heal.

2. The events that followed upon Christ's descent
from the mountain. The disciples were impotent to
deal with the trouble before them. Yet at hand, surrounded by a glory which they might almost have
seen where they stood, was One who, if He would come
down, would not fail. And He came down. "And
straightway all the multitude, when they saw Him, were
greatly amazed, and running to Him saluted Him."
This is very strange. The crowd had no faith in the
disciples, but they had not lost their faith in Christ; they
ran to Him, and saluted Him. Here was the miracle-

worker Himself. After all, may not the state of things be something like this still? There are loud laments over the decay of faith throughout the world; may it not be that the world has not lost its faith in Christ, but only in His disciples? Deep down in its heart, does not faith in Him still live? Under the ashes, are there not embers that slumber? If we could suppose Him to appear, would it not throw aside all, and rise and run to Him, and salute Him? And if His disciples could persuade the world that He *is* present with them, would they not see something like the same sight?

However this may be, our Lord immediately addressed Himself to the disputants, asking the scribes: What question ye with them? But the scribes did not care to pursue the contention, and thought it wiser to retreat into the background. And the father of the child came forward with his story. It is not in the least surprising that a paroxysm or fit attacked the child at this critical moment. Whatever the nature of his complaint, it was periodic. It was perhaps from foreseeing a near attack, that the father at this time brought the child. And, at any rate, the excitement, the crowd, the scrutiny of all eyes upon him, and all the unwonted tumult and circumstances of the situation, easily account for the fit of the child at this moment.

Our Lord entered into a conversation with the father, asking how long the child had suffered in this way, and other details of the case. Probably He wished not only to inform Himself, but to affect Himself. He wished to have brought home to Him the full extent of this great human misery. He did not hurry the case out of His sight, healing the child with a word, and having done with the uncomfortable business. He looked steadfastly at the terrible sorrow with an unruffled demeanour. But under His unruffled demeanour what compassions were struggling in His heart! He encouraged the father to enlarge upon the subject.

The father was a strong man, and went over the details with an unfaltering voice. I daresay he had left those at home whose voice would have choked in giving the first symptoms of the case. For the real sorrow of such parents as these is apt to escape us. Whatever the actual malady was, it is plain enough what they thought it was. Their poor child was taken possession of by an evil spirit, and his destiny and fate would be that of the spirit which possessed him. It was but a question of time. The spirit was doomed, and his poor victim would share his doom, the thought of which might awaken compassion even for the unclean spirit. "Art Thou come to torment us before the time?" Let any father suppose himself this father. Suppose your child were not only the prey of a terrible malady, which convulsed him and left him as dead, but suppose, if it were supposable, that he was also given over to every wickedness, the subject of every vice, a very child of the devil. This was how that father and mother thought about their child. They had no outlook for him, or if an outlook, only one—a certain fearful looking for of judgment.

What a household that was! Yet the father went over the details with great fortitude. He even shows a certain loquaciousness which is very true to nature. Sometimes when we are sick, and seriously alarmed, and consult the physician, we go over our symptoms to him, putting him in full possession of them. He is satisfied, and sits down to write out his remedy. When the pen is in his hand, he looks up and asks a question. We answer it; but it starts us anew upon our experiences, and we bring up something that we had forgotten, or dwell afresh on what seem to us the critical points. And thus the father, though he had fully described the child's history already, is started afresh by Christ's question: "How long is it since this came to him?" and he goes over the distressing incidents again, ending with the appeal: "If Thou canst do anything, have compassion on us, and help us."

The last and most singular turn in the whole incident hinges on this, "If Thou canst." In the old version the reading of Christ's reply is, "If thou canst believe, all things are possible to him that believeth." In the Revised Version Christ's words are shorter. The father had said, If thou canst do anything, to which Christ replies, re-echoing his words: "If thou canst! All things can be to him that believeth." To the father this was an altogether unexpected turn that the case had taken. He thought he had done all that a father could do. He had brought his son to Christ; he had exposed the miseries of his home to the eye of the crowd; he had gone over the sorrowful history fully, and with deep feeling he had besought the compassion of Jesus. Could he do more? And now he was told that the poor child's recovery depended on him. It was attached to a condition which was perhaps beyond him, which he did not know whether he could fulfil or not. Hitherto his demeanour had been that of a sorrowful man, but one strong enough to speak with composure of his sorrow. But this new view of things unmanned him. To think that his child's recovery depended on him, that he might be the obstacle to his well-being, this completely shattered him. He cried out with tears: "Lord, I believe; help Thou mine unbelief." Lord, I believe; help me, though I don't believe.

The man's mind went through, in a moment, experiences and phases of feeling which make up the lives and whole histories of some minds. When he said, "I believe," he was not, as we might say, merely making an effort. He really had faith to some extent. His conduct showed it. He spoke with truth so far when he said, "I believe." But his own mind almost spontaneously and with an inborn honesty immediately represented to him that his faith hardly deserved the name. His mind said to him, You don't believe. But then his faith, no doubt stimulated and mixed with his human sorrow, reasserted itself practically in his cry, Help me! and he combined both his mental feelings in one, Help me, even though unbelieving. He showed the strength of his faith in Christ by beseeching

Christ not to make his faith a condition of helping him.

There are many who anxiously put to themselves the question whether they believe in Christ. They debate it with themselves as an abstract or general question —this anxious question. Perhaps no man will ever answer the question satisfactorily, either one way or another, when he puts it in this abstract and general way. For our minds go through such various conditions. We have double experiences. And sometimes when, founding on one set of experiences, we say, 'I believe,' our minds, with a movement which we really cannot control, but resting, no doubt, on a different set of experiences, will immediately say to us, 'You don't believe.' The question is not to be solved in a general or abstract way, but practically. For why do we wish to assure ourselves that we believe in Christ? Is it not for some practical reason? Is it not that we may make sure of His help to conquer some sin, or attain to some virtue, or have strength given to us to accomplish some task or bear some sorrow, or to see some child or other one dear to us healed by the Great Healer? There will always be some practical point; and our wisdom is not to debate with our own minds the theoretical or general question of our belief, for we may depend upon it our own minds will get the better of us, and land us in complete perplexity. The wiser plan is to throw ourselves into the practical point, and let our faith assert itself in it. This man's example is the one practically to follow: I believe, I don't believe; Lord, help me, though unbelieving. Let us sink ourselves always deep enough in the practical and pressing evil in which we are, and for the sake of which we would like to know whether we have faith,—whether it be the greatest practical question of all, the question of our whole being as living men, having a life of which we would know the destiny, or whether it be some lesser crisis and evil,—let us sink ourselves deep enough in the practical evil, and though our minds may answer with two voices, I believe, I don't believe, yet practically our faith will put its foot on the neck of our unbelief, and rise victorious in the cry, Lord, help me, though unbelieving.

For why did our Lord always insist on faith, before working any of His miracles for men's good? There may be reasons which are beyond us to guess. It is said about Himself that He could there—in some place or other—do no mighty works because of their unbelief. There may be something in the nature of faith which is altogether mysterious. But we can see certain reasons at least. We find that Christ always gave way to men; He receded or advanced according to the temper they showed. He did not cry, nor lift up, nor use compulsion, but invariably gave place before men's free will. In His own country He could do no works because of their unbelief, and He left it and went over the sea to the country of

the Gadarenes. There He performed His great miracle
of healing the lunatic who dwelt among the tombs;
but when the people besought Him to depart out of
their coasts He departed, and returned again to His
own country. Men's reception of Him must be of
their own free minds. And it was for the same reason
that He always endeavoured to secure faith, before
working His miracles. He did not come to work
miracles. What good would miracles, however many
and stupendous, do to us? He came to save men
from their sins, and His miracles were only part of
the means He employed. He came to get hold of
men's minds. Sometimes He worked a miracle and
trusted to its after effect. But usually it was the
other way. He sought to get hold of the mind first,
and His miracle was only a seal put on the inner
mental change, which He had succeeded in creating.

Christ's teaching of Christianity was practical, and
so must our learning of it be. He went on historic-
ally, treating case after case as they came up, seeking
always to have the mind of His patients engaged.
And our own history must really be a series of cases
of experience and practical faith. It is well for us
to be in earnest about ourselves and our faith; and if
we are in earnest, we will, no doubt, often ask ourselves whether we be of the faith, whether we believe.
But this abstract question, if we dwell on it much,
will only perplex us. We shall never be satisfied that
we have faith; our minds, founding on our histories,

12

will whisper to us that we do not believe. Therefore
it is better for us to try to realise our need, our sin,
—to feel this deeply enough,—and then we shall be
assured that we cannot keep ourselves, that none but
Christ can help us, and we shall have recourse to
Him, even though feeling that we have not faith. Our
cry will be like that of this man, Lord, help me,
even though unbelieving.

There is one point, in conclusion, deserving an allusion.
This story is about a father. Fathers have many
sorrows from their children, as this one had; but there
is a compensation from the sorrows and griefs. If
there were fewer fathers, there would be fewer good
men,—thoughtful, reverent men, with their natures
ploughed deep, not the soil of them only, but the
subsoil. But the point worth repeating is this. This
father brought his child to Jesus to be healed of Him,
and saved by Him. He performed all the external
duties with faithfulness—put his child in the way, was
anxious for him and his welfare. He even besought
Christ in his behalf; but in spite of all this the chain
between Christ and the child was not complete. There
was a link wanting. And the father himself was that
link. The current of healing virtue had to pass from
Jesus through the father to the child. The Lord demanded personal faith on the father's part. The
demand, when he realised it, shook the strong man's
nature to its base. It is, indeed, fitted to do this. But
the truth is a serious one. It is not enough for you

to bring your child where Jesus is, to put him in the way of good, to send him to the Sabbath school, or take him to the church. If you wish Jesus to bless him, to heal him, to save him, He asks that you be a believer yourself. This is the condition. With this condition all things may be looked for: "All things can be to him that believeth."

VIII

CHRIST'S AUTHORITY

VIII

CHRIST'S AUTHORITY

MATTHEW xxi. 23–27

WHEN we read the history of Christ, and especially
when we observe His encounters on many occasions
with His adversaries, we cannot help concluding that
He possessed a very keen and clear intellect. In all
those skirmishes in which He engaged with the Pharisees
and other sects of the Jews, the weapon He uses is
bright and polished, and flashes with the light of mind.
And we are apt sometimes to imagine that, having to
fence with sophists, He satisfied Himself with defeating
them with their own weapons, and, feeling that He
could not reach their heart, was content to cover them
with shame in the encounter of intellect.

The present passage, even more than others, leaves
this impression upon us. On reading it, we at first conclude that the question of the priests as to the authority
of Christ was a captious one, and put with the design
of using the only answer Christ could give for the purpose of ensnaring Him,—the answer that it was by
the authority of God His Father; and that Christ,

perceiving this, availed Himself of the privilege of one
who is questioned to put a question in return, and that
we have consequently a mere skirmish of wits.

But this is not probable.   For, first, such a manner of
bearing Himself does not become Christ, even before
priests and Pharisees. He could not on any occasion
strip off from Himself or forget that which He was, the
Saviour of men ; and therefore no words which He ever
spoke could be mere formal intellectual husks.   They
must have contained in them some body of truth which,
if applied to themselves by the hearers, would prove
saving.   And, second, we must not forget that if any
public or official notice was to be taken of Christ and
His proceedings, the priests and the elders were the
persons to do it.   They were the guardians of the
temple which Christ had just violently invaded, and
where He had overturned the hitherto customary
arrangements.   They were the public and national religious authorities.   They sat in Moses' seat.   They
were responsible for the continuance and the proprieties
of the national worship.

Now Christ had recently taken a very bold step.   He
had begun to proceed from words to actions.   He did
not merely preach, like John, to whoever liked to listen,
making the wilderness His temple and the Jordan His
water of baptism ; but He presumed to correct the
temple ordinances.   He interfered with the national
service.   And all that He did was done with an
air of authority which was very striking.   And this

authority, which was so charming to the common
people, as not only proving His own sincerity and
the strength of His own convictions, but somehow
approving to their consciences His divine mission,
was what was partly aggravating and partly, perhaps,
perplexing to the priests. To some of them who were
mere traditionalists, as, no doubt, most of them were,
crusted over with officialism and with that haughty
assumption which the national priest is so apt to contract, Christ's procedure would be most exasperating.
Contempt and anger, however veiled, must have filled
their minds. To others this whole demeanour of Christ
must have seemed a mystery, and not so easy to be
settled or accounted for as some thought; and it is
possible that among those who put the question: By
what authority doest Thou these things? there may
have been some earnestly looking for light, and hoping
for some direct statement from Christ, which would be
more definite and precise than anything they had yet
heard from Him.

Now I will briefly refer to three things: first, Christ's
pretensions, what they called His authority; second, the
baptism of John, to which He recalled the attention of
those inquiring after His own authority; and, third, His
refusal to go further, and say anything specific about
Himself.

First, His authority. There is nothing more striking
about Christ than His pretensions. No one ever made
so much use of the personal pronoun as He. He put

Himself forward always. Even when He humbled Himself, He drew the attention of His disciples to His own humility. " If I then, your Lord and Master, have washed your feet, ye also ought to wash one another's feet." The rule so well understood by us, that when we refer to our own services to our friends, we rather detract from them, seemed not to be known to Him. "Greater love hath no man than this, that a man lay down his life for his friends: ye are My friends." He seemed to admit nothing to be superior to Himself, or having larger claims in earth or heaven. Once or twice, indeed, He puts Himself below the Father: " My Father is greater than I." Yet even on the occasion when He said this, He does not scruple to indicate how great He is in His own mind. " If ye loved Me,"—and He says it in a tone which implies how much He feels that their love is due to Him,—" if ye loved Me, ye would rejoice, because I said, I go to the Father: for My Father is greater than I."

But ordinarily He joins Himself and the Father together : " I and the Father are one." And whether that refer to oneness of essence, or only to complete moral harmony of will and character and purpose, and to perfect intimacy and fellowship of heart with heart, it is a tremendous assumption. And as to His disciples, though He generously shares all with them, and lifts them up even into the region of His own joy,—that region far above all clouds that hang over earth in the clear sunny atmosphere of the heaven of heavens, with all the thoughts that crowd His own mind and all the sights that fill His own eye, — yet He takes a very lofty place with regard to them : "Without Me ye can do nothing"; and He demands to have all their actions filled out with the thought of Him : "This do in remembrance of Me." He even makes Himself responsible for what might seem an extravagant undertaking regarding them : "Verily, I say unto you, Whatsoever ye shall ask the Father in My name, He will give it you."

Now this assumption is what was characteristic of Christ; it struck everybody, the common people and the Pharisees alike. The latter imperiously, and with, no doubt, an air of piety as well as authority on their side, demanded : "Whom makest Thou Thyself?" and with a feeling of shocked perplexity : "Who is this that forgiveth sins also?" The common people called it His authority, and heard Him gladly; for He taught them as one having authority, and not as the scribes. The scribes, no doubt, did not pretend to be more than expounders, and perhaps their exposition was not very warm. They adhered to what was written; but in Christ there was a well of originality, a new fountain opened up. He expounded the Old Testament certainly, but in His mouth it became fresh and new, as if it had never been uttered before. He stretched it out with a new spirit; and the spirit was so fresh and powerful that, like a new wine, it burst the old letter, and men felt that God was speaking in their ears directly. He even put Himself above the law; He exorcised the spirit of hardness and

selfishness that was in it, and put in its place generosity
and meekness and kindness: "Ye have heard that it
hath been said, An eye for an eye, and a tooth for a
tooth: but *I* say unto you, That ye resist not evil."

It was not merely that Christ went His own way, like
any great religious genius, and declined to act under the
constituted authorities.   Neither was that which He ex-
hibited merely the force of moral character.   For one
often sees great moral power display itself in men quite
uneducated, and who have but little intellectual ability.
And there is generally in those men a sense of their
own power, or, at any rate, the moral earnestness of their
nature impels them to act; and they come to the front,
and brush aside mere formalities of ecclesiastical order,
and take a first place, assuming even in the strength
of their convictions a superiority over the mere dead
ecclesiastical machinery and men of the national belief.
Such men denounce with unsparing invective the
withered formalities of mere paid Christianity, and
demand that reality and life be poured into it again.
And, without doubt, Christ possessed this power ; and this
was largely what made Him so dear to the people, and
so offensive to the authorities.   But there was more.

Christ not only scorned and trampled on their ven-
erable traditions, but He arrogated to Himself an
authority equal to that of the original law.   " A greater
than Moses is here."   As they said, " He had not only
broken the Sabbath, but said that God was His Father,
making Himself equal with God."   There was not

only the extravagance of His claims, but His incon-
sistency; and this, no doubt, while it enraged the
more serious-minded Pharisee, made many a Sadducee
smile. Modern thinkers feel that they cannot dispose
of this peculiarity in Christ so easily; His claims begin
to be felt to be the highest evidence of their own truth.
Men feel that they must make a consistent character
out of Christ. Formerly His assumptions were accounted
for by saying it was an imposture—a conscious fraud.
But this view has long been found untenable. It is
inconsistent with all the rest of Christ's character. His
truthfulness, His earnestness, His humility, His moral
elevation, every attribute of His heart protests loudly
against such an explanation.

More lately the claims of Christ have been accounted
for as those of an enthusiast. But here, again, we are
met by His intellectual character. No one had fewer
elements of a fanatic than He had. No doubt He had
moments of strange joy quite unconnected with all that
lay outside of Him. And He had also awful hours of
depression. But when we think of the keenness of His
intellect, the broad sense with which He discriminated
between things sacred and things secular,—for instance,
the sharpness of insight which He had into the motives
of other men,—we cannot believe that He was ever
deceived as to His own. His own testimony to Himself
is now felt by every one, accustomed to reflect on moral
questions, to be the highest proof of the truth of His
claims. But at all events it was to have some light

thrown on this element in Him, what we should now
call the supernatural element, that these people came
to Him.

Now, second, observe Christ's treatment of the chief
priests and the elders. When they asked concerning
His authority, He answered, "I also will ask you one
question. The baptism of John, whence was it?" I
have already said that it was by no means His intention
to get quit of them by fixing them on a mere dilemma.
He did not mean to thrust them into a corner by calling
attention to a passage in their history rather difficult to
explain. They wished to clear up this point in His
history. Well, He might be permitted to refer to a
small matter in theirs, not undeserving of having some
light thrown on it—their conduct in regard to the baptism of John. This was not His design. He was in
earnest in referring to the baptism of John. Observe,
what they asked about in Him referred to His pretensions to the highest thing about Him—to what was
directly from heaven. He sought to take His stand
with them on a lower platform. You ask about My
authority, about who gave Me the authority, whether,
in a word, I have a commission direct from God; let
us take something less difficult to begin with. Let Me
ascertain from you whether you agree with Me on
certain fundamental principles long in advance of the
question of My authority, principles illustrated in the
baptism of Jordan. Do you admit them to be divine?
The baptism of John, was it from heaven, or of men?

What was this baptism of John? John's preaching, which his baptism symbolised, consisted of a single sentence: "In these days came John the Baptist preaching in the wilderness of Judæa, and saying, Repent ye: for the kingdom of heaven is at hand." Repentance and the kingdom of God. John's baptism was a baptism unto repentance, and unto faith in a coming kingdom of God. There were two things: sin and the remission of it, the kingdom of God and the near approach of it. He was a voice crying in the wilderness: Prepare ye the way of the Lord. Sin, and the kingdom of God—that implies two things, a verdict on our present life, and a hope of another state of things. That which is distinctive about Christ can only be understood, when these two things precede it. The baptism of John, was it from heaven? Was his preaching of repentance true, needful, heavenly? Do you acknowledge the truth of that position which he took, and not merely its truth, but its heavenly origin? And do you look with him for a kingdom of God other than the state of things now existing, when God shall reign, and His will shall be done, and the confusions and evils and pains which now fill the earth shall disappear? Are you dissatisfied with what is within you, and, feeling your sin, do you also feel the need of its remission? do you mourn over the condition of things without, and, mourning, look for the incoming of a better time, when God's kingdom shall be over all?

These questions did put the priests into a dilemma. They were the principles insisted on by John, and the priests had failed to hail him as a necessary reformer. They allowed him to sink out of sight. They did not recognise the truth, partly because they did not feel it, and partly because it did not come from their side nor originate with them. There might be truth in what John said, but they had their own reasons for not acknowledging him, for not taking up the cry he raised. They did not like his mode of raising it. Though the son of a priest, he, too, seemed to be fighting for his own hand. For this, if not for other reasons, they stood aloof. Of course, there were other reasons. They disliked his doctrine as well as his manner. They had ceased to feel the truths proclaimed by John. Their religion had become outward and professional merely ; hence they had no deep sense of sin. Life in their day had become soft and easy, and they saw no great need for any such change as the setting up of a kingdom of God seemed to imply.

Hence they were thrown upon a dilemma. If they admitted that John was a prophet, then they were condemned by their own history. If they denied it, they stood in awe of the convictions of the multitude, who might tolerate an expression of uncertainty, but certainly would not tolerate an unfavourable judgment regarding John.

It is a humiliating position that those priests have brought themselves into. It is, no doubt, the position

into which Christ wished to bring them. He has
thrown them back upon their conscience. Before this,
perhaps, the true reason of their passing by John had
not been felt by themselves. We many a time hide
from ourselves in a cloud of general feelings the real
spring of our actions. It is only some subtle moral
question, such as Christ put, that reveals our own minds
to us. These men felt, no doubt, at this moment the
real reason of their rejecting John. Their encounter
with Christ called them back to the real motives from
which they had acted. They hated John, and they
hated him still; and they would have said so, if they
had dared. But they were cowards as well as recreants.
They feared the multitude. The unsophisticated conscience of the populace was against them, so dead
against them that they were afraid to give expression
to their dislike; and so they took refuge in a plea of
ignorance: "We cannot tell."

It is a singular glimpse that we get into their minds,
and into the minds of the common people. The
common people would not have stoned any of themselves who denied John; but that ecclesiastics should
do it—priests, ministers in God's house—seemed to them
too flagrant an immorality to be endured. John's
baptism coincided so completely with the principles of
morality, with the lessons of the theocratic State, with
all the hopes of every serious person, that to see it
condemned by persons whose part and duty it was to
hail it, was too shameful a thing to be tolerated.

13

As the priests were well aware of this state of the popular mind, and well aware also of the state of their own minds, they declined to answer.

Third, Christ's refusal to say anything about Himself: "Neither tell I you by what authority I do these things."

They said, We cannot tell; and He answered, Neither tell I you. His answer was not, Neither will I tell you; rather, If you will not tell Me, it is useless for Me to tell you. If you will so deny your own convictions, or if you still stand so low that you do not recognise the principles of John's baptism, it is of no use for Me to speak of My pretensions. "If I tell you earthly things, and ye believe not, how shall ye believe if I tell you heavenly things?"

Now this is Christ's invariable way of answering those who come inquiring about His pretensions,—wanting to know whether He really be a supernatural Being. He answers either by silence, or He takes His stand a step or two lower down. He intimates that His claims are to be judged on moral grounds. If those who inquire regarding them be themselves immoral, be not living up to the moral light they have, it is needless discussing His claims; and even if those who come to Him be honest and earnest in their inquiries, He intimates to them that His claims are not matter for mere abstract discussion in themselves. They are the last link in a chain; they are the crowning point of things going before—great moral principles, such as sin, such as baptism for purification, such as the hope of a kingdom of God upon the earth; and it is in connection with such principles that His claims are to be estimated. Unless these principles be admitted as true, He cannot be understood, for He stands upon them. He supplies what they demand. There is no probability in His claims, for there is no necessity for Him, unless these things be already believed and felt.

This, I say, was Christ's way of meeting those who wished direct statements from Him about His mission. He either kept silence, or He drew their attention to moral principles lying in advance of His claims. When men came to Him with no earnestness or real desire to comprehend Him, asking proof of His mission, He was silent: "A wicked and adulterous generation seeketh after a sign: there shall no sign be given them." Even when individuals came, men not wholly bad, but with some good in them, yet allowing the evil to overmaster the good, and not living up to the light they had, He refused to grant any supernatural evidence. Herod was a man not wholly bad. He heard John gladly, he observed him, he did many things because of him. His conscience concurred with the stern preacher's demands; but he was too much involved in a corrupt circle of profligate women and debauched men to be able to act according to his convictions—too weak and dissolute himself to put his better feelings into acts; and when Jesus was sent to him by Pilate and questioned by him, He was silent: "When Herod saw Jesus, he was exceeding glad: for he was desirous to see Him of a long season . . . and he hoped to have seen some miracle done by Him. Then he questioned with Him in many words; but He answered him nothing." The bloodthirsty king, the adulterous husband, the murderer of God's prophets—this was not the kind of man with whom Christ would be confidential on the subject of His mission.

But even men who came to Him with earnestness, seeking some light as to what He really was, He usually did not answer directly, but took His stand with them on some principles of the kingdom of God, some general moral truth, which, if acknowledged, would lead up to His claims. Nicodemus, who came to Him by night, made these the subject of his first remark: "We know that Thou art a teacher come from God: for no man can do these miracles which Thou doest, except God be with him." He inferred from the miracles that Christ was from God; and he came to receive some assurance that his inference was right. Christ silently passed by his inference from miracles; He was silent meantime about His claims, but drew Nicodemus away to fundamental moral principles, the need of regeneration and purifying: "Verily, verily, I say unto you, Except a man be born again, he cannot see the kingdom of God: ye must be born of water and of spirit." This was the true point of view from which to look at Christ's claims; then they became intelligible, natural, needful. These common, broad, fundamental general truths, so well known, so generally admitted, so low, so to speak, that He calls them earthly things, things that men without a revelation may observe,— these are the preliminaries to a true estimate of Christ's claims. Then come the heavenly things: the lifting up of Christ, as Moses lifted up the serpent in the wilderness; the love of God, and the redemption of men.

And, strangely, Christ deals with these captious scribes much as He dealt with Nicodemus. He brought them back to great moral principles,—to the baptism of John—to repentance—to the washing of regeneration —to the kingdom of heaven. Was it that, being so near the end of His career, with His heart open now to all men, a harsh answer, even to Pharisees, was more than He could give? Or is it rather this, that having but one gospel to preach to men, whoever they may be, He stands high above being moved or disturbed by the temper of men; and having but one thing to say, He says it with an unruffled calmness to all alike: "Ye must be born again,"—shining out like a steady light in which is no variableness nor shadow of turning?

Now is not this still the question men are putting, and this still the answer they are receiving? What is every one asking? By what authority doest Thou these things? It is the question of Christ's pretensions. What is He? is He anything more than man? How many are putting that question? and in how many forms? In their own minds many are putting it who have been taught very definite beliefs as to what He is; and others in essays—in books. And in what different spirits is the question put! Some put it like the priests, some in quite another frame of mind. And though Christ may be answering some here and there to their own great joy and peace, He is failing to answer the great majority. His answer is silence ; or it is a throwing of men back in the meantime upon antecedent principles, which perhaps, in a too one-sided devotion to what was supernatural in Him, had been neglected, —back on the baptism of John.

To its inquiries regarding His claims, the public— the world—receives no direct answer from Christ. Is not the reason this, that like the priests, the world has no earnest belief in principles long anterior to His claims —in sin, in repentance, in the kingdom of God? Do we now, any more than they did in those days, hold these beliefs with any seriousness? Do men in general long for the incoming of the kingdom of God? Are they not rather quite contented with the world as it is,—with its business, its society, its movements, its keen political atmosphere, and its sweet incense of intellectual fame? Would not any important change be felt like a breaking in upon a sweet dream, and a waking up to unknown and fearful realities? The claims of Christ require an earnest, deep moral basis to rest upon; and this basis, perhaps, does not exist in the world as it now is. Does it even exist in the Church? Suppose that the kingdom of God were to come upon us, not in terrors at all, but as softly as the morning breaks upon the night,—that we saw it coming down from heaven and flushing all the earth, like the dawn descending the mountain sides,—how should we arise to meet it? Would our occupations, and the aspirations of our hearts, and our affections shade off into it without any shock, so that it would seem to us only a calmer, brighter morning, and we should grasp one another's hands with nothing more than a glad subdued surprise, saying that the kingdom of God was come? or would its advent be felt to be a calamity rather than a blessing? The claims of Christ require a moral basis to rest upon, and that basis does not exist in the world as it is at present.

Even those who in some measure believe in Christ often fail to get an answer from Him. They look for some manifestation of His power on themselves, some exhibition of His heavenly mission, some proof that He is from God; but He answers them nothing. They go from church to church, from meeting to meeting, seeking some proof of His supernatural power, but they come away unimpressed, unconvinced, cold, uncertain, weary, perplexed. The reason? Is all previous knowledge lived up to? Or are the great principles of John's baptism—sin, remission, the kingdom of God—understood and felt with any vividness? How far may some sin be at the bottom of Christ's silence? not an open sin, but a hidden one,—some mode of feeling rather than of thinking, some mode of thinking rather than of speaking or acting? May it not be alienating the mind, unfitting it to receive correct

impressions of Christ, making it *averse*, by passing a
constant current over it in another direction?

How, for instance, the cherishing of an enmity in
the heart may hinder the very essence of Christ's *love
of God* from commending itself to the mind! "If a
man love not his brother whom he hath seen, how
can he love God whom he hath not seen?"

Or how, for instance, the cherishing and keeping
in the mind of impure thoughts, which are too subtle
for human intercourse to detect, which betray themselves only by the hasty glance of the eye, or by the
too great sensitiveness and unwillingness to refer to
what is impure,—how this may make the mind so
averse to the thought of Him who was holy, harmless,
undefiled, that He can find no entrance! Or how that
hauteur which accredited professors of religion are apt
to entertain, that self-satisfied confidence, that sectarian
dislike of others because their ways are different from
ours,—how this may close the eyes of the heart, so
that Christ Himself shall not be recognised, even when
He stands before us, and how we may let some great
work of God go by, because it is not carried on precisely according to our ecclesiastical rules!

The faith of Christ is founded on morality. It is not
morality, but it is based on it, on the common facts
of our life and its needs—on sin, on the miseries and
evils of life. It presupposes these, and is received by
minds alive to these, by open, candid, simple, earnest
minds. To these Jesus unfolds His claims. "I thank

Thee, Father, Lord of heaven and earth, that Thou hast hid these things from the wise and prudent, and hast revealed them unto babes." Through these things we rise up to Him.

Christ is not a supernatural fact out of all connection with life, but His claims base themselves upon life as it is. And that which hinders His divine claims from being admitted is oftenest some sin, some neglect of a duty which we know, some giving way to a vice which we are aware of, which disturbs and alienates the mind from Christ; some pride which makes us feel we have nothing to learn; some thing of this kind which puts the mind out of harmony with Christ and His claims, and makes it hard for them to commend themselves to the heart. I say oftenest, let me not say *always*; for there are mysteries here, especially, which no theory of ours will take in. There are earnest, pure minds on whom the light has not yet broken; yet these are not far from the kingdom of God, though they may think themselves to be; and it will sometimes happen to them that in some moment of thought or feeling the partition wall that confined their view will be suddenly gone, and they will wonder what it was that hindered them; for they are unchanged, except that the light is about them. "If any man will do His will, he shall know of the doctrine, whether it be of God, or whether I speak of Myself." But when I say *oftenest*, I am surely standing on ground on which He stood Himself.

IX

THE GROWTH OF THE KINGDOM
OF GOD

IX

THE GROWTH OF THE KINGDOM OF GOD

MARK iv. 26–29

AND He said, So is the kingdom of God, as if a man should cast seed upon the earth; and should sleep, and rise night and day, and the seed should spring and grow up, he knoweth not how. For the earth bringeth forth fruit of herself; first the blade, then the ear, after that the full corn in the ear. But when the fruit is ripe, immediately he putteth in the sickle, because the harvest is come.

This short parable is found only in Mark. The thought which it contains is one of the most remarkable ever expressed by our Lord. Nothing that He ever said suggests to us so directly that Jesus was something altogether new; that His thoughts and Himself were the entrance of a new factor and element into the life and minds of men. At first sight, His words here seem to be clean in the face of all that Scripture had hitherto taught. For no idea pervades the Old Testament so completely as the idea that the kingdom of God is brought into the world all at

206 THE GROWTH OF THE KINGDOM OF GOD

once by a direct act of God's interposition; it is not a growth but a creation, the almost instantaneous act of immediate divine operation, where men are not agents but spectators. But our Lord says, "The earth bringeth forth fruit of itself." Mankind has powers of its own, and the kingdom of God in its fulness is the effect of the operation of these powers. And they operate slowly, first the blade, then the ear, after that the full corn in the ear. The kingdom of God in its perfection is not an immediate creation of God apart from men; it is not a great miraculous interference and exhibition of divine power; it is a slow growth of the mind of mankind, through generation after generation of its life, and cycle after cycle of its history. Our Lord transfers the kingdom of God from heaven into the mind of mankind; and He translates it out of a sudden divine operation into a growth and progress of the human mind.

In endeavouring to understand the words of our Lord, and, above all, His parables, there is nothing that needs so much to be attended to as the historical situation in which they were spoken. That is, we must transfer ourselves back into the age and times in which Jesus lived, and into the circumstances amidst which He stood. Above all, we must endeavour always to keep before our minds what might be called His consciousness of Himself, His idea of what He was. For in His parables especially He begins with Himself, and looks out into the future of mankind. He and

His words and His work are the new starting-point in
the history of man, and from this He looks out and
surveys this history to the end of all earthly life. When
He speaks of the sower going forth to sow, He Himself
is the sower; and His word, which comprehends all
that He was and did, is the seed. In like manner, His
word, His life, and all that He was, is the leaven that
leavens the lump of mankind. He is the householder
who hires labourers for his vineyard ; the lord who
gives his servants the talents or the pound, and goes into
the far country, to return again and reckon with them.

The teaching of His parables is apt to be missed
through our desire to make them directly practical and
edifying. But many of them are meant less for edifi-
cation than for instruction. They project before us
great general principles regarding His kingdom, which
do not inform us what to do, but how to think. In
particular, there are two elements which He is always
setting in relation to one another, showing how the one
influences the other, and how the second behaves under
the influence exerted on it by the first, and what the
issue of the relation will be: these two elements are
Himself on the one hand and mankind on the other.
He regards Himself as a new power brought into the
world of men, as a seed flung upon the soil of the
human mind; and He is occupied with the thought
how this soil will receive it, how it will grow and cover
the field, and what the great harvest will be.

This is obviously the general meaning of the present

parable—"the kingdom of God is as if a man cast seed upon the earth." There are three steps indicated in the similitude.

First, the husbandman sows his seed on the soil. This is a time of anxious and strenuous activity on his part. He interferes with nature. He brings in a distinct power, different from the powers of the soil. He takes a seed which has certain capacities, and commits it to a soil which has also certain powers. His interposition is of a higher kind than the powers either of the seed or of the soil. There is will, intuition, foresight; he is a power altogether unlike those other natural forces which he interferes with, and calls into operation.

Secondly, having done his part, he can do no more. His period of work is over. He sleeps, and rises night and day, sleeps by night and rises by day. He leads an ordinary life. It may be a busy or an indolent life. So far as the work which he was engaged in before is concerned, he does nothing; he can do nothing. He has committed the seed to the soil, and it is out of his hands. His extraordinary interference with the laws of nature was a thing done once for all; now he must leave natural law to do its part. And it will not fail. "The earth bringeth forth fruit of itself; first the blade, then the ear, after that the full corn in the ear." Not he any more, but the earth operates. It has powers which it puts forth, and the husbandman waits for its operation.

Then, thirdly, when the fruit is ripe the husbandman again comes upon the scene. He puts in the sickle and reaps the harvest.

Our Lord is the husbandman. His manifestation on the earth, during the brief time He lived on it, with all its meaning,—His word, His life, His death, and rising,— the whole circle of thoughts and deeds connected with His appearance on earth and contained in it, the whole meaning of this was the sowing of the seed. He committed it to the earth; He flung it upon the soil of the mind of man; He threw it as a fruitful germ into the life and thought of mankind. And then His work was done. He departed from the earth. He sits on high. The scene of operation now is another—the soil, the earth, the bosom of mankind. It has to put forth its powers; having received the seed, it must nourish it. Its powers must come into play.

Finally, when the whole process has been gone through, the blade, the ear, the full corn in the ear, the Lord the husbandman will once more come upon the field; He will put in His sickle and reap the harvest, which so long ago He had sown. But between His sowing and His reaping He will not any more interpose. As the husbandman, having committed the seed to the soil, *can* do no more, but must leave nature to do all; so the Lord *will* do nothing more, but will leave the powers of the human mind, the forces of the human heart, the capabilities of the soul of man, and all the expanding activities of human society and

14

life, with its ideal inspirations and its practical operation, to do the rest. There will be no more miracle, no more treading of the earth by divine feet, no more intervention and breaking in upon the ordinary development of the human mind and the ordinary progress of human life. The intervention has taken place; and henceforth, until the harvest, the progress will, as it were, be normal. This seems the general meaning of the parable. And it only remains to allude to one or two points in it a little more fully.

1. Let us notice, first, the inactivity of the husbandman, and the operation of the powers of the ground during the period of growth from seedtime to harvest. The husbandman sleeps, and rises night and day, and the earth brings forth fruit of herself. The husbandman's work is done, and he cannot add to it. So far from being able to do anything more, he is represented as not even knowing how the seed grows: "the earth bringeth forth fruit of herself, he knoweth not how." When he has sown the seed, his part is completed. He may be active in other departments of work, but in this department his inactivity is enforced until the harvest, when he can again interfere. He waits till the fruit be ripe. Of course, his mind may be active enough, but his hands are tied. He may anxiously watch the progress of his field, as the delicate blade rises above the ground, as it passes into stalk and ear with the advancing months, and as the leaf drops and the yellow tinge shows itself here and there, until,

finally, all is one blaze of gold. He will anxiously scan the heavens when they seem like brass, and the field cracks and gapes with thirst for the refreshing shower; and will rejoice when the cloud, like a man's hand, rises from the sea, giving promise of rain. By day and night his thoughts will be occupied with the prospects of his harvest. Not only through the week, but even on the Sabbath his mind will fall at times upon his fields; and after returning from the house of God, he will sometimes in the still Sabbath eve, when the sun sends his slanting rays across the earth, and the voices of the flocks are heard answering one another from hillside to hillside, saunter along by the edge of his fields, and, as he surveys them, be filled with thankfulness or with concern. He is far from indifferent, though he knows that he is helpless.

In like manner the heavenly husbandman, having sown His seed, scattered His great truths and principles, both of thought and life upon the soil of the mind of man, and gone unto the Father, though He will not again do any such work as He has done, nor be seen again upon the earth till the harvest, is not without interest or concern in the growth of the seed. It is, no doubt, His chief concern ; its growth and progress lies on His heart. Yet as the law of nature is that the earth bringeth forth fruit of herself ; first the blade, then the ear, so it is the law of His kingdom that, being planted among men, men will advance it.

The earth bringeth forth fruit of herself. Yet we

know how. The earth, without doubt, has powers, and in virtue of these powers it turns the seed committed to it into a harvest. Yet it is the earth wrapped round with heaven, swaddled in the clouds, or clad in the light of the sun, that is fertile. It is the earth subject to all the moods, acted on by all the influences of the skies, daylight and darkness, shadow and sun, the dark and cloudy day, and the clear shining after rain; it is the earth thus quickened, warmed, vitalised by the heavens, that brings forth fruit of herself. Without these influences she would be as barren as the sands. It is the heavens that evoke her powers, that might even seem to confer them. It is under all these sweet influences from above that she ripens her harvest.

And the analogy holds in regard to the spiritual harvest. It is upon the mind of man that Christ has sown His seed. It is on the mind, the heart, the life of man, where He will reap His harvest. To that the seed has been committed, and that will yield the fruit. Yet not of its own natural powers alone, but under the continual influence of heaven. Only with heaven close around them, enshrouding them, quickening them, transfiguring them in its light,—only then will mankind mature a harvest for the Lord. Otherwise, mankind will be as barren as the earth would be without the skies; otherwise, the seed committed to it will wither and rot under the clods. It is true that our Lord will not again appear upon the field until the harvest. But all progress of the seed is under His influence from on high. It is He that sends down the quickening rains of the spirit. He is the Sun of righteousness. He has all power in heaven and on earth. It is in fellowship with Him that the harvest of mankind grows and ripens. "Because I live, ye shall live also."

2. And this suggests, secondly, a word or two upon the great significance of His earthly appearance, and upon the weight which He lays upon it. It is a common thing to see a husbandman going forth bearing precious seed in spring, scattering it upon the bosom of the earth. It is so usual that it awakens little reflection. Yet if we think of it, it will appear to us a thing altogether of a different character from the operations of nature, the blind efforts of the soil into which the seed is cast which follow upon it.

The husbandman is an agent wholly unlike the soil. In his operation and interposition, characteristics appear which belong to a sphere much loftier than that to which the natural laws of the soil belong. He is free, conscious, above the laws of nature in his great act of sowing. He brings in among them a new force which does not belong to them. He does not contradict or supersede the laws of nature; but he does interfere among them, giving them a new direction. If we could suppose the earth endowed with an understanding of the nature of its own operations and how it deals with the seed committed to it, mysterious and effectual as its operations are, we cannot doubt that it would regard the interposition of the husbandman as from its point of view miraculous, and altogether transcending the sphere to which its own powers belong. And without any doubt our Lord Himself regards, and desires us to regard, His appearance and work upon the earth as a thing out of the course of mankind's natural development. It is as much beyond and above the natural progress of human life as the husbandman's work in sowing the seed is above the natural laws of the soil. It is a break in upon the natural progress of mankind.

Whatever powers men had, whatever scope lay open to mankind naturally, our Lord's coming threw something altogether new into it, started it upon new lines, and set a new goal before it. The end which He has now set before it, mankind could no more have reached apart from His coming, than the earth could of itself bring a harvest to ripeness, unless the seed were committed to it by one who was altogether above it. The husbandman commits to the earth the seed, without which it would have lain for ever fallow and barren ; for however great the powers of the soil be, however infallibly it will give life to that which falls into its bosom, and carry it through all its stages of growth to maturity and to harvest, the soil cannot sow itself. Every seed which it quickens must be deposited on it by forces external to itself. It cannot spontaneously bring forth fruit, unless it be sown. And the husbandman who sows belongs to a sphere high above it. So the mind of mankind cannot sow itself; it can only bring to maturity what

another deposits on it.   And the Lord, who scatters
His divine seed there, is not of mankind, but comes into
it from on high.

It is not necessary to dwell on the seed which the
heavenly husbandman has sown in the bosom of mankind.   The parable does not refer to what the seed is.
It only dwells upon the fact that the Lord's manifestation on the earth was the seedtime of mankind,
the new creative hour of its history, the great supernatural interposition which sowed in its bosom the
seed of which all the future ages of its history would
be only the quickening and ripening, and of which
the end of its history would be the harvest,   If we
were to think what the seed sown by Jesus was, we
should hardly know where to begin.   We might reflect
on the new thoughts of God which He taught men
to entertain, and remember that it is through Him
that we have learned to say, Our Father in heaven.
Or here we might think of that life with God and
toward God which He lived, and by His example
left with us to grow in our minds and be an ideal
to reach up to.

Or, turning in another direction, we might think of
the astonishing law which He introduced, and which
He declared to be the law of His own life, even
the law that he that saveth his life shall lose it,
and he that loseth his life shall find it; the law of
self-negation; the law that life is through death; that
unless a corn of wheat die it abideth alone, but if

it die it bringeth forth much fruit. This new law, no new one to Him, under the influence of which, when in the form of God He came down to earth, and when on earth humbled Himself unto death,—this new law is pre-eminently the law of His kingdom, the mother of all deeds of mercy, of all pity to the poor and the wretched, the founder of all homes of charity, of all forgetfulness of ourselves and all memory of others—the great law that elevates us above ourselves. This was a novelty indeed, something divine and nothing less; a law, if we are to believe men of science, which runs sheer in the teeth of the laws of nature, and the laws which rule in the lower creation. There the law is that each organism or creature thinks only of itself; its efforts are directed to maintain its own existence, and the strong tramples the weak to death. In Christ's kingdom, the strong exhausts himself to support the weak,—a law, we may say, which none but God Himself could have conceived or illustrated in Himself.

Or we might think of this, how Christ's manifestation on the earth not only told us the nature of God, that He is love, and not only revealed to us the law of human life, even self-forgetfulness, but solved the problem that pressed in all previous ages on the hearts of men—the problem of our relation to that heaven which is above us. The best of men in all ages and in every nation have felt that they were not altogether right, and have been haunted with strange

terrors of a vengeance before them that was only
slumbering. They have looked into the future with
dread, and with anxious painfulness have sought to
avert that evil which lay on them with a dark presentiment. And the smoke of altars has gone up for
ever to heaven, and the dearest blood they knew has
been shed by them in the agony of their fear. The
evil that they knew lay on them—their own evil—
they knew not how to be relieved from. The Lord
has solved the problem for men. He has done so,
not by denying the evil, and telling us that what
haunted us was only a phantom of our own imagination; not by extenuating the evil, as if it were
inevitable in frail creatures such as we. He recognised
the evil, and showed it to be tenfold greater than men's
worst fears ever pictured it. And the way of relief
from it was this: that God had resolved to take our
evil upon Himself and invalidate it. " He was made
sin for us, who knew no sin ; in whom we have redemption through His blood, even the forgiveness
of sins."

3. The only other thing I shall allude to is the great
place which the Lord assigns to mankind. The relation
of mankind to His work is like that of the soil to the
sowing of the husbandman: " the earth bringeth forth
fruit of itself; first the blade, and then the ear, and
after that the full corn in the ear." The earth matures
the seed committed to it ; and it does so very gradually,
stage after stage, till at last comes the harvest. And

thus will it be with mankind, and the seed sown on its soil by Christ. It has received the seed, and beyond all doubt it will mature it, not speedily nor at once, but gradually through the epochs of its history, according to the laws of its progress, stage after stage, each following the other not by chance and not by necessity, but according to the law of the free activity of the human mind, till the harvest be ripe.

I apprehend that when the Lord says the kingdom of God is as if a man should cast seed into the ground, He has not in His mind at the moment any particular organisation, such as the visible Church, which gradually broadens out till mankind are embraced within it. He rather just thinks of men as men, with minds and hearts, with needs and aspirations, with powers and capabilities. He and mankind are the two factors which He has in view; He in contact with mankind, mankind in contact with Him; He and His word and all that He was, flung right upon the soil of the human mind. He speaks altogether generally, and without respect to such institutions as Churches. And this fact makes it probable that the parable maintains this general view throughout, and that there is no allusion in it to the growth of the kingdom of God, as we might call it, in the life of individual persons.

Of course, it might be true that the law of growth in the individual would be the same as that of the whole ; each particular stalk of grain advancing by the same stages as the whole field. And in this point of view many useful lessons for the individual life might be drawn from the parable. But such lessons, being hardly intended by the author of the parable, would be greatly coloured by the mind of the person who drew them. One mind would be found dwelling on the beauty of the grain at each separate stage of its growth, or on the delicacy and tender grace and sweet perfume of the early blade as it rises above the soil, fit emblem of the tenderness, the lovely lowliness, the delicate sensibility of the young Christian mind, with its freshness yet untarnished. Again, the sturdy stalks, the rank luxuriance, the healthy succulence, the rich resources, and the great promise of the corn in the ear, might be admired. And, last of all, the full corn, bending its head as if by the very weight of grace ; its roots now loose in the soil, as if feeling itself ready to be transported into the garner. To such a mind all seems fair ; every stage has its own charm, and God has made everything beautiful in its season. And if we are to reflect in this direction at all upon the parable, this is, no doubt, the right view to take of it.

But another mind of a pessimistic type would draw lessons of an opposite kind. He would point to the canker and the worm that fastens on the early blade, to the trailing slime of the slug and the withering bite of its loathsome tooth, and remind you of the blight and ruin that thus often overtakes early faith. To him the rankness and green luxuriance of the corn in the ear, that delighted the eyes of the former observer, would be offensive immaturity, which he would designate lank-ness and flabbiness in the Christian mind. Then, on the day of harvest he would observe with pain how many green stalks were falling before the sickle, very far from full or ripe; and even on the richest and most golden heads he would finger many a grain and find it light, and sorrowfully presage that, when the great winnower took his fan into his hand, many and many a one would be carried away before the wind with the chaff. Such reflections, though unlike one another, may have their own use. But perhaps the parable was not meant to suggest them. He that observeth the wind, saith the preacher, will not sow; and he that regardeth the clouds will not reap. Amidst droughts, or frosts, or tempests, we tremble for the harvest, deeming the season unpropitious, and fearing that it will be disastrous. Yet one day with another, and one time taken with another, through sunshine and shower, storm and calm, the grain matures, coming forth from all vicissitudes at last a plenteous harvest. So in like manner with the individual life. We dread the chills, the droughts that wither, and the storms that shake; yet we find that the Christian ripens in all weathers, and at last out of multiplied change of experience is ready for the garner.

Perhaps the thing in the parable that charms us most is what might be called the outlook of our Lord,—and it is especially consoling and encourag-ing to those who are entering on a new enterprise

in His name and in His cause,—His surprising and
generous faith in mankind, and in the final result of
man's history: "The earth bringeth forth fruit of herself; first the blade, then the ear, after that the full
corn in the ear," and then comes harvest. The more
we read of Christ, I think, the more we are inclined
to repose absolutely on His judgment; the more
exactly we can place ourselves in His point of view,
the surer we are that our point of view is right. I
do not mean so much that we trust Him because
He is God or the Son of God. Even before we
have come that length, He seems to us trustworthy.
Judging Him just by our ordinary standards, He
impresses us as being the absolute truth. No mind
ever was so well balanced as His; none so free from
passion, prejudice, narrowness, one-sidedness. His
judgment seemed like the going forth of rays of
light. And when to this we add His perfect moral
life, we are constrained to say, Here is the absolutely
true life and thought. And we fall back upon Him
in all things. We believe in God because He believed
in God. And we believe in Him because He believed
in Himself. And we believe in the destiny of mankind now that He has come into it, because He had
great hopes of it, and looked forward to a great
harvest of the seed which He sowed.

If there is any lesson for the individual contained in
this parable, it is the lesson of the gradualness of the
growth of the kingdom of God; the fact that it will not

hurry, will not push; that its growth has degrees, has a progress through stages. Yet this is rather an inference from the parable than strictly anything said in it. Our Lord is speaking of His kingdom among men on the great field of the world, the human mind. And He informs us that its growth must be gradual, that the harvest is not to be looked for at once; because the seed, flung upon the mind of man, into a sphere where the principle of progress or advance operates, will be brought under this operation. But all that He here says is merely that not at once, not immediately, but after patient waiting, the harvest will come. When He speaks of the blade, the ear, and the full corn in the ear, He does not mean that the kingdom of God must go through stages exactly corresponding to these. That is but a general analogy. The ripe harvest does not immediately follow the sowing of the seed; and no more will the perfect kingdom appear at once as the fruit of Christ's work on the earth.

And in transferring to the individual mind what He says of the kingdom of God, we must be very cautious. In speaking of God and His ways, we must always leave room for exceptions. The wine which our Lord usually drank had been planted, fed on the rains of heaven, ripened in the grape, and trodden in the wine-press; but on one occasion He made it in an instant out of water. The bread He usually ate had gone through the blade, the ear, and the full corn in the ear; but on several occasions He created it apart from any such process. Still, no doubt, truth also in the individual mind has a progress, and will not hurry. Its harvest has to be waited for. And the truth is one which perhaps is more helpful to us when considering the case of others than when considering ourselves. Even in regard to ourselves it may on occasions be useful; it may allay our bitterness against ourselves, or it may rouse us again out of the despair with ourselves into which we have sunk. But, above all, it gives us patience, and teaches us consideration and hopefulness in regard to others. Perhaps you should not strain the childish mind in order to hasten its growth in religion. Perhaps you should not press the sweet flower, in order to bring out the aroma of godliness which you are so eager to enjoy. Let the truth unite with the unfolding powers, with the expanding mind, with the increasing manliness, with the more subdued and less impulsive affections, with the character filling out and rounding on all its sides. Live as you would like to see the child live, and wait.

For what is the harvest, the crop? The crop is just the soil,—the powers of the soil changed by the sowing of the seed, and transmuted. And the harvest which the Lord will reap will be our minds, with all their capacities on all sides, changed by the seed which He has sown upon them,—our minds determining all their powers towards one fruit. And when we consider our minds, this may well be a work of time. When we think of the all-sided subtlety of our minds, the crowds of thoughts and feelings that rise in our hearts as we meet with men and women and the world, it cannot usually be soon that each of these thoughts and feelings will be sanctified. The husbandman waiteth long for the fruits of the earth. The Lord waits, and we must wait.

When we read our Lord's history we are often surprised at His hearty recognition of faith among men, and the unexpectedness of the joy it seemed to bring Him. O woman, great is thy faith. Daughter, thy faith hath made thee whole. I have not found such great faith, no, not in Israel. Let her alone, she hath done what she could. It almost seems as if there lay on our Lord a sense of gloom, an oppression of sombreness, due, perhaps, to what He foresaw before Him, which made Him hardly anticipate such things among men; and when He found them, they broke the gloom and overjoyed Him. He was certainly, in His view of mankind, no pessimist. Hence we ought never to be pessimistic in our views of human progress; for, as already said, the more exactly we place ourselves in Christ's point of view, the surer we are that our own point of view is right. And so amidst all the conflicting uncertainties about us and the noise of contending combatants, when we see former speculations on man, and life, and destiny chased away by newer speculations, and principles by which men once lived laughed off the stage by those now held,—amidst all this we fall back on Him. And we believe in the destiny of mankind now that He has come into it, and look forward with assurance to the harvest of the seed which He has sown.

But this seed He has committed to us. He has entrusted us with it; His dearest wishes He leaves us to fulfil. The fruit of the travail of His soul depends on us—not unaided, for He is with us always unto the end of the world. And He is confident we will not fail Him; that we will enter into the spirit of His work; that we will fill up, if need be, that which remains of His sufferings, for His body's sake, which is the Church.

The harvest of the world may be yet far off, but in our own selves it is always near. And even the former can be hastened. Do not let us read this parable, when it speaks of the blade, the ear, and the full corn, as meaning that the growth of the kingdom is under fixed, unalterable laws like those of nature, which we can do nothing to control, or vary, or hasten. Do not let us suppose that the parable is the first page in the literature of evolution. We begin to be afraid of what is called Law. Law threatens to push God from His throne, and the conscious freedom of the human mind from her seat. No, with God's help we have the harvest of the world in our own hands. It is we that must place the crown of glory on Christ's head. But what is His glory? What do you count glory? Is it not influence over others? that your mind reflects itself in theirs? that you are repeated, multiplied in others? And this is

15

Christ's glory—where He is reflected, repeated in each of us, when His mind is in us, and in the universal mind of man. Then He is Lord. If there is a rational universe of spectators to look on, I think they would call this glory. Yet if this be the glory which we give, it is not quite that which He seeks—except as a means. If He seeks the glory of being formed in each of us, it is because this is the way to our blessedness. His glory is His goodness realising itself in our redemption. The ancient seer said, Show me Thy glory; and he was answered, I will make all My goodness pass before thee—not as a substitute, but as the glory in truth.

To God on high, who can overlook the whole field, and has mankind in His hand, it is possible that the laws of human progress seem as fixed and definite as the laws of the soil in maturing the harvest. To God who has given freedom and self-consciousness to our minds, the laws according to which these will operate may be perfectly clear; but to us below such a view is scarcely possible. If we believe in such laws, we cannot discover them. To speak of evolution where there is will and freedom seems out of place. Perhaps the only law which the parable teaches us to recognise is just the law of growth from less to more, and that the growth is gradual and slow. And from the nature of the case it could not be otherwise. But it is not blind or unconscious, it depends upon our own free will. It is a progress carried on by minds which can foresee, and labour, and wait, and which if they must wait can long, and pray, and look that the sun and the rain of heaven will not be withholden. The Lord has committed His kingdom to us. The success of all the travail of His soul depends on us, not unaided, as we saw, but under heaven. He believes that we will love Him who first loved us. May the love of Christ constrain us not to live unto ourselves, but unto Him that died for us, and rose again.

The thought of the parable is wide. Christ brings Himself and mankind together, and He forecasts what His appearing among men will eventually make men, a kingdom of God over all. He enables us to look across present confusions, the conflicts of mind with mind and system with system, the opposing cries and rival banners of contending parties,—across all that to the time when He shall triumph, and the kingdom be the Lord's. That may be further away than our life shall extend. But the hope is large and animating. And meantime the part of each of us is to see that he is in the kingdom, and when the harvest is ultimately reaped, he too shall be gathered into the garner of God.

X

BID ME COME UNTO THEE

X

BID ME COME UNTO THEE

MATTHEW xiv. 22-33

I ASSUME that this incident in Peter's history may be read in a spiritual sense. All Christ's history may be so read. He went through the work of salvation outwardly to body it out to our sight, so that we might not fail to understand it. He opened blind eyes, and He gives spiritual sight—He is the light of men. He fed the multitudes, and He cried, I am the bread of life. He raised the dead, saying, I am the resurrection and the life. He lived among men, He went into their homes, He sat at their table; and after His ascension He says to the Churches, Behold, I stand at the door and knock: if any man hear My voice, and open the door, I will come in to him, and will sup with him, and he with Me. In His life He acted the truth of the gospel. This does not mean that His material actions in common life were typical of spiritual things—suggestive analogies of what was deeper. The truth is rather that all that He did, He did as the Saviour. Just as all the evils under which we suffer—our sorrow,

231

our want, our dying—are not to be called accidents or
incidents, but are at bottom to be connected with something fundamentally wrong in our relation to God ; so
when He comforted sorrow, and fed the hungry, and
raised the dead, He did all this as redeemer, as one who
had gone down to touch the evil of the world at its
sources ; and His special wonders were only the ways
in which He met this fundamental evil in the forms
in which it presented itself.   He did not work His
miracles or do His works as God Almighty, but as
God the redeemer ; and they were all acts or parts of
His redemptive work.   It was Messianic virtue that
went out of Him—" Himself took our infirmities and
bare our sicknesses."   His works were all parts of one
whole, and their interest does not lie so much in themselves—their interest lies in this, that they show what
He was who performed them, and what upon the whole
He was engaged in doing.   And this consideration for-
bids our regarding the present incident as a mere
singular or curious adventure on the part of one of
His apostles.

Now of the many truths suggested by the passage,
I may mention two or three.

1. The first is, that one gets one's first view of God or
Christ, or gets a new view many times, in the midst of
trials.   It was when the tempest had come down upon
the disciples, when they were toiling in rowing against
contrary winds, and had toiled for long, that Jesus
appeared in the fourth watch of the night walking

upon the sea.   Perhaps it would be fairest not to
regard the incident as illustrating how Christ first
shows Himself to men, but rather how, when He has
laid some command upon them, and they find it
beyond their power to carry it out, He appears to
help them.   He had constrained them to get into a
ship and go to the other side; and when they obeyed,
the storm arose against them, and He appeared to their
help.   But perhaps before looking at any of the details
of the transaction we should look at the whole horizon
of it, at what might be called the sky of the picture,
at the lights which fall upon the figures from a higher
region.   Men upon the earth and their actions have
little meaning, when looked at merely as upon the
earth.   It is the light from above, from an overhanging
heaven, that throws them out into relief, and gives
them their significance.   Corresponding to this scene
in the history of the disciples there was another scene.

The Lord, who had just fed the disciples with miraculous bread, when He sent the multitudes away, went
up into a mountain to pray.   Whether in the fellowship of His Father He was replenishing the fountains
of His power and grace, which had just been drawn
upon by His great miracle, we do not know; if it was
so, it was for the sake of His disciples; or whether, which
is more likely, it was just the destiny of His disciples
—their trials, their progress, and the best means to it,
their training and education for the time when they
should be left alone in the world—that was the subject

of His prayers.   In any case what we learn is this : that our life here has another side.   There is a reflection of it on high ; there is a rehearsal of it between the Father and the Son, before we are called upon to enact it.   As we weave the web of life, the pattern through which the threads are shot is being constantly let down into the loom from above.

The truth that it is oftentimes in trouble that we first get a view of God, or get a new sight of Him, is familiar, and it is natural.   It is when defeated by the world or by evil, and overcome, that we feel the need of another arm than our own to save us.   It is when we are pierced through with a wound which no balm of time or man will heal, that we turn to another Physician, and desire a divine hand to probe our sore.   It is when groping amidst a darkness which no sun that rises on sea or land will clear away, that we cry for the true light, the light of the world. All this reveals us to ourselves, and makes us feel that we are not of ourselves sufficient for ourselves ; that we need God ; that we cannot do without God ; that unless we are strengthened, comforted, enlightened by Him, life is beyond us, and more than we can encounter.

There is, however, another way in which trial, or trouble, or anything that affects us deeply brings us near to God and Him near to us.   These trials stir our nature to its depths.   That which is frivolous, or commonplace, or conventional, or in any way superficial in us, is broken through ; and the deeper elements of our life and nature are laid bare. Our deeper feelings, the more serious side of our being, gains for the time the upper hand. And, of course, it is this side that has in it most affinity for God and the things of God. And thus we are even unconsciously brought near to Him, and may readily be made to see Him. In such conditions He is not far from any one of us.

You remember the history of Jacob wrestling with the angel. This wrestling was an entirely personal thing, a thing between Jacob himself and God. But that which preceded it, and no doubt led up to it, was an anxiety on Jacob's part not for himself at all, but for others very dear to him. Having made all the dispositions that prudence could suggest, having divided his family and possessions into groups, and placed that which he felt he could easiest spare first and that which he loved most hindmost,—having made all these arrangements, he has to wait for the morning, and the events which it will bring. He would thankfully act, if any action were open to him; but there is none. He must wait inactive. And as he waits, deeper thoughts begin to crowd in upon him. His anxiety and earnestness in regard to others becomes an anxiety in regard to himself. An indescribable sensation comes over him, he feels himself seized in a supernatural grasp —"there wrestled a man with him until the morning."

Or you remember when you yourself were in circum-

stances similar. You sat by the bedside waiting for
the turn of the disease in one very close to you. You
had done all, used all means, called in all aid ; nothing
more could be done, and you sat down to wait the
issue. And as you waited, your thoughts about the
patient seemed to be reflected into yourself. Fountains
began to open in your heart which had long been
sealed ; the horizon seemed to widen, and views opened
up that had not been seen before ; there came out of
the past voices and words long forgotten; human life
assumed a greatness not felt before ; you felt in the
presence of something greater and higher than belonged
to the earth—it was the presence of God.

There is a small point in the narrative before us
which perhaps should not be missed. When the
disciples saw Jesus walking on the water, they
thought it was a spirit, an apparition, and cried out
for fear. He came to them in the fourth watch,
when possibly the dawn had begun to break, and
the light behind Him may have given gigantic pro-
portions to His form, or the driving mists of the
storm may have so enveloped Him, that in the
imperfect light He seemed unnatural. At all events,
the conclusion which the disciples came to shows
how highly their minds were strung and agitated.
But the point to be observed is that, when God or
Christ appears to men in the midst of afflictions or
trials, the view which they first receive of Him is
sometimes distorted and not true. It is God, but

He has to speak, before He be recognised. Jacob
wrestled long before he knew fully whom he was
wrestling with. And the patriarch Job in his sore
afflictions, though he knew he was confronted with
God in his trials, had a view of God far from true.
God appeared to him a cruel spectre, though at the
last he knew Him as He is. And the experience
of these men no doubt holds true still. Men are
by their sorrows or their troubles brought near to
God. It is God or Christ whose face breaks in upon
them, though in the darkness it may seem distorted
and terrible, and not divine. Yet there is a reality
in it—it is He; and He comes nearer and reveals
Himself. He speaks and interprets Himself: "It is
I; be not afraid."

2. A second idea which the passage suggests is the
irresistible attractiveness of God, when He is thus
seen, the irresistible power with which Christ draws
men to Himself and into His life, when He appears
to them as they struggle with the hard trials of
their own life. Peter cried, Lord, if it be Thou, bid
me come unto Thee upon the water. I, if I be lifted
up, said Christ, will draw all men unto me. How
obscured through so many centuries has God's countenance been! Many have doubted whether that which
they saw was God at all, whether it was anything but
an ideal reflection of themselves, which they named
God. But be it what it might, its attractiveness was
overpowering. Always when it has been seen it has

drawn men. They have sought God's face. It has been their desire to see His face in righteousness. They have thought that if they could but behold His face, they would be satisfied: "Show us the Father, and it sufficeth us." "When I awake, I shall be satisfied with Thy likeness." Even when seen imperfectly, and but as a star through the clouds, it has drawn men irresistibly. We know its attractiveness on men like Abraham, how he followed it from land to land; and on all the patriarchs, the secret of whose life lay here, that God appeared to them; on David and the singers of Israel: "My soul thirsteth for God: when shall I come near, and appear before God? One thing have I sought after, that I may dwell in the house of the Lord all the days of my life, that I may see the beauty of the Lord." We know its attractiveness even among men in the heathen world. How many sought after God, and worshipped before Him, though in many false ways, catching glimpses of His brightness through many mists, and singing hymns to the glory of Him whom they ignorantly worshipped! When God's face breaks in on a man, it seizes him with an irresistible attractiveness. He longs to be near God, to enter into the life of God.

Naturally, all this is even more true of Christ, because His life is not an abstract conception, but a human life. When He is once seen, when He once does receive our attention, the attraction of Himself and His life cannot be resisted. And the attraction

which He exerts differs from that exerted by others.
Any original power draws multitudes within the circle
of its fascination. Imitators of a power or gift, as of
oratory or poetry, are numerous. And perhaps Christ
found, so far as was possible, imitators in this way.
Not His disciples only, but others seem to have
emulated His works: "We saw one casting out devils
in Thy name; and we forbade him, because he
followed not us."

The influence of Christ must have been wider than
is at first apparent. Outside the circle of those influ-
enced unto salvation, there was a large movement that
went on among others, as there is still. "Many will
say to Me in that day, Lord, Lord, have we not prophe-
sied in Thy name? and In Thy name have cast out
devils? and in Thy name done many wonderful works?"
These felt only the indirect agitation which ran out in
eddies from the great central current. But all those
who catch a glimpse of the face of Christ are attracted
by it, and desert all other things to follow it.

You perhaps remember how you became a disciple.
It was in the same way as one did of old. You sat
at the receipt of custom. You were eagerly plying
your calling — more eagerly because it was not a
calling that brought in much at once. What came
in, came in littles. And you had to give it all your
mind. And as you sat anxiously accumulating penny
after penny, and thinking how long at this rate it
should be ere you were rich, suddenly a face pre-

sented itself before you, a divine face, so glorious
that all other thoughts vanished from your mind but
the thought of it; and when the voice came, saying,
Follow Me, you arose and followed Him. Or perhaps
you remember how that face rose upon you again,
if not with greater power, in a way that agitated
you more. It was not now serene and calm, but
blurred and languid. It was the moment of the
world's triumph. Her judges had given sentence
against Him. A crowd of eager, hateful faces glared
upon Him. The contemptuous swagger of the
soldiery, and the subservient, sycophantish conduct
of the servants and the crowd overawed and frightened
you. And at a distance from the Master, you became
confused, and were coward enough to deny Him.
Then far away, and in the hands of His enemies,
the Lord turned and looked upon you. You beheld
the torn and bleeding face,—most divine when torn
and bleeding,—and you went out and wept bitterly.
Ah! brethren, if we ever live well at all, it is only
as we catch glimpses of this divine face; if we ever
repent, it is when we see Him faint and weary for
us, and think how we have been unfaithful to Him;
or when we have sinned, and remember how He said:
"If ye love Me, keep My commandments." If we ever
have an earnest desire to do well, it is when that
pure and holy human face breaks in upon our sight,
and we think of the life which He lived upon the
earth, so different from that of men. If ever, amidst

the mysteries of this life and the riddles of the painful earth, we feel any content and peace, it is when He says: "Come unto Me, and I will give you rest"; and when, coming to Him, we hear Him in His sore distress say: "Even so, Father: for so it hath seemed good in Thy sight." Let us strive to have this face ever before us. Thus a godly life is lived, when we see Him; thus it is better lived, as we see Him more; thus shall it be perfect, when we shall see Him as He is.

The apostle said: "Bid me come unto Thee upon the waters." Two things appear here. There rose in his mind an impulse to enter into the fellowship of Christ, and to rise up into His life,—an impulse which could not be resisted. And there was created also a feeling of power which could not be measured. Perhaps the mind at such a moment does feel that it can do more than really it can do. Peter walked on the water to go to Jesus. He both went down into the sea, and made some way in going to Jesus. But seeing the wind boisterous, he became afraid. His effort so far corresponded both to his own feeling of what he was able to do, and to the word of Christ elsewhere, that all things are possible to him that believeth.

We might think that Christ, knowing that the apostle could not walk on the sea, still encouraged him by saying *Come*, partly because enthusiasm in His behalf is welcome, even though it exceed the bounds of possibility, and

16

partly because He would thus teach the somewhat confident and impulsive disciple a lesson of his own weakness, and by saving him let him learn from whom alone
real strength to do any work of faith could be received.

Perhaps such considerations did not influence Christ.
He encouraged Peter to do what he did, because to do it
was not impossible.   Jesus was disappointed that the
apostle failed: "O thou of little faith, wherefore didst thou
doubt?"   Speculations as to how it could have been done
are really useless.   But if by faith Peter could raise the
dead, his faith could equally have sustained him upon
the sea.   In that age, when Christ was upon the earth,
there was granted to faith a power even over the material
world, and there was perhaps no physical limit to what
faith might do; in this age, when miracle is withdrawn,
these physical powers do not come within the scope of
faith, but there is no limit to what it can accomplish in
display of moral power.   It would be out of place for us
to desire or to expect by our faith to remove mountains,
or to touch fire without being burned.   Into this side of
Christ's miraculous life we cannot enter.   But there is
another side, not less miraculous but almost more, in
which our faith may still, and ought still, to perform
wonders.

The greatest miracle of Christ was His sinless life.
This is the most stupendous, the most incredible of
all His miracles.   Just think of your own mind, and
endeavour to conceive of yourself in a state of sinless-
ness.   Consider the crowd of thoughts that rise in your

mind, the crowd of feelings that sweep over your heart, and imagine, if it be possible to imagine it, that none of these thoughts or feelings in all their multitude and variety had anything in the least wrong about it; that when thinking of yourself you never thought selfishly, or above what you ought to think; that when thinking or feeling about others you never thought or felt wrongly, harshly, unjustly, impatiently, peevishly, crossly; that when thinking of God you always thought with due reverence and adoration, and that you thought of God as much as you ought to think; that in all you said or did there never was any excess, and never any defect; that you were holy and without blame before God in love. It is so far beyond us that we cannot even imagine it. Yet this miracle of living was performed by Christ. And though it may be impossible for us to come up to the measure of it, yet our faith is invited to enter into this miraculous region, and it may perform in this region works truly miraculous. We may attain, through faith in Christ, to a patience, a meekness, a purity, a godliness, which deserve to be called miracles; which, when we look at ourselves and our own former evil, and our natural weakness to do such things of ourselves, we are constrained to call miracles. This is the miraculous region open to our faith still.

But to Peter in his day the other region was open; and there is no reason to blame him for attempting to do a thing which, if we attempted it, would be folly. It is not the will of God that our faith should be

directed to such things. And it is no faith that is
directed to anything but the will of God. A few
years ago one of the greatest men of our time was
taken ill; and after consultation his physicians informed him that his malady was incurable. No
remedy could be found for it; it was mortal. This
intimation revealed to him that it was the will of
God he should die. His congregation proposed to
meet to pray for his recovery, and he forbade them.
It was not the part of faith to direct itself towards
that which was clearly contrary to the will of God.

In the apostle's case it was different. It was not
the direction of his faith that was amiss, but the
weakness of it—not its enthusiasm, but its instability.
But his history is one repeated oftentimes in the
lives of all who are disciples. We enter upon great
enterprises, but come short of fulfilling them. A
glorious ideal of a life opens up to us, when Christ
and His life and deeds first break upon our view; but
it ends in failure, or comes to comparatively little, and
would have wholly come to nothing but for His
timely help. Probably no one realises all that he
conceived or thought possible at first, all that was
possible to faith. There is such a power in the
example of Christ; and that word of His, *Come*, raises
such a tumult in the heart, and quickens in such a
way all the powers, that all things seem possible, and
perhaps are possible. "All things are possible to him
that believeth."

This apostle failed to do even what he attempted. But the cause of his failure was his want of faith,—he saw the wind boisterous, and began to sink. He became aware of his natural position and of his natural powers. He sank back into his own natural self. He looked around him and at himself, and failed to continue looking to Christ. His faith failed. For though definitions of faith be hard to give, and though no man can tell another what believing is, no doubt the essence of faith is just to realise the presence of Christ with us, to realise Him in such a way as to feel, as clearly as if we saw Him, that He is beside us, does see us, is speaking audibly in our ears, and is ever ready to stretch out His hand to help us. This is faith — true, saving faith. With such a faith, all things are undoubtedly possible. What is there that we should not be able to accomplish, if we had every moment and on all occasions, when undertaking any work or resisting any evil, this vivid sense of Christ's being beside us? Could we sin or do evil, with Christ standing at our right hand? Could we be harsh in temper, unlovely in demeanour, sulky in behaviour to another person, if Jesus Christ were one of the three? Should we feel weak before any duty, though it might seem casting ourselves into the sea, if we saw Him in the midst of the duty, and heard Him audibly saying to us, Come?

In the circumstances, this word of Christ, *Come*, has much meaning. It sanctions all efforts to make our life or deeds like His,—all means to put ourselves nearer to Him, beside Him. We may be inclined to judge or criticise the conduct of the apostle, to see in it a new illustration of what we suppose, with all its attractiveness, was the defect of his character. Perhaps the other disciples felt in the same way. They may have thought his act extravagant, foolhardy, or presumptuous; they probably remarked of it that it was Peter all over. It is of no consequence what their remarks were. The Lord said, *Come.* He was neither jealous of His own prerogative, nor inclined to quench the ardour of the apostle's heart. His act might be very like him; but this, that it was like him, was just what made it dear to Christ. Its value in His eyes lay in its being spontaneous, the natural out-come of His disciple's temperament. Peter expressed himself in such actions. And this is just what pleased the Lord in them; and other things He overlooked, or did not care to see.

Is not this just what pleases us, that what others do for us should be natural to them, the expression of themselves? Do you school your child, and rigidly ordain that it shall show affection to you only in ways which you have carefully taught it? Does it not please you rather when it has original ways of showing love to you? when it breaks through what is customary, and invents, in the force of its affection, new methods? What we desire, what Christ desires, is love, spon-taneous love,—let it be awkward, singular, unusual in its acts, if natural and genuine, we care little. If genuine, though it may be awkward, it will never be vulgar. Its awkwardness will be due rather to its delicacy, to the confusing effect of the very strength of its emotions. The devotion of one who flung himself into the sea to be beside his Master is not the kind of devotion which the Master will readily cast away. A calculating, cool, judicious devotion to the Lord was far from being in the manner of the early disciples. There was something in their hearts that got the better of their calculations. Their displays of reverence and love might be called extravagant. Witness this action of Peter's. Witness the liberality of Zaccheus—"the half of my goods I give to the poor." Witness the passionate penitence of the woman who washed the Lord's feet with her tears. Witness the prodigality of that other woman who broke the precious box of ointment. Witness the last pious act of Nicodemus, who embalmed the dead body of the Lord with an hundred pound weight of spices. Impulsive women! Extravagant men! If we had but some of the sorrow for sin that caused these tears to flow! some of the reverent love that prompted such unbounded expenditure!

3. Peter cried: Lord, save me. And immediately Jesus stretched forth His hand, and caught him.

The truths suggested by these words are various. One may be that the life of faith must be wholly of faith. You cannot mix up the new and the old. Peter's natural resources as a fisherman did not avail him at all in his extremity; he had no help but cry to the Lord to save him.

Or another truth may be this: when a man fails in any act of faith which he has undertaken, it needs more divine help to put him on his way again than it originally required to start him. The word of the Lord, *Come*, was sufficient at first; now His very hand is needed,— "Jesus stretched out His hand, and caught him." And it is not amiss for us to reflect on this, that we may be on our guard against falling.

But possibly it is better not to take the incident to pieces in this way, but to look at it as a whole. The passage, at any rate, teaches us this, that it is much easier to imagine a high ideal of life, and obedience, and work, much easier to desire and to attempt to imitate Christ, than it is actually to accomplish it. It is not the idea, but the practice, that is hard. Our enthusiasm will meet obstacles, the buoyancy of hope and idea with which we set out will desert us, and, becoming heavy, we will sink. The word and the example of Christ may raise enthusiasms within us, and cause us to throw out great purposes; but only the help of Christ, His hand, will enable us to perform the least of them.

Ideals are, no doubt, very valuable things; they may sustain us often amidst the worry and confusions of our commonplace life. An enthusiasm, an ideal enthusiasm, is what we need—provided it be a practical enthusiasm,

and not enthusiasm for abstractions. If there is anything against which in religion we should be on our
guard, it is against abstractions—against theories about
life. They are dangerous, because we are apt to take up
with the beautiful abstract theory, the generalisation,
the ideal, and to feel that, being possessed of the theory,
we are in possession of all that is needful. Now, talking
about what is called *the* Christian life, and forming a
fine ideal of it, will not help you much, but it may do
you infinite mischief. Going about uttering great swell-
ing words about being *true* men, so far from making
you true men, will obliterate the small remnants of
truth that are in you. You will identify doing the truth
with having a theory of it. Give me the man who never
had a theory in his life either of Christian life or true
manliness, who never had an abstract conception about
duty all his days, but who doggedly faces his duty, and
does it whenever the particular duty has to be done.
To be true men is to do the truth on each particular
occasion when the truth has to be done.

Yet, though the very great difference between the idea
and the actual practice be taught by the passage, it
teaches more. It reminds us of the truth of Christ's
words on another occasion, the literal truth of them, for
the more we put them in practice, the more shall we
become convinced of their exact literality,—we are re-
minded, I say, of His words: "Without Me ye can do
nothing." Peter's experience is but a type of that which
all experience. The strength to obey Christ is given by

Christ. The deliverance out of danger is found when
He stretches out His hand.

But the real truth of the incident is best seen by
taking it as a whole,—from the beginning of it on the
other side of the sea, when Jesus constrained the disciples to get into the ship, to the end of it, when He
grasped Peter's hand, and came into the ship, and they
worshipped Him. The truth has the two sides; on the
one hand the faith, the obedience, of the apostle rises
step by step, each step leading to something higher,
to something greater; and, on the other, Jesus develops,
as we might say, new resources of power to save : first
giving bread from heaven, and then general commands,
next, by His word, *Come*, encouraging to great undertakings, and then by His hand enabling the failing
disciple really to accomplish his daring act of faith.
The little incident is fitted to be a glass to us, in which
we may see both what we should be, going on from
strength unto strength, and that which Christ is, in all
things able to help, mighty to save.

And the result of it all was they worshipped Him.
"When they were come into the ship, they worshipped
Him, saying, Of a truth Thou art the Son of God."
More and more they felt His greatness, His divine
power, His divine goodness. He laid His commands
on them; He came to their aid, and enabled them to
carry these out; they felt Him in their life, and that
what they were able to do was due to Him; and they
worshipped Him.

The man who is stimulated to attempt any act of faith, who is enabled to perform it, who is rescued from sinking amidst the waves of evils within and without, will feel that the impulses came from Christ, that the strength was not his own but Christ's, and that it was Christ who stretched out His hand and delivered him. And being certain of this, he will also feel more and more that Christ is not of this world, but is the Son of God. May this be the end of all our experience and all our history, to know more and more what Christ is, and to worship Him with a fuller and more thankful heart.

XI

"IT IS FINISHED"

XI

"IT IS FINISHED"

JOHN xix. 30

THESE words were uttered nineteen hundred years ago by a man on a cross at Jerusalem,—a man whom a lawless and fanatical mob had arrested, and after a mock trial, under the eyes of a feeble and time-serving governor more fearful of losing popularity than of spilling innocent blood, had carried, with every circumstance of brutal cruelty and barbarous licence, to the place of execution, and there, amidst the insulting sneers of the wretched bystanders, nailed to the cursed tree. More than once the Crucified One had spoken from the Cross; and these were the last words He uttered. "Knowing that all things were now accomplished, that the Scripture might be fulfilled, He said, I thirst. When Jesus, therefore, had received the vinegar, He said, It is finished: and He bowed His head, and gave up the ghost."

There is a certain mysterious fulness in these words. The Sufferer does not say what is finished; it is something filling His mind and heart, something that has filled His mind and heart for long, some great familiar thing which He does not need to name, something the end of which has come at last—an end hard to reach and greatly wished for; and He both describes this great thing, and expresses His relief at its completion when He says, "It is finished." Now, though it be one great thing to which Christ refers when He says, It is finished,—a thing which He elsewhere speaks of as His work, as the work given Him to do,—we must, in order to understand it at all, take it to pieces and look at its parts separately, and, indeed, on this occasion at only a very few of them, and these perhaps not of the deepest meaning.

And, first, His death agonies are finished. Were this an ordinary death of an ordinary man and nothing more, would it not speak very significantly to us? It is not a thing, Death, that we have no concern with; it is before us all: "It is appointed unto men once to die, and after this the judgment"; and as the old tyrant asked some of his slaves to kill themselves, to show him how to die, we see here a death scene, which we might well covet as our own. He was a young man this, to have to die, the blood being yet full and firm in His veins. The world was very fresh and lovely to Him; no man had ever such an eye for the freshness of nature and the warm realities and vigour of life as He had. He hardly ever spoke, but He spoke of something real and living: "Consider the lilies of the field." He had often gazed on the flowers; and they were not only beautiful in His eyes, but full of lessons of the wisdom and goodness of His father in heaven. "Whereunto shall I liken this generation? They are like children sitting in the market-place." His eye had strayed, too, among the children practising their games, celebrating mock marriages and mock funerals. Alas! He saw that soon enough their mock diversions would become very real, and the world would care as little about their joys and their mourning then, as their sulky companions care about them now. Or again, casting His eye over the earth in spring, He says, "A sower went forth to sow," or in autumn, "The fields are white unto harvest." You see how all nature fastens itself upon Him with its deep beauties, and all life with its stirring animation; and His heavenly truth comes forth clothed in the warm, rich drapery of earth and human life.

And yet this Son of man, thirty years of age or little more, dying in the bloom of manhood with such deep feeling of all that is fair on earth, has no regret at leaving it. At first, indeed, the terrors of the death He had to die did overcome Him for a time, and the thought rose in His heart that, if it were only possible, He would stop short of entering the waters of that dark flood that now rolled close at His feet; and with great submissiveness He did in His agony approach His Father, hazarding the question whether it might not be possible to escape the cup that was now to be put into His hand,—a thought that, perhaps, only the terrors of such an hour could have raised in His mind.

17

But it was not possible, and He went forward with gladness and strength to that which was His Father's will. He has no regrets at leaving all that He loved on earth. He has loved ones whom He is leaving; He has a mother, but He calmly provides for her. Bringing the beloved disciple and her together, He commends her to his care, calling her his mother and him her son; and this done, He says, "It is finished," and dies. And so, on the other hand, as there is no regret, there is no triumph. Even when, in the moment of His greatest weakness, still showing Himself to be the power of God unto salvation, and converting the dying thief, it is with no excitement, but a certain calmness, that He addresses him: "To-day shalt thou be with Me in paradise." And there is the same calmness and faith in His words about Himself: "Father, into Thy hands I commend My spirit."

How many of us could face death in this clear, calm way, with all our faculties about us, our hearts and consciences and memories all alive, and speaking out what is on them; and yet our memories able to draw up nothing from the past to terrify us, and our imaginations to conjure up nothing in the future to dismay us, knowing in whom we have believed? Oh, may we die the death of the righteous! and may our last end be like His! But to die His death, we must live His life.

And this leads me to say, in the second place, that these words of Christ, "It is finished," cannot refer merely to His death agonies. They refer to the whole

sorrows of His life.   There is a depth about the words,
and the sufferer speaks out from beneath a load of
oppression that has lain on Him far longer than these
hours upon the Cross.   The sufferings of the Cross were
perhaps, in some respects, less than those in the Garden ;
and those in the Garden were not alone.   Often during
His life, He would become strange-like to the bystanders,
being carried away by other thoughts than the things
about Him ; and He retired, and wrestled on a mountain
apart, and came back calm again.   The words, " It is
finished," refer to some deep lifelong oppression that
lay on Him,—that lay always on Him, though only now
and then rising up so as to overmaster Him, and of
which the Cross was but the end,—an oppression that
lay on Him from His childhood, crushing Him down,
pressing out of His heart all mirth, giving His whole life
such a solitariness and grand sublimity, that at last His
disciples hardly dared to speak to Him.   " After that
durst no man ask Him any more questions."

What wondrous man is this that rises before us, so
calm in death, so strange, and meek, and sorrowful when
living ?   It is the man of sorrows ; and when He says, " It
is finished," He means that all this sorrow is over at last.

> " Now sorrow and pain
> Come never again."

You speak in the same way yourselves, when any
tremendous tension is removed from you.   You sit
for weeks by a troubled bedside, and are familiar with
racking pain and cries of, Would God it were morning !

and tossings till the day dawn, and restlessness till it
close. At last the symptoms aggravate; it has been
coming on, gradually but surely; you have been looking
for it long, and when the last convulsion is past, you
throw the load off you, and say, It is over—he is at rest.
" It is finished." This oppressive sorrow of Christ's that
had lain like a burden on Him, He has now thrown off
for ever.

But wherein consisted this sorrow of Christ's?
Sorrow is a thing of the mind. And although Christ's
bodily sufferings were perhaps greater, and His horror
of death more intense than in the case of any mere man,
yet His sorrows came mainly from His mental sufferings. I think His bodily sufferings must have been
keener than those of any mere man would have been,
for this reason, that He was sinless; and thus His frame
must have been more keenly and wondrously sensitive
to suffering than our bodies are, which are dulled and
deadened by the effects of sin. Even in life we are in
death. From our birth we are becoming the gradual
prey of death, and every pain that we suffer, and every
day's hard labour that we endure, and every disease
that leaves us so much feebler than it found us, blunts
our feeling and makes the last pains of dying less sharp
to us. But Christ met death with the sensibilities of His
frame blunted by none of all these things.

Again, His shrinking from death must have been very
intense. For He was the life. " In Him was life." By
the time we come to die, death has oftentimes little to

do. We are born with the seeds of death in us, and they gradually ripen; and so strong a hold have feebleness and disease often got of us already, that death is natural, and almost welcome. We have been dying all our life. But He had no sin, and death no hold of Him. He met it in the full flush of life,—a life that would have been immortal, but for His voluntarily laying it down. And even this, apart from the terrible circumstances of His death, arising from its being in the place of sinners, may have made *dying*, to Him, a thing of unspeakable horror.

But, not to speak of His death and its sorrows, mere living must have been full of sorrow to Him. He must have been a man of sorrows, and acquainted with grief, if He was to live upon this earth at all. Just think a moment. What is it that makes your life lovely to you? Is it the food that you eat, or the raiment that you put on, or the property that you acquire? Is it even the joy of health, and the gladsomeness of youth and activity, and of seeing things prosper and go well with you? These things do add something. But is not the main thing this, the knowledge that there are beings who love you, to whom you are everything, who understand you, and sympathise with you and with your struggles, and rejoice in your victories over what is without you, and still more in your victories over yourself? Give you the whole world, and leave you alone in it, and where would your happiness be?

But Christ was alone in the world. "He came unto

His own, and His own received Him not. He was in the world, and the world was made by Him, and the world knew Him not." Though its Creator, it knew Him not; no secret sympathy, as we might have thought, betrayed Him to it; it understood Him not, gave Him no credit for what He was, saw no love in Him, no compassion in Him, no salvation in Him. In a word, it had nothing in common with Him, and thus could not recognise Him. He was alone in the world.

Even the few chosen ones were far from knowing Him. Though He took them with Him on many great occasions, yet they were rather like strangers about Him; they never, till He had gone up into heaven, knew Him. They were dull and slow of heart, and found themselves beside one who was quite beyond them, so far beyond them often, that they did not suspect what unfathomable meaning lay in some of the things they saw Him go through. Thus, on the Mount of Transfiguration, they were merely confused; and Peter spoke, "not knowing what he said." When admitted to behold some of His greatest miracles, they only wondered, but did not understand. When He went down into His last great trial, they sorrowed, but still could not accompany Him; and when He plunged into the dark stream alone, they fell exhausted on the bank. He was alone. "They knew Him not." You take a child with you into the churchyard, but what does it know of all that you feel? You are convulsed with old memories of those you have laid there,—their voices are again in your ears, you

hear and see them, and remember your former happiness and your present bareness; but the child, where
is it? Chasing insects over your graves, pulling wild
flowers, none the less beautiful to it, that they grow
on the dust of those whom you once clasped living to
your breast. It knows nothing of your griefs. So it
was with Christ. The world pursued its butterflies,
and plucked its flowers, and heeded Him not, while
He stood with His heart rent, overawed Himself by
the riot of evil things like ugly weeds about Him.

May we not see now some way into His sorrows?
and how to Him mere life was full of griefs. And
may we not see something of the meaning of those
sudden escapes He often made to the seashore or the
mountain side, just to be away from men, and to flee
from the loneliness which He felt in the society of the
best of them? There was One with whom He could
commune there,—riding on the storm, or thundering
on the mountain top; "and He continued all night in
prayer to God." That heart was deep enough to comprehend Him; and He poured out His soul in His
Father's ears, and came back refreshed and strengthened.
His life having been filled with sorrow, you can understand the relief with which He left it, to go to His Father,
when He cried, "It is finished."

But surely this is going but a little way into the real
sorrows of His life and death. It was, no doubt, a sharp
grief to Him to be despised and rejected of men; to
come and make such offers to men, and be repulsed

by them; to meet in so many cases only scorn in
return for such love, and in so many cases more
neglect. And to this pain, coming from men's ingrati-
tude, was added also the sorrow which He must have
felt, when He considered the fate to which they were
consigning themselves by their rejection of Him, as He
says: "Ye will not come unto Me, that ye might have
life." And the apostle, who knew His feelings best,
has added: "He that hath the Son hath life: he that
hath not the Son hath not life; but the wrath of God
abideth on him."

But there was a heavier sorrow than all this which
lay on Him—the weight of sin. His sorrows were
not for Himself, they were thrown upon Him by those
about Him, as you have seen a mountain throw its
dark frowning shadow across the bosom of some clear,
smiling lake. Christ's heart was itself clear, only the
gloom of sin darkened it. He became involved in men's
sin. He came to bear it. No doubt this rejection by
men, His little success among them when on earth,
their little sympathy with Him, and His solitariness
among them, were all fragments of the great burden of
sin which He had to bear. These evils were part of
the sorrows of His state of humiliation, and due to sin.
They were the *penumbra*, the commencing shadow of
the eclipse — not its full darkness. But what I am
saying now is not merely that He felt the consequences
of sin, but that in some way He came in contact with
sin itself. "He bore our sins in His own body on the

tree." Now that, no doubt, means that He suffered severe physical pains due to them, but it also must mean that He endured grievous sorrows in His soul. He bore our sins. But who shall say in what way He felt sin? How did this substitute, who was guiltless, feel the guilt of those for whom He suffered? Clearly He could not feel it as we do, as bitter remorse, stinging us and eating out like a cancer our happiness and life. He could not feel it as regret for wrong done; it could not come upon Him in passionate waves of memory, as it comes upon us, when we remember our former evil, and our unkindness to those who loved us, and how we seduced weakness, and initiated innocence, by our corrupting talk or actions, into a career of vice; or how we have been guilty of degrading actions, of which only God and we are conscious. It could not take this form, because Christ was Himself holy and undefiled; but it cannot be supposed that His sufferings in body were the whole of what is meant by bearing our sins. They somehow came home to His own mind.

Christ, being our substitute, felt in some way both the pollution of our sins that were laid on Him, and also the guilt of them. It was not mere punishment that He felt; but He felt how deserving of punishment our sins that were laid on Him were, how foul and unholy they were, and how hateful to God. He, lying under our sins, felt Himself lying under the pollution of them, and under the anger of God due to all this. We cannot tell how all this should be, but here lay His chiefest sorrow.

"He was made sin for us, who knew no sin." We must not make too much nor too little of such expressions. He was made sin for us—He was not made sinful for us. He took sin, but never sinned. But, on the other hand, He did not merely suffer certain bodily evils as penalty of our sins. We are fond of saying He paid our debts; He was our surety, our cautioner ; He paid the smart of our arrears and defalcations. And so He did. But with a certain difference. The man who permits himself to be drawn into such a position for another among men, whether voluntarily or by unforeseen implication, shares not a whit in the dishonour of the other. The defaulter's disgrace is all his own. The surety goes abroad among his fellows, bowed down by no load of reproach from without. He is a humane man, an honourable man, a man unselfish, at least, whether wise or no ; and men esteem and exalt him. But our surety stood closer to us than that. Our sins came home to Him. He felt their dishonour, their awful pollution, their heinous guilt, and felt it somehow as His own.

We cannot understand this. And we need not. We know that thus He bore our sins, that thus He made an end of sin. And we know that it was this sin-bearing which made up more than anything else the sadness of His life : "Now is My soul troubled; and what shall I say ? Father, save Me from this hour." Did it ever strike you that Christ was never a child ? He was one in years; but He was always saying startling things, bringing out words from a great deep somewhere, that none dared to look into. He was always looking forward; and the sense of something to come saddened Him, and He trod the earth under a shadow. You do not fancy Him a child like your children, gay, and free of concern; He was grave, retired, and sad. He moved about with a weight upon Him. It is not anywhere recorded of Him that He smiled. He was as one with his face steadfastly set to pass along a way, at the end of which stands some object of great terror, dimly erect. That way was His life; that dim, terrible object was the Cross. It was no romantic, moss-grown, ivy-clothed cross, relic of some splendid temple, beautiful with age, and sacred as the symbol of a hereditary religion. The Cross before Him was the green, fresh, bitter Cross—the first and shameful Cross. And ever as He walked along the way, His eye caught it, and it threw its great dark shadow all along the path, even to His feet when a child. And it saddened Him, and He could not repress allusions to it many times among His disciples. You hardly fancy that Christ was ever youthful-looking. You think of Him, do you not, as of some young man whom you have seen, who has suffered from a painful malady a long time? At first this man was peevish and fretful; no hand could smooth his pillow enough, or make his posture easy enough, and he complained, and was envious of the health of those about him. But by and by all this goes, and he becomes subdued and submissive. Suffering makes his brow clear and white, and his face is sad and chastened; but his eye is clear, and looks forward full into the grave without turning aside; for he has looked there often, and knows what is in it. I think this last is how you think of Christ, composed and submissive, calmly looking forward, yet oppressed and laden by the sense of what was before and about Him; and when He passes through the fire, and sin closes around Him, you understand the energy of relief which He feels, as He casts it off, and cries, " It is finished ! "

Now these are rather things personal to Christ. But I think it right to dwell on things personal to Him. For His coming out from the Father and living among men, and dying for them, were not mere pieces of mechanical acting, without exercise of will, or emotion, or feeling. They were not mere official actings. We do speak of the offices of Christ, and say He performed the offices of a prophet and a priest. But that is merely a way of grouping together certain of the things He did, and certain of the relations in which He stood, in order to help ourselves to a clearer understanding of them. All about Christ was personal, real. He was the Son of God and of man, and all He did He did as Son of God and of man. His relations were not official, but natural.

But, before closing, I wish to refer to one other thing now finished. I might refer to many things. Thus His ideal of a godly human life was finished. He was the author and the finisher of the faith. The first and only faithful life lived upon the earth was His. And that splendid, spotless, godly life of faith, the track of which circles the earth like a bow of light, was now finished. Again, His preparation to be the eternal mediator was complete. "Having been made perfect, He became the author of eternal salvation unto all them that obey Him. And, not to enter into details, who can imagine what processes of divine intentions from the beginning were now, on the Cross, brought to an end, for He was the Lamb slain from the foundation of the world? What strivings and yearnings of God's heart were now come to an issue! and what feeling, as of a stilled tempest when warring elements are hushed, passed over all worlds, when His cry, "It is finished," was heard loud above the disorder of the universe, even as before, on the Sea of Galilee, His voice rose above the waves, when He said, "Peace! be still," and there was a great calm. "For it was resolved that in Him should all the fulness dwell; and, having made peace through the blood of His Cross, by Him to reconcile all things unto Himself; by Him, I say, whether they be things in earth or things in heaven."

All this they mean. For it would be alogether a defective view of our Lord's words to hold them merely a cry of relief. They are a cry of triumph—a long drawn out shout of a satisfied and filled benevolence, of a goodness and love that at last has gained its object, the redemption of a *world*. It is a moment this, when even a Creator's heart may not restrain its joy, feeding upon it in silence, but may give it out—"It is finished"; a shout not only of a satisfied and filled benevolence, but of a filial joy that could not be repressed, in having glorified His Father: "I have glorified Thee upon the earth: I have finished the work Thou gavest Me to do!" But the one point I wished to bring before you at last was, that His revelation of the Father is finished. When He spoke of going to the Father, a disciple exclaimed: "Show us the Father, and it sufficeth us!" Having seen Him, they would be content. Ah, we should all be content then. All hearts would hush, and turn to the Father who made us in love. This is the cry of the heart, Show us the Father. It is around Him that the darkness gathers. It is against this darkness that we grope in anguish, and fear, and terrible longing. This is the cry, if only articulated, of all the unrest of men; and their wars, and their migrations, and their art and science, and their many times irreverent thronging the threshold of the Unrevealed, and impious guessing of what is within: "Show us the Father, and it sufficeth us!" Let us hear the words of Christ: "He that hath seen Me hath seen the Father" —seen the Father!

Now I admit that these words might have a lower meaning than they seem to have. They might mean merely: He that hath seen Me, and the relations between the Father and Me, may learn what the Father is. When two things are closely related to one another, and one of them and all its relations is known, you can infer what the other must be, although it be not the object of direct knowledge itself. As you have a knowledge of that which is infinite, not in itself, but because it lies about the outer rim of that which is finite, you move around that circumference of light and feel a knowledge, too, of the outer darkness. And God the Father may thus be very really known, if we would consider the Son's relations to Him in the world, how He lived with Him and walked with Him. We shall then see both what God requires from His children, and what He gives them. God requires much. "Father, if it be possible; nevertheless, not as I will, but as Thou wilt! He went out into a mountain to pray, and continued all night in prayer to God. The Son doeth nothing of Himself, but what He seeth the Father do." But God also gives much. He rewards His children openly. The thunders of heaven proclaim: "This is My beloved Son in whom I am well pleased." "Ye shall be scattered, and leave Me alone; and yet I am not alone, because the Father is with Me."

Yet this is certainly not what Christ means, when He says: "He that hath seen Me hath seen the Father." He means that He is the likeness of the Father. The Son is the image of the invisible God. The Son bears the likeness of the Father. He is the brightness of His glory, and the express image of His person. It is not merely that He is God as the Father is, that He shares the divine nature: He is the likeness of the Father. The personal character of the one shows itself in the other. You see not only God in Christ, but

God the Father in Christ; for the Son bears the likeness of the Father.

And now men need say no more, Show us the Father. He that hath the Son hath the Father also. And when this was shown, He said, "It is finished."

Now three concluding remarks.

All is finished—whatever it was—for which Christ came into the world. He made an end of sin. He brought in everlasting righteousness.

1. Whatever Christ came into the world for was finished. His work was not cut short by death. Death did not come on Him, as it comes on us, paralysing us in the midst of our work, so that the tools fall from our hands, and we are changed and carried away. How many pieces of human work are thus for ever suspended, and hands that have acquired skill through a lifetime's exercised pliancy become rigid, and the work that was all but executed is postponed for ever, and humanity fails to reap a portion of its destined harvest of beauty or of goodness! But death did not surprise Him, nor suspend His work; it came to perfect Him, and to finish His work. All that is expressed in Christ's appearance—the coming nigh of God to men, the unveiling of the mysteries of our life, the reaching back to the hidden springs of all that God does,—all this was but sealed in Christ's death. "God hath commended His love to us, in that while we were yet sinners Christ died for us." That which He came to do but reached its end in His death; He

made an end of sin, and brought in everlasting righteousness. He became obedient unto death, even the
death of the Cross.

2. Is not this also a fair inference from the passage
—that we may and should take our impressions of
God the Father from Christ the Son? The Son is the
likeness of the Father: He that hath seen Me hath
seen the Father. Fasten, then, your eyes upon Christ
in all His intercourse with men,—in its tenderness, and
patience, and compassion,—and at every new movement,
as He frequents the feast of joy and ministers to it, or
stands at the grave and weeps, and restores the dead;
as He lets Himself be stealthily touched by the fearful,
and heals; as He stands over the bier and says, Thy
sins be forgiven thee; as He lifts the little child and
blesses it—keep saying to yourself, This is God; this
is the Father of all; this is how He thinks of men,
and walks among them, and shows Himself to them,
and pities them; this is how He thinks of me, and
looks on my sorrow and my sin,—my Father! God
over all, be blessed for ever!

3. The lesson of the apostle. "The love of Christ
constraineth us; because we thus judge that if one died
for all, then were all dead; and that He died for all,
that they which live should not live unto themselves,
but unto Him who died for them."

He seeks by dying for you that you should live
unto Him. It is not a little thing that He seeks; it
is that all that is embraced in that one thing *life*

18

should be His. It is not a little thing, it is everything. It never and nowhere has been Christ's way to depreciate Himself, or ask little of those whom He has benefited. There is One, indeed, whom He sets before Himself at least, if not above Himself, the Father; the Father first, but Himself always next, and along with Him. "Herein is My Father glorified, that ye bring forth much fruit, and ye shall be disciples to Me." He, in a word, demands everything from those for whom He died. Whether it be reasonable that He should ask the life He gave you to be devoted to Him, you can yourselves conclude. Whether, apart altogether from its reasonableness, your blessedness does not lie simply there, in giving yourselves to Him, you also know. "Blessed are all they that put their trust in Him."

> "'Tis finished—The Messiah dies
> For sins, but not His own;
> The great redemption is complete,
> And Satan's power o'erthrown.
> 'Tis finished—Legal worship ends,
> And gospel ages run;
> All old things now are past away
> And a new world begun."

XII

THE POWER OF HIS RESURRECTION

XII

THE POWER OF HIS RESURRECTION

PHILIPPIANS iii. 10–11

"THAT I may know Him, and the power of His resurrection, and the fellowship of His sufferings, being made conformable unto His death; if by any means I might attain unto the resurrection of the dead."

It is remarkable that it is in the Epistles written from Rome that the apostle speaks so much about knowledge, namely, in this Epistle, and in the two Epistles so closely related to one another, that to the Ephesians and that to the Colossians, and in the brief letter to Philemon. Writing to the Ephesians, he prays that God would give unto them the spirit of wisdom and revelation in the knowledge of Him, that they might know what was the hope of His calling; and again, that they might be able to comprehend with all saints what is the breadth, and length, and depth, and height; and to know the love of Christ, which passeth knowledge. And to the Colossians he writes that he prays for them without ceasing that they may be filled with the knowledge of His will in all wisdom and spiritual understanding. And the word *know* is very frequently met with in the present Epistle: " Yea, doubtless, and I count all things but loss for the excellency of the knowledge of Christ Jesus my Lord."

Had the apostle then, in his enforced retirement in prison, leisure to *contemplate*, and had he then in his solitude, when no man stood by him in his bonds, *felt* Christ more? There is no doubt that, as a subject of contemplation, of reflection, Christ is very profound, and that years of calm thought, though they may have the effect of opening up surprising mysteries, will be far from exhausting Him. There is also no doubt that in the midst of afflictions, such as Paul then endured, a very special knowledge of Christ might be attained. In the ordinary life of preaching, with the necessity lying on the preacher of finding what in Christ was applicable on each occasion, and with the many hardships and persecutions which this life entailed, he must have reached to a profound knowledge of Christ through both the channels of reflection and experience. But in his two years' imprisonment he had opportunity of long, continuous, connected thought on Christ, and to while away the tedium of the weary hours this must have been his chief resource; and he had also, in his tribulation and bonds, long experience of what resources of consolation and strength were in Him. But all this knowledge did not satisfy him. It rather spurred him on to long for more. There were treasures of wisdom and knowledge not yet opened up to him;

there was a depth of feeling to which he had not yet attained. And his prayer is that he might know Christ in a more all-sided way—penetrate further into Him by his thoughts, and feel Him more profoundly in his emotions: "That I may know Him, and the power of His resurrection, and the fellowship of His sufferings."

The expression 'to know Him, *and* the power of His resurrection,' does not mean to know Him, *even* the power of His resurrection; as if it were not *He* strictly that was known, but only the effects of certain things about Him felt, such as His resurrection. The meaning is rather the reverse, namely, to know Him *in* the power of His resurrection, to reach through knowing the power of His resurrection to a knowledge of Him, to be brought close to Him through all that He has done and all that has happened to Him, so as to know Himself.

The object of all that He did and of all that happens to us is to bring us and Him close together, so that we may behold His glory, and be satisfied with His likeness; so that, in a word, we may know Him. Now we need helps to this. We learn to know Him through the experience of our soul and life, each of which enables us to add something to our realising of what He is. We realise anything great only slowly. It is through living that we enter into anything, whether it be a great sorrow or a great joy. When we lose one that was much, or, as we say, all to us, the loss becomes real to us only as we live, as we enter into the scenes and relations in which he filled so great a place. As we sit by the fire, and he is not there, our loss comes home to us ; or as we gather about the footstool of God, and he is not there, our loss comes home to us anew with a hallowed sadness. In our mirth he does not share, and so that mirth is cheerless. Step by step only, as we live,—as we enter into the various aspects of life,—does the feeling of how it is with us now become real. And in like manner when any great joy or honour has fallen to us, we do not realise it at once in itself ; we realise it best when we see it reflected in men's faces, or feel it in the more cordial hand they give us, or observe it in the slight, though to us not imperceptible, change in their demeanour or increase in their respect. And thus it is, no doubt, also with the knowledge of Christ. We learn to know Him as we live. We know Him in knowing the power of His resurrection and the fellowship of His sufferings. We know Him by experiencing those successive energies of power that make up the manifold power of His resurrection, and by entering into those various conditions of endurance, from temptation, from the evil that is in the world, and from the throes and agonies of death, which make up the fellowship of His sufferings.

The verses under consideration seem to contain the same idea stated twice ; once more compendiously, and then drawn out into detail. " To know Him, and the power of His resurrection," embraces all. For we must not forget what place the resurrection of Christ held in the preaching and thinking of Paul. It was his gospel. He staked all upon it. He had not known Christ after the flesh. His first sight of Christ was a sight of the risen Lord. On the way to Damascus he first knew Christ, and it was in the power of His resurrection. And this first sight gave a direction to all the thoughts he had about Him; and, like all men who have profound experiences and a mental history, he started from that which made the crisis in his own life, and put the resurrection in the forefront of his preaching. Among the philosophers on Mars' hill he preached the resurrection,—an idea so foreign to Greek speculation, that they could not understand him, and they thought 'resurrection' was a deity which he wished to introduce; and in some perplexity they canvassed his sermon, saying: He seemeth to be a setter forth of strange gods. With the Corinthians, who were inclined to doubt the bodily resurrection, he could come to no compromise. He pushed the question to the extreme. He showed how if this was lost all was lost. "If Christ be not risen, then is our preaching vain, and your faith is also vain. Ye are yet in your sins." And his words were not the words of a mere enthusiast, who had had a vision which a fervid temperament took for a reality; and who, amidst the spiritual excitement produced by it, sought to turn the world upside down. He reflected on the question. He set it in all lights, and, look at it how he would, the resurrection took its place as the corner-stone of his faith. No man was less inclined to be carried away by a heated brain than he was. In spite of the eminence to which he has been elevated, as pre-eminently the theologian of the New Testament, no man probably has fewer theories than he has. He plants his foot down everywhere on facts,—either on facts of history, or on undoubted facts of human experience. When, for instance, he has to lay a foundation for his great doctrine of justification by faith, he lays that foundation in human experience.

He appeals to men's consciousness whether any one individual can hope to be justified before God in any other way; whether anyone will sist himself before the judgment-seat of God, demand that the books recording every deed and thought of his life be opened, and challenge a verdict upon it. "By the works of the law shall no flesh be justified." If there is to be justification at all, if God is to express His satisfaction with men, it will not be with men standing before Him with the blurred and blotted scroll of their own life in their hands. In a similar way Paul sets his foot down on the resurrection as a fact of history. This had a meaning to him, not because he was an enthusiast, the victim of a diseased imagination, but precisely the reverse, because he was a man of reflection. For the resurrection, first of all, was proof to him that Jesus was the Messiah. But it entered into his system in a far profounder way than that. It furnished to him what he felt was needed, a new departure in the history of mankind. It gave him the ideal and the reality of a new man, not an earthy man, such as Adam was, before he fell, nor even as Christ was upon the earth, but a heavenly and spiritual man.

It is only the spiritual man that can have perfect fellowship with God—"flesh and blood cannot enter into the kingdom of God." Now Christ on earth was not wholly a spiritual man. He had a body of flesh. But on His resurrection He became wholly spiritual, He assumed a spiritual body. Then He was wholly, in mind and body, the spiritual man, the new man—head of the new humanity, and the second Adam. Then, too, He was constituted Son of God in power by the resurrection from the dead. He was the new man, the Lord from heaven; and being elevated on high, was in a position as new man to put forth all His power to save men—His power, which was the power of His resurrection. And it is this power which the apostle desires to know. Therefore, when he says the power of His resurrection, he means all the power which He now puts forth, and all the power which thinking of Him, as He now is, exerts on men's minds.

The other expressions, 'fellowship of His sufferings,' 'being made conformable to His death,' and the like, perhaps break up into details the compressed expression, 'power of His resurrection.' And therefore, in the remarks I am going to make, I shall throw out this expression 'power of His resurrection,' and read the passage thus: That I may know Him, and the fellowship of His sufferings, being made conformable unto His death; if by any means I may attain unto the resurrection of the dead.

Now the expressions, His sufferings, His death, may be taken, first of all, to mean the actual sufferings and death which Christ Himself experienced. And in that light we may look for a moment at the statement made by the apostle—"that I may know Him, and the fellowship of His sufferings, being made conformable to His death; if by any means I might attain unto the resurrection of the dead."

First, a certain knowledge of Christ and the fellowship of His sufferings and conformity to His death might come from sympathy.

His story is familiar to you, and it excites your liveliest interest. It is a record of sorrows such as you can read nowhere else. Suffering everywhere awakens a response, even when the sufferer does not suffer altogether blamelessly; we pity and feel with one even who has brought great sorrows on himself. But here is One whose great sufferings were uncaused by anything in Himself, except, it would seem, His very goodness,—sufferings of the sharpest kind, borne with the most uncomplaining meekness. You read His story; you enter into it all,—the fury and falsehood of His enemies, the pusillanimity of His friends, His meek endurance, His thought of those depending on Him, even on the Cross, His tears over the misguided men who were hasting to be His murderers. You know every

step of the history from Bethlehem to Nazareth, and
from Nazareth to Calvary; you go along with Him, you
feel for Him, you feel with Him, you pity, you wonder,
you admire, you almost adore.   Indeed, so much are
you one with Him, that you almost feel it is yourself,
and not another of whom you read.   You *know* Him,
and the fellowship of His sufferings.   And, what is
strange, this sympathy awakens, or at all events there
goes along with it, a strange feeling of self-surrender,
and a strange feeling of a new power arising within
you; you are in some way made conformable to His
death, and attain in a sense to a resurrection of the dead.

This life of His was a high life.   You feel it to be
very far above your own.   It is the true human life.
And His sufferings and death were endured that He
might remain true, and in no thing, not even the least,
prove false to this ideal of life.   You are insensibly
drawn after Him.   You also conceive, and long to live,
the life which He lived.   You, too, feel that you would
suffer rather than do evil, and die like Him rather
than sin, and do unworthy deeds.   You feel something
going on within you, a reaction against vice, a change
of sentiment, a readiness to submit to all things rather
than pander to a low craving; you are in some manner
made conformable unto His death.   And this is not
all.   There is not only a readiness to deny evil and
die to it, but there is awakened within you a certain
sense of power, as if faculties long dead were stirring
in their graves, and coming forth.   You are conscious

for the first time for long years, perhaps, of impulses towards what is higher, and a rising up within your soul of energies that are like the beginning of a new life. Ancient founts of inspiration well through all your being. There is a moral awakening, a return to better days, before passion or business, or the dulling effects of life and age, had brought down a spiritual stupefaction upon you; you attain in some degree to the resurrection of the dead.

This is a knowledge of Christ and the fellowship of His sufferings, and an experience of resurrection which may be produced by sympathy, for this sympathy becomes religious. But, second, something far closer in the way of knowing the fellowship of His sufferings and reaching the resurrection of the dead may come from *faith*. In your first reading of His life, that reading of it which awoke your sympathy so deeply, and changed you at least for a moment, and roused you out of the mere dull routine of a busy commercial or literary life, and unsealed the deeper fountains of feeling and sent them streaming through all your spirit, — in that first reading of His story, which was rather superficial, what you were fascinated by was the nobility of the Man, His high moral aims, and His unwearied labour in seeking to awaken men to the same aims as He pursued Himself, and the sad, ungrateful requital which men gave Him. You caught the infection of His life and His manner, He did you good, you were better for knowing Him, you had the fellowship of His sufferings, and felt a power stirring in you like a resurrection ; just as, on a lower level, you are still quickened and strung and made strong by the stirring tones and lofty example of any eloquent and noble mind. But you did not enter much into deeper questions, or ask yourself very closely as to the meaning of such a thing in the history of mankind as this life of Christ. Or if you did, you pursued the inquiry more in an objective, external way, as a general question that had little direct bearing on yourself. You speculated, perhaps, over the causes of such sufferings ; over the nature of one who suffered in such a way, and so undeservedly ; over the ends He might have in view, and over the meaning in the history of the human race, the moral meaning of such an incident as this, both on the side of Him who suffered, and on the side of those who inflicted the sufferings, and even on the side of God, in whose providence this was an event so outstanding. You concluded that such things must have a deep enough meaning, if you understood them ; they must either be the introduction into human history of some wonderful new thing or force, or they must be designed to show that human history and our ordinary life is a far deeper thing than we ordinarily think. But the only effect of this reflection was to throw a shade of mystery around the life of Christ, to make it more fascinating, and to increase your sympathy. You still remained outside its real meaning.

But now you go to the history again with a resolution to see, if not all that is in it, at least more of what is in it. And you hear one who stood near the beginning of it, looking forward to it, himself a great figure in the moral history of mankind, greater than any of the prophets, second only to Christ—you hear him saying to those about him and to you, Behold the Lamb of God, which taketh away the sin of the world. And towards the end of His history you hear Jesus Himself saying, in words that sum up the meaning of His life : The Son of man is come not to be ministered unto, but to minister, and to give His life a ransom for many. Here then is the key to His sufferings. They were sufferings endured for sin. They were part of the consequences of God's anger against the sins of men. " He was wounded for our transgressions and bruised for our iniquity ; the Lord made to fall upon Him the iniquity of us all." This is the meaning of His sufferings.

Here you enter a deeper region, and move among elements that have a profounder meaning. And there is something in your nature which constrains you to enter into the fellowship of sufferings having this meaning. Perhaps it is as yet more in an intellectual way, but the exercise of the mind on such questions tends to move the heart. You realise to yourself the condition of Jesus amidst such sufferings,—how He felt, how He looked at the situation, what views He might have of sin and its deserts at the hand of God, how

He felt the righteousness of God, and sympathised with it, and with God's anger against sin, and could say, even when feeling its awful weight: Even so, Father; just and true are Thy ways, Thou King of saints. And as you strive to enter into His feelings, the feelings become your own.

These tremendous things, 'sin of the world,' 'anger of God,' and the like, come to be not so much things outside of you as things that belong to you. They do not look any more like distant mountain-tops which you gaze at from afar. They are near to you, they over-hang you. The situation of Jesus among them becomes your situation. That sin of the world which He bore is your sin, and you feel towards it as He felt. That anger of God which He lay under is anger against you; and you are alarmed at it as He was, and go through, in your own way, the agony which He suffered. Whatever views He had of these things you share. Most heartily you acquiesce both in the sufferings, and in His enduring of them for you. You know Him and the fellowship of His sufferings, and are made conformable unto His death. Far enough, indeed, may you be from feeling altogether as He felt; from offering up to God that mind, that human mind, with its due feelings in such circumstances, which He offered up. The heart of man is too shallow for such tides of feeling to roll in it as rolled in His, the mind of man too narrow to gauge the meaning of the situation in which He found Himself placed. Yet as a child has

19

some points of contact with the greatest man,—as the little mourner sits in the house dumb, his mouth shut by the same sad loss that makes the grown-up mourner mute,—so you, however feebly, think as Christ thought amidst His sufferings, and feel as He felt.

This is to enter by faith into the fellowship of His sufferings, and be made conformable unto His death; to feel how righteous God is, and to bow in meek submission to His ways; to have such a sense of sin and what it deserves, as to be almost willing to place yourself under the punishment due to it, yet thankfully to accept His placing of Himself under it instead of you,—this, I say, is to know the fellowship of His sufferings, and to be made conformable unto His death. And then, indeed, you attain unto the resurrection of the dead. Then that change, which even sympathy in some measure produced, becomes real and permanent. A new life begins to stir in you. Buried with Him by baptism into His death, like as Christ was raised from the dead, you walk with Him in newness of life. Buried with Him in baptism, wherein also ye are risen with Him through the faith of the operation of God, who hath raised Him from the dead, you feel the working of the mighty power which God wrought in Christ, when He raised Him from the dead.

These are thoughts suggested by the text, when the expressions 'His sufferings' and 'His death' are taken to mean Christ's own sufferings and death. But this is not the usual meaning of the words. To have fellowship with Christ's sufferings does not usually mean to enter by sympathy or faith into the sufferings which He Himself actually endured; it means to endure oneself sufferings like to His, to bear them in the same cause, and with the same mind, and thus to have fellowship with Him. This is most probably what the apostle means. And this is both possible and necessary. This appears to be the meaning which the expression 'sufferings of Christ' has in the New Testament, as when the apostle says, " For as the sufferings of Christ abound in us, so our consolation also aboundeth by Christ."

For what really were Christ's sufferings and death? It is said : " In that He died, He died unto sin once; in that He liveth, He liveth unto God for ever." And it is said that He *condemned sin in the flesh.* What do such words mean? They may mean that He *died unto sin* in that He bore the penalty due unto sin. And in so far as this is the meaning, I have already referred to it. But this is not all the meaning. To die unto sin even in His case is the same as to be dead unto sin, that is, to be insensible to it, to deny it. To condemn sin in the flesh is to live in the flesh a sinless life,—once for all to repudiate the claims and the solicitations and the power of sin,—to pass a sentence of impotence, of annihilation, upon it. There at the end of Christ's life stood sin, once for all beaten, a powerless thing, not indeed expelled from

Christ's flesh, but refused admission into it,—that human flesh, where all its triumphs had been gained before, pure from it, unconquered by it, nay, conqueror over it,—the activity and shameless pressing of itself upon Him during His life ended,—there, I say, it stood, paralysed and covered with confusion, confessedly vanquished and dethroned, even stripped naked and flung out in utter degradation. Christ died unto sin, in that He lived every moment of His life free from it, in active conflict with it, suffering on all sides its countless evils, each an incentive to sin, a temptation to evil or an obstacle to righteousness, and at last laid down His life in conflict with it.

For we must not make Christ's life an unnatural thing, or lift it out of the conditions of God's ordinary providence. That it was lived in these conditions is what gives it its value. There was He in the world, in the Jewish nation, under its economy, in a time when powerful currents of opinion were running, currents that crossed one another,—there, I say, He stood, as any one of us stands now, exposed to influences, with various desirable things set before Him, some higher and others lower, and various things most undesirable, which yet He felt He must choose,—compassed about with infirmities, tried by incertitudes, on a sea, indeed, of troubles from moral and social and political tides rougher even than that on which we ourselves have ever been cast, and with only His sense of duty and God's will to guide Him,—there

He stood in the midst of providences which all con-
spired to try Him, whether He would live sinlessly,
and in obedience unto God and His mission; and all
converged to bringing Him to the Cross, if He should
be found without sin, and because He was without sin.
And thus He died—He who did no sin, neither was
guile found in His mouth.

Now in all this region we may have real fellowship in Christ's sufferings. To know Him and the
fellowship of His sufferings must be to suffer as He
suffered, and to have the same mind amidst suffering
that He had; and while suffering, to remember that
He also suffered, and thus, like the three children in
the furnace, to feel beside us another like the Son of
God. This is certainly what Paul means, and particularly in this passage. He refers principally to external
sufferings, to persecutions and probable martyrdom,
which lay before him, and which at the last overtook
him. In his trials he was knowing Christ and the
fellowship of His sufferings; in his martyrdom he
was made conformable unto His death. But, though
not exactly in the same way, every Christian in his
life partakes of the sufferings of Christ, and in dying
is made conformable to His death. We must go over
again what Christ went through. It is given us not
only to believe in Him, but also to suffer because
of Him, having the same conflict which we saw in
Him,—"to bear in our body the marks of the Lord
Jesus." The early Christians speak very much of

sufferings. The life of hardship which they lived
naturally drew their attention to Christ's sufferings.
" Though He were a son, yet learned He obedience
by the things which He suffered. Heirs of God, and
joint-heirs with Christ; if so be that we suffer with
Him, that we may be also glorified together. Let
none of you suffer as a murderer; but if any one
suffer as a Christian, let him not be ashamed. Now
do I rejoice in my sufferings for you, and fill up
that which is behind of the afflictions of Christ in
my flesh for His body's sake, which is the Church."
They knew Him and the fellowship of His sufferings.

And it is thus that we must all know Him and the
fellowship of His sufferings, being made conformable
to His death. At this point it is that our knowledge
of Him begins. Our first real knowledge of Him
consists of, or is gained in, our dying to sin. When
we give sin up, when, so far as it is concerned, we
become dead men, our senses gone, our feelings frozen
in death, when our ear is deaf to it, our eye glazed,
our face unmoved before it, our heart untouched,—
then our first real knowledge of Him begins. For
we then begin to live to Him, our eye opens on
Him, our ear catches His word and His voice, our
heart fashions Him in His glory, we are drawn into
the community of His life. And all our career is but
a repetition of this many hundred times a day, a
repetition so frequent that it becomes a connected
line of dying to sin, of knowing Him and the

fellowship of His sufferings, being conformed to His death.

But this *dying* is not altogether a figurative expression. That insensibility of our whole nature to sin, which we call *dying* to it, is really a death, and is really only perfect in death, in actual death. As Christ died to sin all His life and on the Cross, so we die to sin all our life, and at last in death. Our death is the last and most glorious act of dying to sin. Then is sin condemned in the flesh outright. That body of death which held sin in it, and fed it, and ministered to it, and where it once reigned, and always with more or less pertinacity sought a footing, is dissolved, its elements severed and dissipated, that sin may no more have a foothold in it. Your dying, my brother, is but the highest act of your whole life, the necessary close of a life of denial of sin ; then you most deeply deny it; then you cast it off, and cast it out wholly. This is the meaning of a believer's death, it is the crown of his life—he dies unto sin. All his life through, he knew Christ, and the fellowship of His sufferings, being conformed to His death ; now at last he knows Him fully, now at last, in truth, he is conformed unto His death.

Thus do you know Christ and the fellowship of His sufferings, being conformed to His death ; you know the fellowship of His sufferings, till you go to the length of being like Him in His death. You are not alone in suffering or in dying. "Count it not strange as though some strange thing happened to you." Neither was Christ alone in His suffering and death. There is a fellowship, a sameness. It is the same conflict with sin in Him and in you, the same great moral struggle. It is the same world, the same life, the conditions of which never greatly alter. It is the same providence of God. There is a oneness all through, a moral oneness, so that even the reproach of Christ could be spoken of in Moses' days. That was not reproach for the sake of Christ,—nor strictly the same reproach as Christ suffered or was to suffer,—it was a reproach common to all God's saints, which may be called the reproach of Christ, because in a pre-eminent sense He endured it and gave it meaning, and therefore it is named after Him. That great tide of evil that rose so far back, and rolled so high, and in its whole dark height broke on Him, is the same in whose foaming broken waves you are now tossing, and in which you shall yet one day be submerged. Strive to realise this fellowship. Would it not give your life a grandness and a meaning which it can in no other way attain? Every act and thought would be filled with a meaning, both backward and forward, of inexhaustible amount. What consolation it would minister to a life of misery, and what joy and sense of power to a life of temptation, when it was overcome! And how it would set death in its true light, in which it would no more be the valley of shadows, but the dawn of victory for ever!

Was it not realising this sameness, and entering into

this fellowship of Christ's sufferings, that led many of the early Christians to seek a martyr's death? They desired to have even outwardly the same suffering as He. Do you wonder at it? We shudder in our feeble, sensitive, nervous way at the stake and the lions. Does it matter much how we die—whether suddenly or slowly, whether by violence or of lingering decay? Is not the former better? No doubt, the calm sentiment of great bodies of men prompts them to pray that they may be preserved from sudden death, lest unprepared they be hurried, with all their sins thick upon them, before the Judge. And there is some truth in the sentiment. It allows due weight to what we call a decision of the mind, a determination in favour of God and truth.

And this is a thing of the highest moment and worth —the only thing in man of worth—this voluntary decision in favour of God; and sudden death may leave the mind without the time which slower removal gives for making this decision, or making it anew, and assuring ourselves that we have made it. And again, I say, this decision is a thing of the highest meaning in itself and in the estimation of all, even of men and God alike. But the fear of sudden death has, for this reason, something of sentiment in it. For the Judge is wise. Allowance will be made. Account of all will be taken. He will not judge as men judge. If you are concerned over one dear to you, suddenly hurried away thus, of whom you cannot say with certainty that his mind ever had decided, you do not sorrow as those that have no hope.

Influences for good are rarely without some effect. And the movements of the mind are not always seen or conscious. And the Judge is wise.

But whether violent death be better or no, cannot we conceive how the early Christians should think so? Thus were they most conformed to Christ's death; then they had an assurance that they knew Him and the fellowship of His sufferings; they felt after Him in the fire. This being in the same circumstances with Him verified to them the feeling that they were His, that they knew Him and were one with Him. They did not seek the stake out of fanaticism; but they welcomed it, because it brought home to them that they were one with Christ, and knew Him. Even the great apostle was not too great for this. It was a mistake, we say; it was not needful, it was no better than a superstition, little better than a fanaticism. Perhaps. And it is surprising how high, in this age, our standard of Christian judgment is.

It is possible we may be in danger of condemning Paul as overdoing somewhat his Christianity. He certainly did so long to be like Christ, to enter into all that He entered into, to suffer as He suffered, and even to die on a Cross as He died. We may think this was not needful, that it was an enthusiasm, profoundly religious, no doubt, but carried to excess. There is no proof that Paul or any of the early Christians courted martyrdom. They did not seek it, yet it had its joys when it came to them. They sought to enter in such a

way into all that Christ was, and go through all that He
went through; to have to such a degree the fellowship of
His sufferings, that it was a joy to them to die as He
died rather than in any other way. " Yea, and if I be
offered upon the sacrifice of your faith, I joy and rejoice
with you all: for the same cause also do ye joy and
rejoice with me." Let us look away from the manner of
feeling peculiar to them, to the thought that lay under it,
which was this: the worth and the meaning of the fellowship of Christ—that nothing but the assurance of being
one with Him can give us peace—and the gladness with
which we may seize on anything that will make us
realise that we are one with Him in His life and in His
death.

It must have been a strange thing to the apostle to
think that he could not die like Christ, that he could not
be conformed to His death, that there was an ignominy
in that Master's death, whom he so loved and so adored,
that he could not sink to. There was no power on earth
that could, that dared, so treat him, the citizen of Rome,
as that blessed Lord had been treated. He must have
wondered and adored the more, when he thought that
the world of which he was a citizen would not allow him,
who was so far behind his Lord, to sink so low, and
suffer the ignominy He suffered. But so far as was
possible, he longed to be like Him, and counted all
things but loss for the excellency of the knowledge of
Christ Jesus the Lord,—that He might know Him and
the fellowship of His sufferings, being made conformable

unto His death, if by any means he might attain unto the resurrection of the dead.

When he says: "If by any means I might attain unto the resurrection of the dead," he does not express doubt as to his actually attaining to it. What he expresses is wonder, and awe, and joy before the grandeur of such a prospect, and the feeling how alone such a joyful grandeur is to be reached, which is only through fellowship in the sufferings of Christ, and by being conformed unto His death. Perhaps we should think of it in this way. Christ, in that He died, died unto sin. His death was for sin, unto sin. But He put away sin by the sacrifice of Himself. When He died to sin, His connection with sin was over. And He rose by virtue of His own native life. He could not be holden of death. His dying was, one might say, a special thing; it was unnatural. His rising was natural, it was a rebound; it was the life in Him asserting itself.

And so the believer, having died to sin, having in death put it away, rises in virtue of his new life. "The body, indeed, is dead because of sin, but the spirit is life because of righteousness." Being conformed to Christ in death, we attain unto the resurrection of the dead. Sin is altogether put off, and the spirit of life asserts itself, and draws the body to itself. The resurrection is a mystery to us—a miracle. Yet is not life a mystery? Is it not a miracle that the living spirit gathers a body about it at all? It is life that raises up around us the structure of the body, that appropriates outside things, that converts them, that assimilates them, that turns them into its own organs.   It is the life in us that does all this.   And may not the powerful, all-conquering life do the same on the resurrection day? do in a moment, in the twinkling of an eye, what our more feeble life here on earth takes many long years to accomplish? Just as Christ by His powerful word made water wine, effected in a moment all those changes of the rain which otherwise needs many months to pass through the vine as sap, and ripen as juice in the grape, and ferment as wine in the vats,—effected by His power in a moment those changes which nature is so long in performing; so may the mighty energy of life in us, of spiritual life, do in a moment what needs many years here,—gather a new and glorious body around us; not another from that which we now have, yet how different, fashioned like unto Christ's glorious body.

But I do not ask you to rest in uncertain speculations.   How the body shall be resumed may be doubtful. But the way whereby you can attain that awful glory and joy, the resurrection of the dead, is certain.   It is by knowing Christ and the fellowship of His sufferings; it is by denying sin and dying to it, till at last you die to it altogether, and put it off, being made conformable unto the death of Christ.

XIII

A GREAT CLOUD OF WITNESSES

XIII

A GREAT CLOUD OF WITNESSES

HEBREWS xii. 1–2

THE life of the godly upon the earth is often described in Scripture by words that represent it as a thing of difficulty. It is difficult even to make a beginning of it, for the Lord Himself says, "Strive to enter in at the strait gate"; and, as it is a thing attained to but by few, He adds: "Few there be that find it." And when begun the difficulty seems hardly to decrease. For the only idea we can gather from the terms applied to it is, that it is a struggle both severe and protracted. Paul says of himself when now ready to be offered, the time of his departure being at hand, and all his past career lying beneath his eye: "I have fought a good fight, I have finished the course, I have kept the faith." And thus he exhorts his son Timothy : "Fight the good fight of faith, lay hold of eternal life." And similarly in the present passage : "Let us run with patience the race set before us."

All these words, race, fight, strife, suggest the same general idea, the same idea as is suggested by the term

20

used of the Lord Himself in the height of His conflict, the night in which He was betrayed, when it is said of Him that, being in an agony, He prayed more earnestly.

It costs a struggle to begin a godly life upon the earth. And it costs a struggle to maintain it. And the struggle is not soon over, but protracted,—even till the time of one's departure is at hand. Sometimes, as at the close of a race, or the sharp decisive moment in a battle, the conflict is severest at the end. Sometimes it is otherwise, as with Paul. Even when a living man, he could say, "I have finished the course." The race once set before him now lay all behind him. He knew he was victorious. He had fought the good fight. What might yet befall him in life, he knew not. But whatever it was, it could make no alteration. He had finished the work given him to do. He could not now be called on to do much, and much could not now be done to him. And he was secure against change. "Henceforth there is laid up for me a crown of righteousness, which the Lord, the righteous judge, shall give unto me at that day."

These verses set forth the life of a Christian man upon the earth, under the figure of a race, more fully, perhaps, than any other passage; and the figure may suggest to our minds its nature more clearly. The verses enumerate all its circumstances and conditions—the preparation for the race, "laying aside every weight, and the sin that doth so easily beset us"; the race itself and the manner of it—"let us run with patience the race set before us"; the great model and victorious leader whom we are to

keep ever before us—"looking unto Jesus the author and
the finisher of the faith"; and, finally, the great cloud of
those who have already run victoriously, and whom we
are to feel near us and around us—"seeing we are compassed about with so great a cloud of witnesses." Thus
before entering upon the race, or always when entering
anew upon it, you lay aside every weight, and strip off
from you the sin that doth so easily beset; so disen-
cumbered, you run with patient endurance; running, you
look unto Jesus, the leader and finisher of the faith; you
look unto Him, and you feel that all the foregone dead,
who have already finished the course, are present with
you, and are as if looking unto you.

First, we must not misunderstand what is meant by
the race set before us. It is not any distinguished and
very splendid career of Christian enterprise, which only
some apostle or missionary or reformer might be supposed able to undertake. The people to whom the
apostle writes were ordinary Christians, poor Jewish
converts most probably, people of less than the average
means and pretensions. They had no resources at their
command. Their names are unknown. They were
mere Hebrews. Their career and influence, whatever
it was, must have been confined to the narrowest limits.
And though the apostle speaks somewhat grandly of
what was set before them, and brings them into connection with Jesus, and the great forefathers of their race
who subdued kingdoms and wrought righteousness, they
were probably very pitiable persons, so far as the world's

judgment would go; and some of you might have been
rather shy of associating much with them. Therefore
the race set before them cannot have had anything very
extraordinary in it.

Nevertheless, it was the same race as that run by the
Lord Himself—the race of faith. In His case it was
faith in God, the God of salvation; the faith of One
conscious of being the Messiah, the Redeemer, entering
with the Father into the great and merciful purpose of
salvation, which He could accomplish in no other way
than by coming down into the race of men, and running
this race of faith as their forerunner and the leader of
their salvation. In the case of the Hebrews it was faith
in God the Saviour, and in His Son the Redeemer, as
the leader in salvation, and the author and finisher of
the faith. Even the faith of Jesus, who for the joy
that was set before Him endured the Cross, was not
the isolated faith of a mere individual out of connection
with other men. It was the faith of the Messiah, one
with men, the leader of their salvation conscious of
His relations to men, their forerunner, the author and
finisher of the faith. And thus the course of the
Hebrews, though nothing but the ordinary believing
life of very mean persons, becomes to the apostle's mind
something great, and even one with the life of the Lord
Himself.

Second, now before running this race the Hebrews are
exhorted to lay aside every weight, and the sin that
so easily beset them. A race is a swift, speedily decided

conflict. The lengthened strain is gathered into a few moments. And this compression of all into a brief space makes the apostle speak as if laying aside weights and sin were a thing to be done once for all before beginning. But, as we know that what is meant by the race is a long drawn-out effort, even that of a lifetime, it is evident that what he represents as needing to be done once for all at the beginning, is a thing which we must be continually doing. We must be ever laying aside every weight, and the sin that doth so easily beset us.

It is not quite easy, with our habits of thinking, to enter into the apostle's manner of speaking. He speaks of the race, and then he distinguishes between that and the things which he calls weights and sin, and bids us rid ourselves of the one, before beginning to run the other. Now, to our minds, the race, the struggle, is just mainly, alas! with the sin that doth so easily beset us, and our greatest conflict lies in laying down those weights which we know will encumber us. We must make allowance for the change that has occurred between our circumstances and those of the Hebrews. They were a pitiful and despised community. The current of external events bore hard on them. They ran the risk of afflictions at the hands of their countrymen, and of the heathen alike. The world, with all its external forces, contempt, loss of goods, persecutions, imprisonments, bonds, was against them. In this they were like the Lord Himself, who endured such con-

tradiction of sinners against Himself.   And these things
the apostle regards as the difficulties of the race, the
obstacles to be surmounted.   In our case the conflict
is more inward.   The world is not violently opposed.
The obstacles are not outward hardships but seductions,
the life of pleasure, the keen competitions of business,
the place in society, the influence that comes of being
wealthy, the prestige of learning, or eminence in science
or art.   These are our obstacles.   And thus, perhaps,
in our case the obstacles in our way, and the weights
which we must lay down, do not greatly differ.

By the race itself the apostle seems always to mean
faith in Jesus as the Saviour, or faith in God as redeeming men through Jesus Christ   This was the real
crux to the Hebrews, as it begins to be with us.   To
keep this faith was the struggle, the race.   All other
things are obstacles, or weights, or sin.   Now the
apostle says that, in order to keep this faith, to run
this race, to hold alive and true and strong our faith
in Jesus Christ as our Saviour, lest it die out, lest we
falter in the race, or stumble, or fall exhausted, or
halt, we must lay aside every weight, and the sin that
doth so easily beset us.

He distinguishes between sin and weights.   Of the
last there may be many, the first is one.   The sin
that doth so easily beset us is a peculiar expression.
The phrase, that doth so easily beset us, is one word in
the apostle's mouth.   It means, that stands well round
about us, or that is well stood round about.   In the

one case—in either case, indeed—the comparison is probably to a garment which the runner is supposed to wear. This either stands well round about us, that is, is like a loose, limp robe that will cling closely to our limbs, and bring our running to a halt, or it is a closely fitting garment that will compress our chest or limbs, preventing freedom of motion; or it is much stood round about, that is, people crowd round it in admiration. It is a gaudy, many-coloured thing, attracting the eye, but fatal to the wearer in the race. It is more probable that the former is the meaning.

Reference can only be made to one or two things.

First, the sin which so easily besets us.

By the sin which doth so easily beset us, the apostle hardly means what we call our besetting sin. He rather speaks of sin as a whole. No doubt, most men have some one sin more natural to them than other sins, into which from temper or circumstances they most readily fall, into which they are more easily led by some bias in their nature or some one-sidedness in their upbringing. And thus what we call sin in general usually comes to the light in them in this form, or prominently in this shape. Here at least they are conscious of their weakness. And though it is probable that the apostle means to describe sin in general, the nature of which is to fling itself, like a loose robe, around the limbs of the runner, and bring him to a halt, and which must therefore be laid aside, practically it will have to be laid aside in the shape in which it most encumbers us,—our besetting sin,

—in the shape in which we know it. The great idea which the apostle brings forward is that when we attempt to run the race of faith, to live a Christian life, then concurrently with our faith in Jesus Christ, if that faith is not to fail, there must be a continuous laying down of the thing called sin. There must always be, ere beginning, a renunciation of sin, a denying of all that is called sin.

The apostle doubtless means that faith in Christ is a disposition of the mind incompatible with that other disposition of the mind which sinning produces. For every sin, even an unwitting one, exerts an influence on the mind. It is said that the electric current, though invisible and to our senses inappreciable, when passed through a wire or substance, disposes every one of its particles differently from what they were before. It is wholly altered, though to the eye the same. And the subtle influence of sin, even when unknown, gives a new disposition to the powers of the mind, puts it into a frame incompatible with that other frame which is faith in Christ. The two cannot exist together. And, therefore, in order to faith, sin must be laid aside.

Who can understand his errors? cries the Psalmist. Much may be in us that is sin that we do not know. Our sense of touch is dull, and we do not feel it. Our thoughts crowd on one another, and their true nature eludes us. We are often, in circumstances of difficulty, surprised into actions about which we have not time to think, and many times forced to do things in the exigencies of life, or the sudden crises of business, of the true nature of which we may have doubts. Life is not a simple thing, but, whether we take our own minds, or the actions we have, as members of an intricate social condition, to perform, very complicated; and so we have doubts as to what is sinful. All that is true; yet the general principle remains, we must lay down what we know to be sin, if we mean to run the race of faith in Christ. The two are incompatible.

Every evil act which we do weakens our vigour in the race, shortens our power of endurance. It is like a drug which unnerves us, and enfeebles our power of running; or, to keep to the figure of the apostle, cramps our motion, and leads to our being exhausted. Nay, everything which we suspect to be evil paralyses us. "Blessed is the man whose sin is covered, in whose spirit there is no guile"—nothing covered over, everything explicit, open between God and himself,—when a judgment, definite and without reserve, is passed by a man himself upon his every action before God. Of open sins we may not be guilty. But are there not many of our actions which we do not care to scrutinise too closely ourselves, which we leave obscure to our own minds, having an uncomfortable dislike to review them too nearly? It is perhaps impossible but that such things should sometimes be in our complicated social and business life. Yet it is impossible to doubt that such things come into collision with the faith of Christ, and hamper it, and stifle it more or less. Its

essence is explicitness, heart to heart openness between
God and ourselves. We must lie on the breast of Jesus
like the apostle, seeing what is in His heart and showing
all that is in ours.

We complain of the languor of our Christian life,
of our doubts and uncertainties, of the feeling of perplexity which we sometimes have in regard to the
faith of Christ. Some of this is due to the currents
of thought now running. But is not some of it also
due to the habits of the time, the commercial and social
customs, following which we do things which we are
not sure about, which we have doubts of, which we are
uneasy about at first? Such a condition of mind and
conscience will infallibly kill, or greatly impair, the faith
of Christ. It will act in a hundred ways upon our
faith, often without our being able perhaps to see the
connection. We must lay aside sin, if we would run
the race of faith.

Secondly, the apostle says we must lay aside every
weight. The weights are not sins. They are things
not sinful in themselves, but yet, if we mean to run,
things which will burden us, and which must be laid
down, if we would not come short in the race. This
comes closer to us than the other. The comparison
with the runner shows us what is meant. Before he
thought of entering upon the race, he went through a
course of hard training. He cleansed and refined himself by hard exercise and abstemiousness, and frequent
purifications, and abstinence from indulgence, and self-

restraint, and command on all sides, till thus all weights, all superfluities of flesh, were cleared away from him, and all degeneration of tissue removed, and every muscle and sinew stood out hard and clean, and the form was perfect in lightness, and strung for the race. This is the figure. But what lengths of self-denial or of self-command it may imply in the Christian, is rather hinted at than expressed.

That habit of body which the runner so laboured to rid himself of was quite innocent. It might be comely even. Only if he meant to run, it must be purged out of him. And what is pointed at as needing to be laid aside must be things quite common among men, harmless it may be in themselves, respectable, very comfortable, not altogether unbecoming perhaps, but still things that make themselves felt as weights, that will burden you in the race of faith, and slack your speed, and even bring your motion to a halt. It will not be easy beforehand to say what such things may be, nor will one man be able to tell his brother what are weights. A thing may be a weight to me, though not to you, some indulgence of appetite perhaps, lawful in itself but very keenly relished, moderately gratified at first, but growing by what it feeds on, till it gradually overmaster and enfeeble the spiritual energies, and deaden the spiritual sensibilities, and the runner grow weary of the race.

Or it may be something higher, devotion to business, or some private pursuit of art, or taste, or self-culture.

It is keen at first, though not excessive. But it gains
on you. By and by, it rises to the power of a passion,
and draws the whole mind within its sweep. You
grow weary of other things, though it may be the race
of faith is the last thing you weary of. Yet this, too,
is swallowed up at last in the fascination of the pursuit.
Or it may be something higher still, some affection
which absorbs the heart. For here the peculiarity of
the life of faith comes in, arising just from the fact that
it is a life, and that all things touch it. It is acted on,
on every hand; and there is nothing which does not
either foster it, or impair it. The faith of Christ is not
conducted by rules, but by experience. In this respect
it resembles our natural life. No man can tell us how
to live, except in general. Our own experience tells us.
We are speedily our own best physicians. We know
what harms us, and what promotes our health. When
we sit down before a repast, we know what things
we can allow ourselves, and what we should pass by.
Others about us may indulge where we cannot, or we
may where they cannot. Or we know how far we can
venture to expose ourselves to the inclemencies of the
season. Experience and reflection tell us how things
act upon our health. The rules of the world are good,
but the verdict of our own experience is better. And
so, in great degree, is the life of faith.

We cannot learn beforehand, except in the most
general way, what things are weights. We shall discover, when we enter upon the race. And here comes

in the peculiarity of Christianity, its ennobling character. It puts us in trust of ourselves. It lays on us the task of judging what is good for us. No doubt it gives us precepts and examples; it bids us run, looking unto Jesus, and remembering the cloud of witnesses. But it leaves us free to judge in particulars what advances, and what impairs, our spiritual life. But this freedom, while it ennobles us, while it entrusts all to us, leaves a heavy responsibility upon us. It expects us to be true, to be watchful, to work out our salvation with fear and trembling, to be scrupulous, to be on the outlook if aught be a weight upon us; and, as soon as we feel it to be that, to be conscientious, nay, to be faithful to Him that loved us, and to lay it down. "All things are lawful to me," said the apostle; "all things are lawful, but I will not be brought under the power of any." This is the test.

Is our Christian life always having the upper hand, bringing all things into subjection to it, and brought into subjection by nothing? Is it the great main stream of our being, drawing all other streams unto itself, and giving them its own colour, fed by them, but absorbing them? No man can help his brother here. No doubt we may observe one another, and may caution one another. Sometimes we may be unable to say why it is that our soul cleaves to the dust, and an outside eye may see the weight upon us, the effects of which we felt, though we did not know to what to attribute the effects, and may warn us of it.

But in the main we must be left to ourselves and to God. "Search me and try me, and see if there be any wicked way in me; and lead me in the way everlasting."

Perhaps, one of the things which in the present day is particularly apt to absorb the mind, especially among the young, is amusement,—competitive amusements. These things are apt so to fascinate and absorb the mind, and to preoccupy it, that it loses relish for other things,— for the highest things as well as for others. And sometimes it goes even further; and, under the strong fascination of the amusement or the exercise, would like to devote to it those times, which the experience of the Christian mind has hitherto thought needful to devote more particularly to religion. This newer aspect of things does tend to create uneasiness in the minds of those of an older generation, who in their youth were accustomed to a different way of thinking. It does raise the question whether there be not passing over the minds of men at present a certain wave of religious indifference; whether the sense of God be not becoming relaxed; whether the feeling be not creeping in, that this bodily, physical life of ours is all our life.

It is possible that these fears may be excessive. What we see may be but a temporary revolt, a reaction against what was felt to be excessive and one-sided in former modes of thinking. Its own excesses will by and by be corrected also. Whatever way we are to look at it, I daresay the best way for those who feel the claims of religion, and the duty as well as the joy of living

unto God, and the difficulty of it,—the best way will
be to show how necessary they feel the ordinances of
God's house to be, as well as the weekly rest both
from business and from amusement, in order that
their religious life may be maintained, and that they
may walk worthy of the vocation wherewith they
are called. Their seriousness and their example will
eventually tell; it will do more than argument. And
when they endeavour to show that they feel how
difficult and hard it is to live to God as they should
do, they have the words of our Lord on their side:
"Strive to enter in at the strait gate: for strait is the
gate and narrow is the way which leadeth unto life." And
they have also the experience of the life of Christians in
all ages, in the cloud of witnesses that surrounds us.

We must be true to ourselves, and watch the least
encroachment on the fulness of our life. Nay, we must
be true to a higher than ourselves, for we are "bought
with a price." When you have engaged in any of the
things referred to, bring yourselves at once to this test,
Is your spiritual pulse as full and strong as it was before?
Is your relish for spiritual things as keen? Is your
spiritual nerve unrelaxed, and your health so robust that
you are ready to take up and carry the Cross? Is your
eye as clear as ever; and can you discern before you,
on the racecourse, Jesus the author and finisher of the
faith? Let every man be persuaded in his own mind.
Happy is he that condemneth not himself in the thing
which he alloweth.

Thirdly, the forerunner in the race, and those we should feel about us. "Looking unto Jesus the author and finisher of our faith, and seeing we are compassed about with so great a cloud of witnesses, let us run with patience."

Jesus is the example both of the race and of the trials of it, and of the manner in which it must be run, and of the reward awaiting the victorious runner, who for the joy that was set before him endured the cross, and is set down at the right hand of God. These are all things to be kept in view by him who runs the race of faith. They are strange things, great things; they lift up our life of faith into a lofty region. It is a great wonder that the Lord should have run the race of faith. And we can hardly say, considering who He was and yet what race He ran, whether it be wonderful or no that He should have run victoriously. The words 'author and finisher of our faith' do not mean he who begins faith in us, and carries it on to an end; who begins a good work, and perfects it to the day of Christ. Such an idea may be included, and whether included or not is true; but the idea here is somewhat different. The word rendered 'author' is elsewhere translated captain, and means leader; Jesus is the leader and finisher of our faith.

Now draw an analogy between Him and yourselves, and compare the circumstances of His life with yours. Mark how He bore Himself under trials unspeakably greater—the Cross, the shame; how He kept before

Him the mark for the prize, the joy set before Him;
and how, having finished His course, He is seated at
the right hand of God. He is in all things the example
we are to keep before us. His life was truly a life
of faith—the work and the joy were set before Him.
He was not cast into a world the issues of which
He could not forecast, nor into a life the meaning of
which was dark to Him. It is probable, however, that
His life, like our own, opened up gradually; that it
was dark before Him, and that light only arose as He
entered upon it step by step. Perhaps trials unfolded
themselves unexpectedly, at least as to their form. He
might not be able to anticipate all the subtlety of evil,
nor the apathy of men, nor the full meaning of enduring
the penalty of sin, till He actually entered into the cloud;
but He knew, on the whole, what lay before Him,—both
the shame on this side and the joy beyond. And thus
amidst all His conditions His life was one of faith, as
our own must be.

And we are to run, looking unto Jesus, the perfect
example of the life of faith. But do we, my brethren,
read and think ourselves into all the details of His
blessed example and life, as we should do? Are we
so familiar with each circumstance of it as we might
be? Be sure every detail of it is full of meaning,—
the motives that shine out as guiding Him, the words
He let fall, the feelings He showed, the steps He took,
how He realised God above Him in all, and how He
thought always of those around Him. It is a great

study for us, as men left largely under Christian freedom to fashion our own lives, having sin and weights which we are honestly and truthfully before God and ourselves to look at and lay aside.

Yet, perhaps, some may feel that this example is no great encouragement to us. This isolated life, if it were isolated, is, no doubt, a marvellous thing,—something in the history of mankind full of wonder. But its very greatness is what makes it fail to touch us. It stands like an isolated peak crowned with snow, its summit lost in heaven; but we dare not scale it, we cannot. It raises great thoughts in us, longings, it may be, to rise,—at certain moments a tumult of emotion in our hearts,—but we fall back before the impossible, and content ourselves with the commonplaces of the life below.

But the words of this apostle forbid you imagining the life of Christ to be a mere isolated thing, and no more than an example. It is an example, but it is an example which is also a fellowship. It is even more. It is an example which is a power, which enters into you, and renews itself in you: "It is not I that live, but Christ that liveth in me." He is not only the author, but the *finisher* of the faith. In some real sense His life contains in it the meaning of all Christian life; it is the sum of the lives of all His followers. The lives of believers are not so much a repetition of His life as an analysis of it; each of them is but a separate thread of the manifold cord which His life was. The apostle uses singular words here—words of large meaning. He says of Jesus, He is the author and finisher *of the faith.* Now, it is not of the faith in each of us, so to say, that he speaks, but of the thing called a life of faith; that new thing which Jesus brought into the world; which He planted among men; which, like a new fire, He brought in His life, and which catches and kindles the dead human life around it. He was the life. Not a living man merely, but a life that seized that about it and communicated itself—the life of faith unto God. And of this life Jesus is the author, the leader, the Captain.

Captain is not a military term here; but the relation of the captain to his troop well illustrates the idea. The captain leads the soldiers, but he is on that account not less, but more, a soldier. He carves the way for them to follow. He steps into the breach first, but his men are at his back. He is only the first soldier of the army,—one of them, one with them, though the first,—to whom falls the dangerous eminence of being the leader and the finisher of the glorious toil. It is his to plan, his to lead in the execution, his to gather up the fruits of the successful enterprise. But he is, after all, but one of the band, one with the band; and the more he makes the band feel that he is one of them, sharing their hardships and sharing with them his honours, the more he is really their captain. Jesus is the Captain of our salvation, the leader of the faith. "For both He that sanctifieth and they that are sanctified are all of one: for which cause He is not ashamed to call them brethren."

Jesus is the Captain in the fight, the Forerunner in the race. Ah! how unlike other captains, behind whom the soldiers press, emulous of their deeds, and eager to share their risks! At how great an interval before us the Captain of our salvation stands! How isolated He seems to go into the conflict! How lonely He looks on the racecourse! And how solitary and great He appears in the moment of His victory! "Who is this that cometh from Edom, with dyed garments from Bozrah? this that is glorious in his apparel, travelling in the greatness of his strength? I that speak in righteousness, mighty to save. Wherefore art thou red in thine apparel, and thy garments like him that treadeth in the winefat? I have trodden the winepress alone; and of the people there was none with me. And I looked, and there was none to help; and I wondered that there was none to uphold: wherefore mine own arm brought salvation unto me; and my fury, it upheld me."

Yet if He seems isolated, we are not. For we run looking unto Jesus, the author and finisher of the faith. We are one with the Captain of our salvation. In His one life, the faith—that new life to God which as Christian men, as the new creation, we have in common —was begun and finished. We but share it. We are about Him who is the Captain. Nay, rather, He is within each of us. Be of good cheer, I have overcome the world. Who is He that overcometh, but He that is born of God? He is not merely an example, He is a power. The life of God was not only manifested in

Him, it was by His coming among us implanted in us. And from the moment it appeared, it became diffused. It caught the surrounding elements of mankind, and quickened them. Men took Him into themselves. They became branches on the vine, and the fruit they bear is the fruit of the true vine.

Finally, we are compassed about with a cloud of witnesses. These are the heroes of faith, whose history is recorded in the previous chapter.

I have but little space to speak of those who compass us about—the cloud of witnesses. They are about us like a cloud. Whether it be to their sanctified splendour, now being made perfect, that the reference is, or to the dense mass which they form, as the spectators did in the amphitheatre, may be doubtful. They are witnesses; for they have all witnessed for the truth, filled history throughout all its ages with their sufferings and glorious deeds. They are, like ourselves, witnesses; and it is to the stimulus which their being so, and the feeling that they and we are one should be to us, that the apostle refers.

Among the crowd of spectators round the course in the Grecian games, none so stimulated the runner as those who in years gone by had run and conquered, and had their brows bound with the crown of victory. Or to take the similar instance at home, those onlookers that stimulate the boy most in the games, are not those dearest to him at home, but those who in former days sat on the form he now occupies, and ran with success the race he is now running, but have passed into the rank of citizens, and are now present as spectators of what they once themselves took part in. It is their encouragement that excites him most, and their applause and congratulations that taste sweetest to him.

I do not know that the apostle means seriously to say that the dead are conscious of us, and are absorbed and fascinated by our struggles, over which they bend and hang with excited interest from their place on high. I think he speaks rather of us than of them,—of what we may conceive and feel, rather than of what is a bare, naked fact. He speaks of our realising our oneness with them, the sameness of our struggle with theirs, the unity of the whole family in heaven and earth, and how we may feel them near us, and be stimulated by their presence. They are present in the memory of their life, in their example, in their spirit, in their principles which they have bequeathed to us,—in the life of God common to us and them, the same yesterday and to-day and for ever, which runs like a stream of light through all history, and which is what gives the history of the world its meaning. It is this which brings the past and the present of the world together, and gathers its meaning into a focus, in the midst of which we stand. It is this which makes the past influential, dear, sacred to us.

The past life of the Church of God is like the memory of one departed that was dear, and on whom we leant for support. We have read of one sometimes, or seen it in the history of our time,—one who had a guide and counsellor from her youth, who took her gradually up very lofty ways, and opened out to her rich glimpses of truth and nobleness, and made the commonplaces of life great, because he filled them out, and showed them to be all instances of thoughtfulness and love, till her soul altogether leant on him and learnt his ways; and when he was taken from her, she followed the bent he had given her, and lived on his counsel as if he were beside her; and when perplexities arose she counselled with herself, and asked what he would have had her do? how he would have done, had he been looking on? And thus, though dead, he spoke, and was beside her, the friend of her youth.

And such should be our feeling towards the Church of God, the heroes of faith of the past. They are one with us and about us,—a multitude which no man can number, the voice of whose praise is as the noise of many waters,—our godly forefathers, whose bones lie scattered on a hundred hills, and those like unto them out of every tribe and tongue, and people and nation. The thought of them gives strength to our heart, and upholds our patience—the thought that we are not an isolated sect of this or that generation, but one with the best, the noblest, and the purest of mankind in all the ages of its history, with that in mankind which has risen to the highest ideal of it, and sought to realise it.

Wherefore, let us exhort one another to run with patience, looking unto Jesus. Have patience; the race is not to be won all at once; it is a long, trying work,

Have patience with the many obstacles; patiently get over them. Have patience with the falls you sustain; patiently gather yourselves up again. A hand will be held out to you, as to Peter sinking in the waves, to lift you up. Have patience with the small progress you make, when the way is dark, and you seem far from home. Forget the things that are behind, and keep the mark for the prize before you. Have patience ever, and with that which it is hardest to have patience with— yourselves. For the apostle says of such as you: "My little children, of whom I have travailed in birth till Christ be formed in you." Run, therefore, with patience, looking unto Jesus not as an example merely, but as your righteousness and strength. Though so far before you as to seem out of sight, He is never really out of sight. There is somehow, though you think the race set before you most solitary, there is somehow always one other figure in sight upon the course,—dim, and distant, and pressing forward,—bent to the ground under some great load that seems to be on Him—Jesus, the Author and Finisher of the faith. Run, therefore, looking unto Jesus.

XIV

AN OPEN DOOR

XIV

AN OPEN DOOR

REVELATION iii. 7-13

PHILADELPHIA is almost the only Church of the seven
to which no blame is attached. It is not greatly praised,
but upon the whole all that is said of it amounts to
praise, the great feature of its epistle being the great
and precious promises given to the Church.

I need hardly mention what you are all familiar
with in these epistles, that the central point in them
is always the state and history of the particular Church
to which the epistle is addressed. Around this condition all the other elements of the epistle are grouped.
First, for example, the epithets bestowed on Christ
who addresses them, the aspects of character, and the
disposition of mind, attributed to Him, have a direct
bearing on the condition and history of the particular
Church. There is a correspondence between that which
He is, that which He has done, or is able to do, and
the state in which the Church is, or the history which
it has passed through. And, secondly, the promises
given have the same close relation to the condition

of mind or circumstances of the Church; they are addressed to this condition, and meet its necessities.

Now the condition of this Church and its history are described very briefly, but clearly. Of its condition it is said: "Thou hast little strength." It was a feeble Church, whether in point of numbers or in point of resources, or most likely in point of spiritual vigour and certainty. It was probably rather in mind that it was feeble; it was a Church of feeble minds. This feeble-mindedness was due to their circumstances. They were surrounded and held down by Jews, aggressive persons, who reposed upon the past and were therefore full of certainty, who called in question the first principle of the religion of these Philadelphian Christians, and sought to show that the foundation on which they were building, even Jesus Christ, was insecure or certain to give way. They thus filled the minds of the Christians of Philadelphia with painful uncertainties, making them irresolute, half ashamed of themselves, of little strength — in a word, feeble - minded. This was their condition; yet their history was this: "Thou hast kept My word, and hast not denied My name." The Church had had to struggle, and the struggle was all the severer that it was a struggle of the mind; but hitherto it had struggled victoriously. It had kept the word, and had not denied the name, of Christ. The very word 'kept' implies the difficulty, the severe effort it had cost. There were fightings without and fears within. If they had been called upon to give an account of how they had kept Christ's word, they would have been quite unable to do so. It was rather it that had kept them, than they that had kept it. They could not answer the arguments of the Jews drawn from the past. When these people said to them, as they said aforetime, " We know that God spake by Moses; but as for this fellow, we know not whence He is," they were dumb, not opening their mouth. They could not explain God's providence, and the way of revelation, and the dispensations.

Yet they were not the kind of persons on whom arguments left no impression. On the contrary, the arguments impressed them. Their minds were sensitive, and everything that had an element of reason in it told upon them. Their minds were only too responsive, showing the effect of every influence as immediately as the mirror shows the breath; and thus they were staggered, unsettled, continually in a state of unstable equilibrium. Yet amidst all this they had kept the word of Christ's patience. Instinctively, rather than with their understanding, they had kept it. If they felt that it was hard to keep, they felt also that it could not be let go. They could not tell why they could not help keeping it, any more than the newborn babe can tell why it desires the sincere milk. Their nature accepted it, and craved for it,—they felt that it was good.

Now it is to people in this state of mind, and who have been passing through this kind of history, that our

Lord speaks. And to this condition of mind and to this history both the character in which He presents Himself, and the promises which He makes, have reference.

The characters in which He presents Himself are these: He is He that is holy, He that is true, He that hath the key of David, He that openeth, and no man shutteth.

And the promises or statements He makes are three:

1. I have set before thee an open door.

2. I will keep thee in the hour of temptation that shall come on all the world.

3. I will make thee a pillar in the temple of My God.

These promises touch the present, the future, and the final.

First, the person who speaks to the Philadelphians, and the character in which He speaks: "He that is holy, He that is true, He that hath the key of David, He that openeth, and no man shutteth." When one comes forward making great promises to us, we desire to know who he is who promises such things. He says, I have set before thee an open door; I will keep thee from the great trial; I will make thee a pillar in the house of My God. May we rely on these things? He that makes them is holy, is true, has the key of David, can set open the entrance to us. These three things are not independent attributes, all of which He possesses; they are connected, and flow from one another. He is true, because He is holy. For what is He speaking to us about? It is about religion, about our relation to God, about the entrance into the kingdom of God, of which He asserts He has the key. In a word, it is just about holiness, about true life unto God.

And He who speaks is holy. He speaks from His own experience that which He knows. He has gone down into the deepest relations of God and men, and risen to the highest. Therefore when He speaks, He is the true. No doubt He has given many guarantees of His truthfulness; He has sealed His testimony with His blood. That is evidence that He is sincere, that He would not lie. But His holiness is the proof that He could not lie. He knows what life unto God is, He has lived it; He judges of it truly. When He speaks to us about it, it is out of His own consciousness that He speaks.

Even the third thing stated, that He has the key of David, that is, the key of the kingdom of God, and can open, and no man can shut, the entrance into it, may be also dependent on His holiness. For what is the kingdom of God? It is righteousness and peace and joy in the Holy Ghost. And our Lord has the key of it. In another place it is said: "He has the key of death, and of the world of the dead." How has He this key? Because He entered into death and the realm of death, and when He came out He left the door open. All there confined can now through Him escape. And if He has the key of death, because He came out and left the door open, He has the key of the kingdom of God, because He went in and left the door open. He unlocked the door, threw it open, and carries the key at His girdle. That which He opened no man can shut.

But how did He force an entrance into heaven? Again, because He was holy: "Thou wilt not give Thine holy One to see corruption; Thou wilt show me the path of life." Thus He comes before these Philadelphians, unfolding to them His consciousness, His history; standing on His own experience; offering to them that which He conquered and took possession of for Himself,—true because holy, possessed of the key of heaven for the same reason,—having passed through what might be called the absolute relations of men to God, able to speak of them, able to act in regard to them.

This, then, is He who speaks to the Philadelphian Christians, and this is the character in which He speaks to them. What now does He say to them?

1. I have set before thee an open door. Now this is usually understood to mean that He had given them great opportunities of doing good, of entering upon large fields of practical work, of carrying the gospel to others outside. But it is obvious that this cannot at least be the primary meaning, because these Philadelphian Christians were persons who needed assurance that they had a gospel to keep to themselves rather than one to carry to others. They had no doubt been able to keep the word of Christ hitherto; but it was amidst many perplexities and vacillations. And it is evident from the title which

our Lord gives to Himself, He that has the key of
David, that when He says, I have set before thee an
open door, He speaks just of entrance into the kingdom of God.   His words do not bear on future external
work, but on past or present confirmation of internal
faith — of entrance and of more abundant entrance.
He says in effect: I have the key of David; entrance
into the kingdom of God is by Me,— and there is
entrance into it. I open, and no man can shut.
Whatever Jews may say, or others may say, however
they may perplex you, unsettle you, enfeeble you,
and paralyse your faith, I have set before you an
open door.   He that is holy, who therefore is true,
who therefore has opened the door for Himself, gone
in and left it open, He affirms, "I have set before
you an open door."

That figure of a door is worth dwelling on. Christ
uses it in a sort of absolute way. There is a door, an
entrance, a way in,—He does not say in from where
nor into what. It is a way in, in where and in from
what, our own hearts will suggest to us. For what
are we men in the world, many men at least, men
who reflect, and who listen to the world? Are we
not people who for long have been walking this way
and that way, pursuing all ways that seemed open to
us of thought and life, but in every case finding that
whatever way we took it carried us but a little
distance; it suddenly stopped, and there rose up before
us a wall, unsurmountable and dead, with no entrance

22

in it, no door, an absolute obstacle to further movement? Before and behind, such walls rise around us,
unsurmountable and dead. Or we are like men in the
outer darkness of night, groping our way, straining
our eyes to catch some rays of light streaming from
an open door. Sometimes, when one comes in youth
from a distant home to a great city where he is
unknown and alone, he walks through the streets
beholding the lighted windows and hearing the
sounds of music and joy within. The sounds but
intensify his own sense of solitude, and he is fain
to hurry away to his own room, lest he should have
to confess to himself his own weakness. We differ
from him in that we see no light and hear no sound
of joy; we only dream of it, and crave for it, saying,
Surely, there is a door out of this outer darkness. Is
there not an open door leading in to where there is
light and joy?[1]

This is not quite the class to whom Christ here
speaks, though what He says: "I have set before
thee an open door," pertains to them also. Those to
whom He speaks had in a certain way entered the
door; they had kept Christ's word, but they had little
strength. They had, in fact, gone in; but they did
not feel as if they had. Though they were within,
they felt as if they were without, or they hardly knew
whether they were within or without. They belonged
to that class of minds which are unduly sensitive to

[1] Cf. *Called of God*, Biographical Introduction, p. 13.

influences from without, like the needle trembling and turning with every current,—minds whose surfaces are crowded with intellectual and moral nerves that feel the faintest touch, unduly sympathetic to every consideration that has an element of truth in it, so that the suggestion of an outside mind breaks in upon and paralyses their own instincts and convictions. Even when such minds are able to keep the word of patience, they have little strength. They are like the light skiff, which, though moored, is carried about with every movement of the water. The truth which they have never reflects itself in their own consciousness, they have no sense of security. Their inward weakness reflects itself in their outward demeanour. They are without courage, apologetic, and creep about as if they had no right to be anywhere.

But I suspect it is not merely minds of this class that find difficulties with this door. All find them more or less. Our efforts to enter seem vain. The light and the joy we looked for within, we do not find. Or rather we find that there is no within—it is all an open door. We make an effort to pass the portal; and when we have done so and look back, we find that what we thought we had passed through has disappeared, and we are still standing without; and before us there is an open door. This experience is so often repeated that we begin to fear our life is going to be nothing but this, always entering but never getting within. And we ask, May not heaven turn out this same kind of thing,—no repose, no peace, no complacency, no satisfied vision,—only an eternal going in, always to find ourselves without?

2. The second great promise which Christ makes to these Philadelphians is this: "Because thou hast kept the word of My patience, I also will keep thee from the hour of trial, which shall come upon all the world." The force of the promise cannot be understood, unless it be remembered to whom it is made. It is to feeble-minded Philadelphians, to irresolute, vacillating minds with little strength,—these shall be kept in the hour of great trial that is to try all them that dwell upon the earth.

It takes a long time to familiarise ourselves with the language of Scripture, and a longer time to learn to translate it into the forms of modern experience and modern life. When John speaks of the trial that is to come upon all the world, he, no doubt, speaks literally. His imagination pictured such a great day of trial rapidly approaching, a day of universal searching and smelting. He idealises good and evil, or, as we might say, polarises them. The evil seems to him to gather itself all together to one pole, and the good to another, and a terrible conflict to arise between them. And perhaps it would help us to conceive how much evil there is in the world, to fancy it all concentrated in this way. Let us suppose the evil that exists in the world, in men's hearts, and lives, and thoughts, their malice and revenge, their cruelty and lust, their ambitions and their selfishness,—let us suppose all this evil now diffused as it were through society, lurking like a subtle influence, dormant and innocuous,—let us suppose it gathered to a point, concentrated towards one pole of the world of man, and breaking out in a terrible tempest. This is how John conceives of evil, and he looks for that day coming on all the inhabitants of the earth, to try them. But in that tempestuous day that tries all, Christ will keep even His feeble-minded servants.

It may be a question whether this terrible ideal picture shall, in the history of the world, be literally realised. Great outbreaks of evil there may be. But perhaps this ideal conception may not be realised, because it is no doubt ideal. John conceives evil as concentrating itself, and breaking out with a concentrated fury. But just as the lightning is conducted by a hundred channels to the earth, and the solid earth receives it into its bosom without being rent, so it may be that this evil which he saw may diffuse itself through society on to the end, just as we see it now. The solid masses of society may receive it; the moral life of men, their faith, may hold it in solution; and it may pass away with no such final convulsion as these words of the prophet would suggest. Standing sometimes on the shore and looking out seaward, you see a wave come rolling in mountain high. It seems as if it would engulf the world. Yet it is met by the

resistance of the stable earth, and when it actually
touches the shore, it rolls in upon it in foam so broken
that a little child may wade in it. And it may be so
with this great tide of evil and of trial which John
saw coming upon all the world. It will be so at least
with all those who are Christ's little ones.

Yet, on the other hand, every influence at present
operating tends to unite men in all lands closer together and make them homogeneous, a single mass
fired by the same enthusiasms, and moved by the
same motives. And in the future, differences will
more and more disappear, and affinities prevail, till
mankind becomes like a fluid, feeling every influence
over all its surface. And then, when great questions
arise, they will in truth agitate the world; and moods
of mind may settle down on men universally, and
currents run that will sweep mankind before them,
as the wind sweeps over a field of grain. And then
there may be a trial that will try all that dwell on
the earth. Who shall live when God doeth this? "I
will keep thee," says Christ to His feeblest minded
follower,—"I will keep thee from the hour of temptation that shall come on all the world."

But with whatever eyes we look out into the future,
it is at least the case that there does come an
hour of temptation to every individual soul, a moment
which is the crisis that decides its history. It may
come at the hour of death with its searching trials,
or it may come in some mood that settles down

on society and you, wrapping you in slumber, and killing the spiritual life within you; or it may come, as it oftenest does, in some private hour of temptation of which the world knows nothing, and which you seal up in your own heart, and divulge to none but God. Such an hour may be before you; or perhaps it lies behind you. You remember it; it is graven with a pen of iron on your heart. You shudder even now to think of it. You stood on the brink of some great sin. You were in act to commit it. But an invisible hand held you back. You were kept in the hour of temptation. Had you not been kept, you who now hold up your face before the world, where would you have been before men, before God? The shame of the felon in the dock would have been little to yours. But some reminiscence of early teaching rushed into your mind and arrested you; some old ideals of purity and truth, that used to haunt your heart, passed like fleeting visions before your eye and deterred you. A certain energy from the past asserted itself, a certain reaction of life as it were in the lethargy of death, and you were saved in the hour of temptation. You know now, when you look back on it, whose hand it was that kept you; but these were the means He made use of. For He does not keep us magically. "Because thou hast kept the word of My patience, I will keep thee in the hour of temptation."

The new keeping is not the reward of the past, but

the result of it. The soldier does not learn war first on the great battlefield. He is a soldier already. He has learnt war on the drill-ground, surrounded by all the arts and monuments of peace. Here he is made a soldier, learns implicit obedience, learns to stand like a rock, or move with his fellows like a machine. And so our ordinary life must be our drill-ground for the great temptation.

In the quiet, uneventful life of these Philadelphian Christians, surrounded by their petty cares, kept down by Jews and others, moving about with no pretensions, doubting, believing, hopeless, cheerful, feeble-minded upon the whole, yet keeping the word of Christ's patience, with little strength, yet gaining their little victories though oppressed always with an inward sense of defeat,—this was the drill-ground that was making soldiers of them, giving them some steadiness, fixing principles, teaching them that the word of Christ could be kept even amidst uncertainties, and that one though thrown down by the wave or the storm may rise and stand erect behind it, giving their minds, upon the whole, a direction that would be found able to face and go through the great temptation. It is thus that Christ would keep them, through their previous keeping of His word: " Because thou hast kept the word of My patience, I also will keep thee from the hour of temptation, that shall try all that dwell upon the earth."

3. The last promise given is the most extraordinary

of all. But it does not need to be dwelt upon. It only
needs to be set in contrast with the kind of person
to whom it is given. To these irresolute, doubtful,
unstable Philadelphians, creeping about through the
world, hardly daring to lift up their hesitating, apologetic Christian faces in the presence of Jews and others
with their loud and positive certainties founded on the
past,—to these feeble-minded men, paralysed by inward
uncertainties, swaying hither and thither, Christ says:
" Him that overcometh will I make a pillar in the
temple of My God." A pillar, massive, erect, lofty,
is the very symbol of stability and strength. It is
strange what inward strength there is even in the
feeblest Christian,—strange to what that strength may
yet be made to attain,—" if ye have faith as a grain of
mustard seed." The point is to have faith. Who can
tell to what position some of those feeble-minded men
whom we see around us may yet attain in the kingdom
of Christ ?

To these Philadelphians, perplexed all their life by
that strange open door, which seemed to them nothing
but a door at which they were always going in and
never getting in, but finding themselves still outside,—
to them Christ says: " I will make you a pillar in the
temple of My God, and ye shall go no more out,"—a
pillar in the temple of God, where His face is seen,
where is the light and the joy and the immediate
vision,—and ye shall go no more out. These Philadelphians had been but a few years converted from

heathenism, most of them; and that which had charmed
them away from their old gods, which were but embodiments in the main of human violence, or human
cunning and intrigue, or human lust, — that which
charmed them away from this was the vision of the
pure and lofty and blessed face of the God of Jesus
Christ, and the hope that He would be their God.

And Christ says: "I will write upon him the name
of My God." The Philadelphian shall have no more
inward misgivings. When he looks at himself, he
shall see inscribed upon his thigh, and feel that it is
written also on his forehead, To the Lord; and he shall
know that God is his God in truth. In another passage
the believer receives a stone with a name written which
none knoweth but himself. The name expresses his
meaning—his meaning to God as one unlike all others;
his consciousness, which differs from every other, for
it reflects his history, his relation to Christ, which is
unlike that of everyone else, having developments none
else could understand, and giving him a place which
none else could fill. This name, unintelligible to all
else, expresses God's heart to him, and his to God.
Many a time, too, he would have given his life to be
assured that he was a citizen even of the Jerusalem
on earth. Though sitting in the dust, she was lofty;
though clad in robes that were stained and tarnished
and outworn, she seemed glorious. He often wondered
if he was worthy to belong to this old Jerusalem.
Himself and others often doubted whether he did

belong to her. But there shall be written on him the name of the new, the fresh Jerusalem, when she has shaken herself from the dust, and put on her beautiful garments; and, looking on himself, he shall read his citizenship of her.

And, finally, Christ says: " I will write upon him My new name." Looking on himself, the Philadelphian Christian shall be conscious that he is Christ's. For the very point of this phrase, " I will write upon him," is to imply that when he looks on himself, thinks of himself, he shall feel that all this is true of him; he is God's, he is a citizen of the New Jerusalem, he is Christ's. What characterised him before was just the opposite of all this — inward feebleness, uncertainty. Now in his consciousness is truly reflected what he is. Christ writes His name on him, not His old, but His new name. This feeble-minded Philadelphian, bowed down all life by an inward weakness, shall know that he is Christ's in truth,—shall see Christ's name written upon himself, not the name by which he used to know Him, but another one, signifying that Christ was to him something other than he had ever dreamed of, greater, of higher meaning, of more glorious idea, of nearer fellowship, conferring something unheard of, undreamed of on earth. " I will write upon him My new name."

" Thus saith He that is holy, He that is true, He that openeth, and no man shutteth, I set before thee an open door." Leave the expression ' an open door' in all its generality,—a door out of all you wish to escape from, into all you desire to realise and enjoy,—a door out of darkness and uncertainties, out of weakness and feeble-mindedness, out of undue sensitiveness to outward influences,—a door into whatsoever you long for, aspire after, dream of in your loftiest hours, and accept the promise in all its marvellous fulness. For so an entrance shall be ministered unto you abundantly into the everlasting kingdom of our Lord and Saviour Jesus Christ.

XV

THE BOOK OF REVELATION

XV

THE BOOK OF REVELATION

THE opening verses of this book tell us very distinctly what the book is. It is the Revelation of Jesus Christ, the revelation made known by Jesus Christ, "the revelation of Jesus Christ which God gave unto Him, to show unto His servants the things which must shortly come to pass. And He sent and signified this revelation to His servant John: who bare witness of the word of God, and of the testimony of Jesus Christ, even of all things that he saw." The book is the word of God, the word spoken by God. It is also the testimony of Jesus Christ, the thing borne witness to by Him who is the true and faithful witness. And it is made known by John to the servants of Christ. God gave the revelation to Christ, who sent and signified it to John, who bore witness of it unto us; and it is a revelation of the things which must shortly come to pass.

Perhaps it may not be considered amiss if I make a few general remarks about the book as a whole, before proceeding to consider the 5th chapter.

351

First, the book consists of two great parts: the epistles to the seven Churches in the first three chapters, and the long series of visions from chap. iv. to the end. Now it is difficult at once to perceive the connection between these two parts, and observe the unity of the book. The relation between the epistles and the body of the book appears to be this. The book proper ("the words of the prophecy" as it is called in chap. i. 3, "the prophecy of this book" or "the book of this prophecy" as it is called in chap. xxii. 18, 19) extends from chap. iv. to the end. This book is the revelation of Jesus Christ, and contains the things which must shortly come to pass. Now this Book of Prophecy, chaps. iv. – xxii., is properly what is sent by John to the Churches, and it is communicated to them all in common. Each of the seven Churches receives this book.

But along with this book, sent to all the Churches, there is sent in each particular case a note or epistle. These notes are appropriate to the circumstances of the several Churches to which they are sent, containing warning or praise, exhortation and encouragement, according to the particular Church's condition, and *in view* of the things revealed in the Book of the Prophecy. The idea is that each Church should receive the general Book of the Prophecy, and its own epistle or note appropriate to its condition,— not the other epistles sent to the other Churches. But, of course, this idea could not be represented in a book, and hence all the epistles are given together before the prophecy.

Again, that which is revealed is called "the Revelation of Jesus Christ, which God gave unto Him." Here are three things, namely, God the original author of the revelation, Jesus Christ to whom He gave it to show unto His servants, and the revelation itself. These three things, or this idea, that God gives His revelation to us through Christ, is symbolically represented in chaps. iv.-v. In chap. iv. there is seen a vision of God, exhibiting His majesty and glory. This is designed to bring before our minds a conception of God, the Author of the revelation. Then in chap. v. there is a similar vision of Christ, and of the revelation given to Him by the Father. The Son beholds on the right hand of God, as He sits upon His throne, a book, sealed with seven seals. Christ, the Lamb slain, receives the book from the Father's hand, opens the seven seals successively, and displays the contents of the book. This book, held out on the Father's right hand, received and opened by Christ, is the Revelation of Jesus Christ, which God gave unto Him, containing the things which must shortly come to pass. And, of course, it is identical with John's Book of Prophecy, chaps. vi.-xxii.; for Christ, to whom the Father gave the Revelation, sent and signified it by His angel unto His servant John, who bare witness of all things which he saw. The book on the Father's right hand is the same as John's Book of Prophecy,

23

that is, it is our present Book of Revelation from chap. vi., where the Lamb begins to open the seals, on to the end of the book.

If this be the case, the successive opening of the seals should lay before us the whole revelation, and the opening of the seventh seal should naturally present the consummation of all things. And so it does in a certain sense. What might be called the skeleton or backbone of the book is made up of three series of visions, the seven seals, the seven trumpets, and the seven vials. Many of those who have written on the book consider that these three series do not strictly follow one another, the last two rather recapitulate the first: the seals go over the whole history of the Church to the end, the trumpets go over the same ground in a different way, and the vials do the same under another aspect still. But this is very improbable.

Unquestionably the opening of the seven seals reveals the whole; but when the seventh seal is opened, and we are expecting to behold the consummation of all things, nothing really is revealed to us. There is silence in heaven for the space of half an hour. There is a lull, a pause, preliminary to another great outbreak of divine judgment upon the earth. Instead of seeing the end, the seer beholds the seven angels who have the seven last trumpets, the sounding of which heralds the end. That is, the seventh seal develops into the seven trumpets. They are all contained in it. And in like manner the seventh trumpet does not reveal a

single event, such as the end of all. It also opens up
into the final series of the seven vials or bowls, which
are characterised (xv. 1) as the seven last plagues, for
in them is finished the wrath of God.

This outline and general progress of the book might
be represented by a very simple illustration, which
younger minds, I think, would understand, and which
older persons will perhaps excuse. A telescope when
drawn out has three sections or divisions; when you
close it, there is only one division. This thick division
then contains the other two within it. The telescope in
this closed form would represent the seven seals; these
contain within them the whole of the visions of the book.
Then, if you draw out one section, this section would
represent the series of the trumpets. This section seems
to come out of the end of the thick part, the seven
trumpets are but the contents of the seventh seal; and
it contains within it the third section. Finally, when
you draw out the third division, the whole is displayed.
This third section represents the seven vials, all of which
are developed out of the last of the seven trumpets.

Such is the general line that runs through the Book
of Revelation. Of course, there is a multitude of visions
which do not seem to fall into this general movement.
They do, however, fall in. They are either preliminary
compends, or they are preparations for the visions that
make up the connected line of progress, or they are
repetitions on a larger scale, exhibiting in fuller breadth
and detail the more compressed scenes given under the

trumpets and the vials. The book contains a progressive movement. It does not cover the same ground several times. It goes over the period from John to the second coming of the Lord, but it goes over this only once. The visions of the seals, the trumpets, and the vials, with the side visions, in many cases more fully representing them, or when necessary bringing on the stage actors in the great drama, and explaining in the manner of a chorus who they are,—for example, chaps. xii., xiii. give us views of the dragon, the beast or Antichrist, and the false prophet,—these visions give us the events that shall intervene, and follow one another in succession, between the time when John wrote and the coming of the Lord, as this coming is described in the 19th and 20th chapters of the book.

Now the question of the interpretation of the book is just this question of the space or period of time between John and the coming of Christ. How are we to think of this period? or rather, how did John think of it? In actual history it has widened out to a period of two thousand years already, and we know not how many thousands more may be added to it. The life of mankind does not show any signs of decay, nor are there any symptoms that human history is played out. The problems before human society are perhaps not new, they are in the main old problems; but it is felt that larger periods of time are needful for their solution, and a wider area, and the co-operation of greater masses of mankind in the experiment. And the solution of these problems is not merely a thing necessary to the perfection and happiness of mankind. The solution of them is the perfection of human society and life; for they are practical, and not merely theoretical questions. And amidst much conflict and confusion, the display of rival banners and the loudness of discordant cries, the thunder of the captains and the shouting, we see perhaps some of these problems, though they are but the edges and fringes of the great central question of human life before God, being solved before our eyes.

But such a view could hardly occur to the mind of John. Neither could he have any idea of the great spaces of time familiar to us, nor of the conditions which human society has assumed in our modern world. He lived in the ancient world, and he was a prophet; and we shall best understand him, if we bring to the interpretation of his book the principles which Old Testament prophecy teaches us. Now, to put it briefly, these principles are three.

First, the prophets all stand amidst the circumstances of human life and the conditions of the world surrounding them in their own day. It is these that they survey, that have significance, infinite significance to them, and that they operate with. The moral and social forces of their own day, the truth of God and those of whose hearts it has taken possession, the evil, the falsehood of the world, the perversities of human thought, the false systems of religion, the immoral principles of life,—systems and principles embodied in the

ruling empires and kingdoms of the earth, in the unclean
rites, in the luxury and voluptuous delicacy of society,
with its cruelty and thirst for blood,—it is these forces
and agents of their own day that all the prophets handle.

Secondly, though the prophets are men of their own
day, they are all men of the future. Though they live
in their own time with an intensity of life to which
nothing now is comparable, with a moral sensitiveness
to the evil and the good about them which subsequent
ages seem to have lost, they do not lose themselves
in the confusions of their day. They possess the key
to the labyrinth in which other men endlessly wander.
Amidst the confused noise of battle, their ear catches
the sound of victory. Behind the pitiless tempest
which rages around them, and blinds other men, they
are able to see a light breaking on the horizon, and a
rainbow on the cloud. The voice which they hear
above the din and clash of systems and of nations
is the voice of the Lord: "I am the Alpha and the
Omega, the first and the last, the Lord God omnipotent,
who has been, is, and will be "—will be more manifestly
and in fuller evidence of presence than ever He has
yet been. There is One on high, an eternal God, the
Creator of the ends of the earth, who fainteth not,
neither is weary, who holds the reins of government in
His hand. There is One who starts and guides, and
who is bringing, and will bring, to an issue the great
movement, the evolution of human history, with all its
breadth of sweep and all its complication of detail; and

the issue is His own, and it will be wise, and good, and
laden with eternal blessing—"Behold, the Lord God
cometh with strong hand, His arm ruling for Him :
behold, His reward is with Him, and His recompense
before Him. He will feed His flock like a shepherd :
He will gather the lambs with His arm, and carry them
in His bosom." The prophets, and John among them,
were all men of their own time; but they were all also
men of the future,—they had an outlook, ordered in all
things and sure.

Thirdly, the important point is, how did they connect their own present time with this future? Now
the answer must be, that it seemed to all the prophets
and to the prophet John that the connection was
virtually immediate. The forces operating around them,
the events transpiring, the conflict waged, would issue
in the incoming of the perfect kingdom of God. A
link or two more, and the chain of events would run
out; a stride or two of God's providence, and the end
would be reached. As this peculiarity can really hardly
be denied, it would be interesting to inquire: (1) into
the origin of it; and (2) into the purpose of it in God's
general revelation. It may be assumed that, in the form
in which His revelation is given, God had reference, in
some respect, to the generations of His people in all
ages. But no doubt, in the particular ages when it was
given, He had special reference to those to whom it was
written.

Now, it is sufficiently evident that, if John had foreseen that a thousand or several thousand years would intervene between his day and the coming of the Lord, his book would never have been written ; he never could have administered to the Church of his day, amidst its terrible sufferings, the consolations which he gives. This form of the revelation, therefore, was a simple necessity for the time it was given. Without it the Scriptures would have had no practical meaning for that time. Men, directed to look for the Lord's coming some thousands of years after their own day, would have fainted in the strife. Reflection was not yet sufficiently ripe to sustain men's minds. But along with this bringing forward of the last great hope almost within their own horizon, the prophets, and John among them, were able to state, in a concrete form, principles which could be taken up in such a form by the Church of that day, and which we are able to generalise and apply to our own and all ages. To John, the Beast, for example, though an actual phenomenon of his own day, or soon to appear in its final form, represented a principle which has not yet been fully overcome, but exists, perhaps, in other forms in our day. And we can apply to the principle in its form in our days his hopes and truths, which are eternal and retain their validity in all ages. It was the same with the prophets. Assyria, Babylon, etc., were successively the enemies of the king-dom of God ; and the victory of His people over them, and the coming of the Lord to destroy them, was the comfort they received.

And thus Peter's statement, that one day is with the Lord as a thousand years, has still its truth. It is a principle which we may apply to the fulfilment of prophecy in a higher sense—looking over the whole history of the world. It is not a principle that will apply, if the question we put be, what is the meaning of the prophet himself? His mind was allowed to remain in darkness as to the times and the seasons. He was allowed to hope, and even to promise, that the time of God's appearing was at hand. The hope was not an intellectual calculation, it was a religious presentiment. And he was enabled to express truths, in terms of his own age and the forces around him, which are true in all ages, and applicable to the forces of each generation, which, in whatever form they appear, are virtually the same. What leads to misinterpretation of the prophets is the failure to recognise that Scripture is practical, written primarily for its own age, though applicable to all ages; that it is not a giving forth of abstract truths, but of messages intended to enable the men, to whom they were given, to live, and to realise that they had present salvation and deliverance.

- The language of every one of the prophets is: "The day of the Lord is at hand." It is not quite easy for us, with our views of time and with history behind us, and that idea of the slow and solemn march of providence which history has taught us present to our minds, to realise this peculiar view of the prophets. Yet perhaps it is not so very difficult. The prophets wrote and spoke

usually amidst very stirring scenes. Great events were
passing around them. In general, it is only amidst the
convulsions that rend society deeply that they speak.
They are the storm birds of providence. It is when the
wind is rising and the storm breaking that their voice
is heard. In the great events about them they felt
the presence of God. He was nearer than usual. The
noise of falling empires, the desolations of the Church,
the revolutions of thought, revealed to their ear His
footsteps,—they heard in them the sound of His goings.
They thought that they could hear, in movements going
on, the fall of the first great drops that strike sharp and
measured on the leaves, when the tempest is about to
burst. God was so near that His full presence appeared
imminent. His footfalls echoed not far away. Speedily
His glory would be revealed, and all flesh would see it
together, as the mouth of the Lord had said. Thus
their belief in the nearness of the Lord's coming was
more a feeling than a thought, more a presentiment
of their heart—a religious presentiment—than a mere
intellectual calculation of time. Still the feeling was
of such a kind that the Lord's coming could not be
imagined to be very long deferred.

Now, in order to understand John's book, we must
take this thought with us. Above all, we must read
ourselves into the history of his time, realise his circumstances,—the thoughts and hopes that then filled the
minds of all Christians, their terrible hardships, the
crushing power of the Roman Empire, whose inhuman

persecutions might well make John represent it as an incarnation of hellish power.

But I have delayed too long over this general subject. We must now turn to the 5th chapter.

It has been said that the 4th and 5th chapters are a symbolical representation of the statement in the first verse of the book: "The Revelation of Jesus Christ, which God gave unto Him, to show unto His servants the things which must shortly come to pass." The book is the revelation; it lies open on the right hand of God; it is held out; Christ the Lamb takes it, and opens the seals with which it is closed, and with the successive opening of the seals reveals to John its contents; and John bare witness of them unto the servants of Christ, even all things which he saw.

The book is a book written; its contents are not haphazard but definite, not fortuitous but determined. It is full: it is written in front and on the back. And it is sealed with seven seals. It is the book of God, the book of the Church's history, of human destiny, of the world's movement onward from groove to wider groove till the end. It is something to us to know that there is such a book on the Father's hand; that the events that transpire on earth are not a confused rush, or a disorderly dance, or a mindless play of forces that mock reason. There is mind and will, there is order and limit, there is a movement and a result. The history of mankind and our history are prescribed.

This thought has been a source of strength to men's

hearts in all times. It has nerved the human will to unbending resoluteness. It has given a moral sternness to the nature, that was inflexible. The thought, the feeling, that they were under God, that He was leading them about alway in triumph as He led Paul, has been a joy to men loftier and more exalted than any other that ever filled the breast of man. Under such a feeling men have not merely faced outward trials, endured hardships at which in other moods human nature would flinch and quiver,—under it they have been able to fight a battle with themselves, to put down their own rebelling natures, to offer themselves living sacrifices unto God with an exalted self-devotion and joy in God which almost looked like possession by a spirit not human.

No doubt many have been content to acquiesce in the thought that there is a book, that their life-history is prescribed, without seeking to know the contents of the prescription, or despairing of the possibility of knowing it. It was doubtless there, this book of an over-ruling, all-determining power; but it was inscrutable. It could not be read. "No one in heaven, nor on earth, neither under the earth, was able to open the book, or to look thereon." Only one thing was left, to endure its decisions, to submit to its determinations, and to preserve under them, as best could be, a dignified human mind,—neither being carried away into immoderate joy when they were kind and bountiful, nor into dejection and despairing complaint when they were cruel and envious.

But others have shown a different mind. They have not been content to know that God has determined all; they have desired to look into His determinations. They have knocked at the door of the mystery; they have fumbled at the seals with their own fingers, making desperate efforts to break them. The thought that they could not be opened has filled them with inexpressible sadness. Like John, they have wept much, when the task seemed hopeless, and none in heaven or in earth could undertake it. For, surely, if it be a joy to serve God blindly, when all we can say is that it is God over all, it is keener joy to serve Him with the eyes open,—to be let into the secret of His operations, to see the gracious motives, to behold, even if afar off, the doubly gracious end.

This is one feeling which the thought of this book of God inspires; there is, however, another. Our heart rises in rebellion at this thought, that our history, or fate, or destiny, has been prescribed, irrespective, as we think, of us; and that we have been sent into existence and into the world with it merely round our necks. And we imagine all kinds of possibilities as concerns ourselves: we may have been overlooked, or excluded from the gracious side of His determination; and in other states of mind we doubt whether we have been included in God's purposes of grace from the beginning. Now in all such moods as this there is a tendency to evacuate God, to empty Him of all His attributes, and leave Him nothing but a

mere unsubstantial will, a mere imponderable force
that disposes of all things. Before thinking of the
book of God's purposes, we should always first think
of God Himself. We ought not to empty Him of
His attributes, reducing Him to a mere will; we should
rather crowd all His attributes together, and clothe
Him in all the riches and brilliancy of them,—justice,
goodness, truth, mercy, compassion, long-suffering, wisdom, forbearance, fatherly pity, love. Thus it is that
John proceeds. Before showing the book of God's
purposes in chap. v., he shows us God Himself in
chap. iv. He is light that no man can approach unto,
shining with the radiance of a jasper stone and a
sardius; but this pure light, upon which created eye
could not look, is tempered and subdued by the radiance of the rainbow, like unto an emerald that bathes
in its colours the eternal light.

Again, look at these beings that surround the throne.
They are mysterious, some of them; but we must suppose them intelligences, or perhaps some of them per-
sonifications of the forms of life in the world, whose
voice, therefore, is the voice of universal creation. If
they be intelligences, their intelligence is more exalted
than ours; they have a deeper insight into God and His
purposes than we can possess. They look upon His
face, and sit in His council. Both the depth and the
sweep of their comprehension of God and His ways
may be inconceivable to us. And yet they are in full
harmony with Him. It is with no dull acquiescence,

but with a passion, a storm of adoration, that they sing the song of His thrice holiness, and fling their golden crowns at His feet.

But whenever fears take possession of our minds, we should remember who it is to whom God commits the book of His purposes to be revealed to us. It is not to some mighty angel, so gigantic that he overstrides the world, placing one foot upon the sea and another upon the earth, whose presence and voice would overawe us; it is to the Lamb that had been slain. The messenger whom God employs to announce the book of His purposes, and who consents to be the messenger, casts light upon the nature of the message. When a king delegates to some distant province a stern soldier, his character announces beforehand his policy; men know he is the herald of a strong repressive rule; he has a chain in his hand, and will lay an iron yoke upon them. But when one is sent renowned for gentleness, who sympathises with popular aspirations, and has already in other fields borne hardships in the cause of men, and striven to widen their privileges and enlarge their freedom, they know that he comes to them with a message of peace and goodwill. And God has given the revelation of the book of His purposes with us to the Son—to the Lamb that was slain. Now these are some of the considerations with which John surrounds the presentation of the Book of God's purposes.

There is another point in the chapter to which I

will only allude, namely, the acclamations that greeted the Lamb when He had taken the book to open it. In vvs. 8 and 9 it is said: "When He had taken the book, the four living creatures and the four and twenty elders fell down before the Lamb. And they sing a new song, saying, Worthy art Thou to take the book, and to open the seals thereof." This ascription of praise is thrice repeated. It is sung, first, by those nearest to God and His throne. Then it is taken up by the multitude of angels that stand around, but further off: "And I saw, and I heard a voice of many angels round about the throne and the living creatures and the elders: and the number of them was ten thousand times ten thousand, and thousands of thousands; saying with a great voice, Worthy is the Lamb that hath been slain to receive the power, and riches, and wisdom, and might, and honour, and glory, and blessing." And, finally, from them the cry is caught up by all creation to its outmost border: "And every created thing which is in the heaven, and on the earth, and under the earth, and on the sea, heard I saying: Unto Him that sitteth upon the throne, and unto the Lamb, be the blessing, and the honour, and the glory, and the dominion, for ever and ever."

No book contains such conceptions as this of John. Oh, if we could realise, if we could even fancy that we hear, this shout of praise, raised first by those around the throne, then caught by the myriads of spirits that stand in wider circles, and then descending till, finally, it is echoed by every mouth in heaven and earth, and on the sea! It is those nearest the throne, the inner circle, those most initiated into the mysteries of God, those that see most deeply and can estimate most truly the meaning of the work of the Lamb, that first raise the cry in His honour. But, finally, all creation is penetrated by it, and repeats it. The things of Christ's life were not done in a corner. They are not of partial significance. The thought of them thrills creation.

The principal thought of the passage, however, is that only the Lamb slain was worthy or able to open the book of God's purposes, and reveal to men its contents. It is possible that 'worthy' means almost the same as able, but the two may be taken separately: He is worthy, and He is able, to open the book.

(1) He is worthy. There is a very important difference of reading in the passage which should be noticed. In our ordinary version it is said: "They sung a new song, saying, Thou art worthy to take the book: for Thou wast slain, and hast redeemed us to God by Thy blood; and hast made us unto our God kings and priests." But in the revision the word 'us' does not occur. It reads: "Worthy art Thou to take the book: for Thou wast slain, and didst purchase unto God with Thy blood men of every tribe, and madest them to be unto our God a kingdom and priests."

24

Those who sing this song have not been themselves redeemed. It is not gratitude that inspires their loud acclamations to the Lamb; it is admiration. They look upon His work from the outside; it does not immediately concern them. They are spectators. His work may not have been without influence upon them. It may have removed perplexities,—if, indeed, they were not endowed with such wisdom as to perceive beforehand that such a work would certainly be accomplished. It may have satisfied the longings of their compassion, as they looked on the miseries of the earth where they often ministered. They may have felt the wave of stillness and peace that passed over the universe, when the Lamb of God was slain, and took away the sin of the world; and they may have felt themselves included, when He made peace and reconciled all things unto God. But, in the main, it is a judgment from the outside that they form. It is a moral verdict that they pass. Their cry is, "Worthy to open the book; worthy to receive power, and riches, and glory, and dominion."

It is sometimes charged on Christians that their religion is selfishness, individual egotism. They love because they have been loved; they serve because they have been delivered. Their care centres each in himself. Their Lord is great, because He has done something for them. Of others they have no thought. The song of the heavenly host cannot be thus charged. They look on the work of Christ dispassionately.

Their praise of Him is that He has redeemed men of every tribe and made them kings. And His work, in their estimation, is the central moral deed of the universe,—He is worthy to stand beside God, and to take the book of His purposes, and unfold it.

(2) He is able to do this. "A strong angel proclaimed with a great voice, Who is able to open the book, and to loose the seals thereof? And no one in the heaven, or on the earth, or under the earth, was able to open the book, or to look thereon." No angel, however strong in power, was able for this; none on earth, however subtle in insight and able to read riddles; none under the earth; even the wisdom that is with death failed. At this impotence of all created minds, John wept much. "And one of the elders said unto me, Weep not: the Lion of the tribe of Judah hath overcome, to open the book. And I saw in the midst of the throne a Lamb, as though it had been slain."

To the heavenly spirit, looking down with ancient memories in his mind perhaps of the strong Son of God, the Son appears a lion; to John, looking up through memories of earth, He appears a lamb. He is both in one; the one because He is the other, a lion because He is a lamb. There are men, some of the brave leaders that command our soldiers, for instance, who are both lions and lambs,—lambs at home, lions in the field. Before the foe they are lions, subtle to watch their opportunity and make their dis-

positions, like lightning when they spring and deliver
their blow, fierce and irresistible in the onset, haughty
and lofty in their demeanour, as becomes men whose
hearts are filled with the thought of the great nation
which they represent; and yet, on another side of their
nature, lambs, to the child or to the woman tender,
to the poor soldier who falls out of the ranks stricken
with the African heat gentle as a nurse, pitiful to the
wounded and fallen foe, and willing to exhaust their
scanty bottle of water to wet his dying lips. These
are lions and also lambs. But the Son of God is
not sometimes one and sometimes another. He is a
lion by being a lamb. It is His weakness that is
power, His meekness and gentleness that overcomes,
His wounds that are a medicine. In the region of
thought, of feeling, of mind—in a word, in the realm
of ideal conduct and spiritual life, the qualities of the
Lamb are leonine. And thus it is that only the Lamb
is able to open the book. For the book is the book
of God's purposes with the world, it is the book of
human history and destiny; it records the varying
fortunes and the issues of the warfare of good and
evil waged upon the earth, of the contest against the
brute force of the beast, against the luxurious dalliance, the seductive voluptuousness of the great harlot,
worldly pleasure, who intoxicates and stupefies the
higher spirit of men with the wine of her fornication.

This is none other than the drama displayed by
John, whose stage is the world; and it is not other

than that played in the life of each of us, even as it was in the life of the Lamb. And the issue will yet be the same: "Be of good cheer; I have overcome the world." For the Lamb slain is able to open the seals and read the book, because He has already in His own life gone through the same history. In the Gospel of John it is said: "No man hath seen God at any time; the only-begotten Son, who is in the bosom of the Father, He has declared Him"; and again: "No man knoweth the Father save the Son, and He to whom the Son will reveal Him." Here Christ is able to reveal, because He is the Son, and knows. But in the present passage He opens the seals, because He was slain. This gave Him the secret. For by dying He gave the world a new direction; He introduced the principles on which the world's history will move. His own experience gives Him insight.

I suspect all insight comes of experience. When we read some of our great dramatic writers, and feel amazed at the subtilty with which they delineate the workings of the human mind in trying circumstances, and the truthfulness to nature and life with which they make men act, we attribute this to a certain instinct, a certain fulness of humanity, in their nature which spontaneously expresses itself, and is independent of observation and experience. There is, no doubt, such a fulness of humanity in them and a creative power. But probably the elements of what they produce have been taken in by observation. The threads of the web which their minds weave have been picked up separately. They have been in situations which suggested their fully wrought - out scene. They have observed traits of human nature which they develop into their great characters. They have heard broken notes of music in life which they unite into their most imposing harmonies. At least this is so with Christ. If with anyone, we might attribute all to instinct or to genius with Him. But it is not so; "He learned obedience by the things which He suffered." "He has the keys of death and of Hades." But if these keys hang at His girdle, it is because He entered into death, and came out of it. He went through death, and carried away the keys of it with Him. He came out of death, and left the door open behind Him. And if He can open and read the book of human destiny, it is because He has gone through it.

We all know how naïve our judgments are of life, before we have experience,—how sharp cut our verdicts of men and things are,—how we condemn and how we acquit on general principles, with no mellowness in our minds, and unable to estimate and weigh considerations which, if we weighed them, would blunt the sharp edge of our verdicts. We know how, when we mix among men, our sharp individuality fuses and melts on its edges, and men and we seem to flow into one another, and become one whole; and instead of the small heart that used to beat in our bosoms, we feel the throbbings of the universal human heart;

and we acquire a sensibility which feels the unseen essential currents of human life, and we become conscious of the true direction in which the stream is moving. The conventional loses its meaning to us, and the true and essential under all the many outward colours reveals itself. And thus our Lord entered into life and learned its meaning, and He is able to look out towards its future, and predict its destiny, able to loose the seals, and open the book in which its destiny is recorded.

But more than this: He brought the true human life with Him into the world. In the life of the Son of man, the essentials of human life and history revealed themselves. He gave the true direction to human life. He threw in principles into it, motives and conditions, of which man's future history is but the unfolding and the issue. And therefore, alone in heaven or on earth, He can disclose what that issue will be. Now we are ready, perhaps, to believe that so far as our individual life is concerned, His life must be the type of it,—the same conflict must be fulfilled in us that we have seen to be in Him. But can we say this of the world, of mankind? Surely the life of the world is but a larger individual life. Mankind is but a universal man. The history of mankind is but the history of one man on a universal scale. Analyse our own individual mind, realise to ourselves the struggles within it of good and evil, the baffling uncertainties, the motives, the impulses,—do we not see that not only other minds, but mankind as a whole, exhibit the same experiences? The elements in our mind, struggling with one another, are but a type of the masses of men, possessed by certain impulses and sentiments, struggling with one another within the bosom of mankind. And this universal life must run the same course, and have the same issue as in the case of the individual.

For what is this book of the Revelation of John? It might be called the drama of Christianity. It is the exhibition of the conflict of the Lamb slain; the world-wide conflict with His enemies, the beast, the false prophet, and the harlot, which are all inspired by Satan, the spirit of evil,—the exhibition of IIis conflict with these, and His victory over them. Men may dispute what, to John's eye, these great enemies of the Lamb were. It is of very little consequence to us what they were in the form which they had in John's day. That form has now passed away. They have in our day become transformed into other external shapes. The particular forms under which they appeared, or seemed to John about to appear, are not likely ever to be seen again. To the eye of the seer the moral and other forces of his time assumed external shapes, but these external shapes have succumbed to time.

But the forces are not dead; they live in other forms. Their meaning to all ages lies in the names they bear: the beast or brute, the false teacher, the harlot, — personification of voluptuous life and worldly pleasure. The beast is the brute in human life, the inhuman, the mere force or power, to which all others are but victims and food, that rends and devours, red in tooth and claw; and the false prophet is the false thought that ministers to this brutal selfish force, that deifies it, and causes men to worship it. The conflict between the Lamb slain and these enemies is the drama displayed by John. Its stage is the world of mankind, as well as the heart of each individual. In the last act of his drama, John shows us these enemies overcome by the Lamb, and cast into the lake of fire.

When we turn from witnessing this drama, surely the most brilliant one ever represented in literature, to the actual world, can we comfort ourselves with the assurance that it is true? Do we see the spirit of the beast, the brute force that raises itself upon the defeat and death of others, the false thought that deifies this spirit and the spirit of the soft, careless, secular life,—do we see this spirit going down before the spirit of the Lamb slain, the spirit of meekness, the spirit of endurance, the spirit of humanity in its holiest sense, the spirit that gives itself for others even unto death?

Whatever we can say of the world, let us make sure that the victory is being won, at least, in our own hearts; that the spirit of the beast—the false thought which ministers to it, and the love of worldly dalliance and delight—is being driven out by the spirit of the Lamb that was slain. Let us see to it that the love of pre-eminence and self-aggrandisement, that desires to rise upon the loss of others, is receding before the spirit of meekness and love, that puts itself at the service of others, — that purity is taking the place of voluptuousness, and dedication to God driving out devotion to the world.

And one thing we must remember. It is not the principles of the Lamb slain, apart from the slain Lamb Himself, that will accomplish this. There are times in our life when abstract ideals have great power over us. They overmaster us, and sweep our whole nature into their current. But this is only for a time. The ideals fade, and lose their brilliancy and their power when taken abstractly. To retain their power, they must be seen in the person who is the embodiment of them. It is fellowship with the slain Lamb Himself that will give us the victory; it is having always at our side Him who has said, " Be of good cheer, I have overcome the world."

Printed by MORRISON & GIBB LIMITED, *Edinburgh*

BY THE LATE PROF. A. B. DAVIDSON, D.D., LL.D., EDINBURGH.

'*Whatever subject Prof. Davidson touched, there are always two epithets which may be applied to his treatment of it: it is masterly and it is judicial. No one had a better power of penetrating to the heart of a subject, no one was more skilful in the discovery of characteristics of an age, the drift of an argument, the aim of a writer. . . . His mastery of a subject was always complete.*'—Canon DRIVER.

An Introductory Hebrew Grammar, with Progressive Exercises in Reading and Writing. By Prof. A. B. DAVIDSON, D.D., LL.D., New College, Edinburgh. Seventeenth Edition. 8vo, price 7s. 6d.

'A text-book which has gone into its tenth [now seventeenth] edition needs no recommendation here. . . . Certain changes, in the introduction of new examples and the enlargement of some parts where brevity tended to obscurity, will add to the already great merits and widely acknowledged usefulness of the book.'—*Critical Review.*
'The best Hebrew Grammar is that of Professor A. B. Davidson.'—*British Weekly.*

Hebrew Syntax. Third Edition. In demy 8vo, price 7s. 6d.

'The whole is, it is needless to say, the work of a master; but it is the work of a master who does not shoot over the learners' heads, one who by long experience knows exactly where help is most needed, and how to give it in the simplest and clearest fashion.'—*Methodist Recorder.*

The Epistle to the Hebrews. (*Handbook Series.*) Cr. 8vo, 2s. 6d.

'For its size and price one of the very best theological handbooks with which I am acquainted—a close grappling with the thought of the epistle by a singularly strong and candid mind.'—Professor SANDAY in the *Academy.*

The Exile and the Restoration. With Map and Plan. (*Bible-Class Primer Series.*) Paper cover, price 6d. ; cloth, 8d.

'A remarkable instance of Professor Davidson's gift of compressed lucid statement. . . . It may be safely said that nowhere within anything like the same narrow limits will one get so vivid a view of that period of Old Testament history.'—*Expository Times.*

Old Testament Prophecy. Edited by Prof. J. A. PATERSON, D.D. One large 8vo Vol. Price 10s. 6d. net.

Old Testament Prophecy was Dr. Davidson's favourite study, and in this volume are contained the final results of forty years' strenuous thinking on this profoundly interesting subject.

Old Testament Theology. Edited by Principal SALMOND, D.D. (In *The International Theological Library.*) [*In the Press.*

The Called of God. With Biographical Introduction by A. TAYLOR INNES, Esq., Advocate, and Portraits. Post 8vo, 6s.

This volume contains a selection of the late Professor Davidson's Sermons, including : The Call of Abraham. Jacob at Bethel. Jacob at Peniel. Moses on Mount Sinai. Saul. Elijah. The Call of Isaiah. The Call of Jeremiah. John the Baptist. Nicodemus. Zacchæus. The Rich Young Ruler. Thomas.

'The biographical introduction is admirable. . . . The sermons have thoughts that startle with their depth, they have passages that thrill us with their suppressed emotion.'—*Aberdeen Free Press.*

A GREAT BIBLICAL ENCYCLOPÆDIA.

'The standard authority for biblical students of the present generation.'—*Times.*

In Four Volumes, imperial 8vo (of nearly 900 pages each).
Price per Volume, in cloth, 28s. ; in half morocco, 34s.,

A DICTIONARY OF THE BIBLE,

Dealing with its Language, Literature, and Contents, including the Biblical Theology.

Edited by JAMES HASTINGS, M.A., D.D., with the Assistance of J. A. SELBIE, D.D., and, chiefly in the Revision of the Proofs, of the late A. B. DAVIDSON, D.D., LL.D., Edinburgh; S. R. DRIVER, D.D., Litt.D., Oxford ; and H. B. SWETE, D.D., Litt.D., Cambridge.

Full Prospectus, with Specimen Pages, from all Booksellers, or from the Publishers.

'We offer Dr. Hastings our sincere congratulations on the publication of the first instalment of this great enterprise. . . . A work was urgently needed which should present the student with the approved results of modern inquiry, and which should also acquaint him with the methods by which theological problems are now approached by the most learned and devout of our theologians.'—*Guardian.*

'We welcome with the utmost cordiality the first volume of Messrs. Clark's great enterprise, "A Dictionary of the Bible." That there was room and need for such a book is unquestionable. . . . We have here all that the student can desire, a work of remarkable fulness, well up to date, and yet at the same time conservative in its general tendency, almost faultlessly accurate, and produced by the publishers in a most excellent and convenient style. We can thoroughly recommend it to our readers as a book which should fully satisfy their anticipations. . . . This new Dictionary is one of the most important aids that have recently been furnished to a true understanding of Scripture, and, properly used, will brighten and enrich the pulpit work of every minister who possesses it. . . . We are greatly struck by the excellence of the short articles. They are better done than in any other work of the kind. We have compared several of them with their sources, and this shows at once the unpretentious labour that is behind them. . . . Dr. A. B. Davidson is a tower of strength, and he shows at his best in the articles on Angels, on Covenant (a masterpiece, full of illumination), and on Eschatology of the Old Testament. His contributions are the chief ornaments and treasure-stores of the Dictionary. . . . We are very conscious of having done most inadequate justice to this very valuable book. Perhaps, however, enough has been said to show our great sense of its worth. It is a book that one is sure to be turning to again and again with increased confidence and gratitude. It will be an evil omen for the Church if ministers do not come forward to make the best of the opportunity now presented them.'—EDITOR, *British Weekly.*

'Will give widespread satisfaction. Every person consulting it may rely upon its trustworthiness. . . . Far away in advance of any other Bible Dictionary that has ever been published in real usefulness for preachers, Bible students, and teachers.'—*Methodist Recorder.*

'This monumental work. It has made a great beginning, and promises to take rank as one of the most important biblical enterprises of the century.'—*Christian World.*

EDINBURGH : **T. & T. CLARK**, 38 GEORGE STREET.